THIS BOOK IS F(

* You are looking to sharpen your fc obstacles
* You suffer from confidence and anxiety issues
* You have made huge mistakes in your life and you feel there is no way back as a result of these
* You have had relationship and marriage breakdowns which have created self-doubt and knocked your confidence in relationships
* Your marriage or relationship breakdown has had an effect on the relationship with your kids
* You have suffered from nasty injuries which have knocked your confidence about getting back out there
* You are a constant worrier and panic like crazy
* You are working towards an important goal and need to power up your tenacity
* You have physical restrictions causing you a lack of confidence in achieving those goals
* You have been through or are going through depression
* You have lost hope in life as a result of suffering from unexpected happenings, such as debts
* You are looking to enhance your self-esteem
* You value giving as a gift and have the desire to give to others
* You have lost a loved one
* You are being put down and told to shrug off your dreams and aspirations

WHAT OTHERS ARE SAYING ABOUT THIS BOOK

"The Challenge in life is to live it the way you want, achieve what you need to, and to be happy long before your short life is complete. There are many words of wisdom and power contained within these pages that will instil huge belief within you, that you really can do all that and much more. Read Sat's book and you will truly understand this."

Michael Khatkar
Writer, Author, Managing Director of VivaMK

"Once we align with our life purpose, we are unstoppable! That's the energy that flows through the book of my dear friend, Satwinder Sagoo. The pain of the past creates us as human beings in the best version of us. It opens new doors of possibilities and the ability to get up and give help to others with words of encouragement, assurance that we are all capable to reach our dreams and goals, and to remind us that we just have to start to believe in our inner potentials. This book broadcasts true greatness as it shows readers how each of us should utilise past experience towards our own growth, spreading good energy, joy and happiness... That is the brilliance of this book – the simplicity of using the sources we all have, the power of good energy you put out to the world, the power of self-love and integrity."

Halyna Chevpilo
Bestselling International Author and Happiness Guru

"Sat Sagoo has created a masterpiece. A true bestseller, this book will lift you when you are down and raise you to new heights when you are on a roll. A must for everyone's book collection."

Mike and Amanda Bibby
Ruby Distributors, Viva MK

"A very passionate, motivational speaker who defiantly speaks from the heart. Satwinder's stunning book shows me that from every adversity come the seeds of equal or greater benefit. His talks are breathtaking, but his book, for me, shows his enthusiastic approach in life that really rubs off. Satwinder has a great way of showing that life is for living and to enjoy everything you do with passion."

Karim Karmali
Bronze Premier Distributor, VivaMK

"Being an avid reader, of all books I have read, this truly captures it all through the heart for MLM professionals and direct sellers. It is packed with inspirational, vital and motivating information. A book to keep revisiting to build you, to propel your business forward, to lift you in times of need as well as taking you to the next level! Highly recommended!"

Amanda Holland
Forever Living Products & Youth Coach

"WOW! What an awesome read. One of the most motivating and inspiring books we have read so far. Truly mesmerising."

Tracy and Dave Sheehan
Network Marketing coaches

"Satwinder has created an inspirational and motivational read, sharing many of his own personal experiences. His passion and energy shine through and will no doubt inspire others to turn their life around just like he has. Bouncing back from adversity many times, Satwinder is proof that a positive mindset is crucial in creating a life of success and happiness."

Adele de Caso
Network Marketing Business Coach, Author of 'Shy People Can Be Successful Too'

"This book offers a healthy wealth of solutions founded with a focused forward mindset that honours the sensitivities of the emotional body while awakening the readers to grace that is birthed from the strength of a supple, tender heart. Satwinder brings to light real-life experiences that we are faced with in a no-nonsense kind of way; offering a multitude of practical and inspirational solutions that work, when integrated into one's daily lives. His expertise is refreshing, richly enlivening and vibrantly nourishing. The assertive passion with which the amazing Sat Sagoo shows up with line for line is undeniably contagious and courageous. Thank you for leading with bravery, for sharing with kindness and for transforming with empowerment. Your leadership style is one of impeccable integrity laced with great vulnerability, and that is where we meet and connect with each other and create space for infinite growth potential."

Samantha Caroline Lavallée
National Bestselling Author of 'Beautiful Disaster' and CEO of Heart Therapy Counselling and Mentoring

ABOUT THE AUTHOR

Satwinder Sagoo is a huge ball of positive energy, projecting hope against the odds and encouraging others to overcome the odds to achieve greatness.

A network marketing leader who empowers others to discover themselves and achieve their dreams, he is also a social media motivational coach who regularly blogs on timelines to instill belief on others that they too can rise up to the hardships of life and achieve happiness.

A martial artist of nearly 30 years, Satwinder holds a black belt in Karate, a black belt in Jujitsu and is currently studying Xtreme Martial Arts, which involves fearlessly executing martial arts techniques merged with acrobatics and gymnastics. From this, he has built a consistent level of discipline in hard work and productivity to see projects through and achieve great success, even from the jaws of failure.

Satwinder's message to the world is simple...you don't have to have a huge profile to achieve great things in life, you just need belief and the determination to have what you want and also the courage to endure life's greatest hardships to see it fully though.

"By the power of truth and light,
by the soul that shines so bright,
withstand adversity's bite,
yet rise up and fight,
life shows no remorse,
So find that positive source.
and be a huge force,
No matter how hard you get hit,
never forfeit,
your life is so worth it."

MY REASON WHY AND WHO THIS BOOK IS FOR

Ever since childhood, I have always dreamt of being a huge motivational figure worldwide, with the opportunity to touch millions of people's lives and make them see that no matter how dark the darkness, there is always light… Whether you eventually see it, or whether you just light up the darkness yourself, there is always hope. When life started hurting me, it would have been easy for me to just sit in one place, freeze and let life pass me by, which would have created a devastating tragedy of not moving anywhere and achieving very little, if anything. I could have lost my house and ended up bankrupt, with no family or friends and most of all….NO SELF-RESPECT.

Instead, what I chose to do was take to social media, talk about my experiences and how I was overcoming them. It was uplifting and touching to see so many people like my status and send me messages of appreciation as I had helped them to see the light. My following just grew and grew, and it encouraged me to help more people, by putting more posts on social media. Even in the toughest of situations, I focused on the Facebook status I would add after I got through my challenges and the potential interaction it would create; this excited me like crazy! Eventually I decided I wanted to take this a step further, by extending out to a wider audience, both in this country and abroad, which brought me to writing this book.

I was 22 years old when my first major life challenge hit me. Once I got over that, I married at the age of 26, started a family and starting living a life which I thought was going to be happily ever after. It was in my early thirties that these challenges really started to come at me, and hence the era in which I truly started to discover myself. Now hitting my forties, I am using the power I have harnessed from these challenges and sharing them with you.

Anyone who has had challenges, no matter when or where or whatever their personal circumstances, will benefit from this book.

A SPECIAL NOTE FROM THE MAN OF SATTITUDE

"Rise above hardship.
Never let life throw its weight around
with you
and take away your one opportunity
to be something special."

BOOOOOOOOOOOOOOOM.....

Hello and thank you for purchasing my book!

Welcome to my crazy, yet unique and temperamental world. As we know, life throws us many obstacles of different sorts and sizes. At times, these challenges are so weary and draining that we lose the will to carry on fighting.....BUT CARRY ON AND FIGHT WE MUST.

In addition, there are times when others need our power to help them fight their own dark clouds, and being there to do that for them is a God's gift. I have often been asked the question 'If you could go back in time, what would you change?' My answer to that is absolutely NOTHING, as it is these huge challenges that define us and make us unique today. If they never happened, we would never grow and discover our true

14

power within, so it is always important to keep the fight going no matter how tough life gets for you, as it is from these grave challenges we are actually given a huge platform to go and create that special lifestyle we have always craved for. If you ever think of giving up on something, or feel your hardships in life will prevent your progress, ask yourself this question...If a holy prophet came to you right now and told you that the only condition for living beyond six months is to achieve that major goal in that time, what would you do then? You would have no choice but to embrace those challenges, simply pull out all the stops and do everything you could, by hook or crook, to achieve that goal, wouldn't you? Why do we wait for the crunch before bringing out the best in ourselves? We all have it in us at all times, no matter how hard life gets, and the time to unleash that tenacious power is NOW.

In this book, I breakdown in detail the notion of 'Sattitude' – a rare and special kind of attitude I chose to accompany me on my journey through my rocky paths in life and the source of power that gave me sheer strength and determination that helped me to relentlessly and defiantly power forward and smooth those paths down. It is also a display of my warm-hearted nature at how I reached out to others in need and waved away their dark clouds, as well as the loyalty and effort I put in to break through sheer nerves and anxiety, to achieve huge and challenging goals.

I sincerely hope you enjoy the book and attain true inspiration to move on and achieve great success in your life

Good luck!

Satwinder

WHAT IS 'SATTITUDE'?

So, we all know that attitude is your emotional response to things that happen to you in life and to people that you meet. So why have I used the term 'Sattitude'? Put simply, it is a unique burst of energy and positivity that is rarely seen, that I show on a regular basis. It involves being one of the craziest nutters alive out there, but a nutter that fuels a special kind of positivity to anyone else I get in contact with. It is, in a nutshell, being the Superman of positivity. Here's my story on this...

When adversity struck me, I started to take to social media explaining what I was going through, and putting a positive twist to each of those posts. For example, when I got stuck in traffic and didn't move, it was just as easy for me to get frustrated and crunch my face up in anger as it was for me to put my music on and dance like a raving lunatic, making other people around me who were also stuck in traffic either laugh or dance along in their car (which I actually do).

When finishing work late at night, it would have been easy to put a Facebook post exclaiming that I was 'tired' and 'had enough'. Instead I took to Facebook and did a live whilst slapping my head in super-excitement and cracking all sorts of crazy jokes.

It was just as easy to ignore strangers in need as it was to go up to them, shake their hand or give them a hug and say 'It'll be OK'. All scenarios have one thing in common...it shows me going the extra mile in my positivity helps me to appear to forget what the challenges are. It shows I am driven by happiness and my energy levels are super high. Any challenge that I encounter does not hurt me in the slightest. I see the opportunity and learning in every challenging situation. In fact, it's as if I have become best of friends with challenge and adversity...they raise me up, they never get me down.

When people saw this, they were left bamboozled by my energy and positivity levels. 'Positive attitude' was too much of an understatement for my strong positivity so many decided to give me the unique name 'Man of Sattitude', with the first bit to reflect my name, to represent my incredibly unique personality and the fact that you could only ever find that type of positivity in Sat Sagoo. Some people even thought I was a Martian as I was that crazy.

I hope you enjoy the craze and energy of 'Sattitude' that this book brings you.

PROLOGUE
WELCOME TO YOUR WORLD

Earth...our beautiful, galactic blue orb, globe of possibilities, and ball of opportunities. She houses many landscapes that form what we know as the world; a world full of many places and many routes to these places. Some routes are smooth and enjoyable, while other routes are rough and bumpy. This world also withstands the temperaments of nature, which we know as the weather. At times, it is warm and sunny and at other times, it is stormy and precarious, yet despite these huge challenges we still march on, we still breathe and the world remains unchanged and still stands in all its glory.

There also resides many species of creatures, and although forms vary, all species have two things in common – a brain and a heart. Among those species are the human race... 'US'. Many people believe we cannot change the state of the world we live in, but you can use your mind and heart to create a different world...YOUR WORLD! The world you seek to create will undoubtedly take you on many treacherous and perilous paths, yet you must find courage in accepting the things in life you cannot change. Take being stuck in a traffic jam. You cannot change the fact that there is a traffic jam but you can change how you respond to being stuck. You can choose to be annoyed or you can choose to accept and whistle a happy tune. At the same time, you can be prepared to mould the things you can change to your satisfaction.

I have had the privilege of accepting many of life's most complicated and, at times, hurtful scenarios. I have also had the privilege of sharing the magic of my fight power to others in distress... I say 'privilege' as it is these challenges and opportunities that have made me the man that I am today. If I hadn't been knocked back many times, I would never have truly discovered and created myself, and also helped others too. Every form of adversity and hardship, either imposed on myself or on others, has given me the platform to undergo change and recreate myself to a more advanced prototype of the previous person that I was, so it is for this reason that I call them privileges...after all, how do we grow if we don't come face-to-face with adversity?

Your mind and your heart are two of the most powerful weapons you will ever possess. They give you the armour to withstand heavy hits, and also the eyes to focus, the drive to move forward with such unstoppable force, and the tenacity to keep fighting for your dreams, so use them to unleash your ferocious power and achieve monumental success.

"Adversity hurts, but not as much as staying where you are and letting the world pass you by."

This book is my story complemented with my own quotes that have evolved from the consistent, positive self-talk I engaged in and kept repeating to myself time and again during my darkest hours; self-talk that drove me to stand up and believe against the almighty denial of the negative prophets brought to me by the empress of life herself. In a nutshell, this book sums up my philosophy in life... Life has its severe storms; you simply have to get on with it and learn to walk through them.

You will notice that I have put these quotes as a break in sections of my story in each chapter. That is the very moment I engaged in that self-talk when I was fighting my battles, or helping others fight theirs. What we say to ourselves or others, and when we say it, greatly affects our behaviours in that situation and hence our attitude.

One more thing I would like to mention – this is my first ever book and it took me two years to write. I had submitted a previous version called *Scripts of Power*, which was just a book of quotes. I had my ISBN and was excited to rock. However, I had a number of knock-backs. I had asked a few well-known motivational personalities to review my book and give me feedback. However, not everyone was able to respond to my request. Additionally, some of the feedback was less than encouraging. I was told that the book would not hack it and that I was not author material. My response... Sheer grit and determination to show them different. I took the book, kept the quotes in, but totally refurbished and changed it, making it more personal and inspirational.

Never let people lead you to believe that you can't do things. I am not a qualified writer, I am not an English super-literate, I don't have the faintest idea about how to sell a book or publish one, yet I did not let that stop me from writing this piece of magic. Academics go out of the window in today's world today, it's all about how well you rise up to the challenge, charge towards it and conquer your fears, doubts and limiting beliefs.

I hope the book inspires you to achieve amazing things in life, as well as rise up and be the true warrior in the challenging episodes of your life.

"My success isn't because I'm super human...
I'm just a super normal guy...
with a super big reason why!"

THE POWER OF QUOTES

Words are so much more than combinations of letters. Words are magical, beautiful and awe-inspiring. Words hold the almighty power of altering landscapes and reshaping the world. Shroud yourself with the power, magnetism and inspiration found in the quotes in this book. There is a chasm of possible difference between where you are today and where you can take your emotions and motivation. Immerse yourself and be soaked in the world of Sat's book; it has the potential to change your life!

Michael Khatkar
Writer, Author, Managing Director of VivaMK

ACKNOWLEDGEMENTS

There are so many people I am indebted to for their immense support, but in particular I would like to thank...

My amazing mum, Satwant Sagoo. You have always been my rock and support at my hardest times; I don't know how I would have coped without you being there. You are absolutely incredible and I love you to the moon and back.

My ex-wife, the mother of my children. The separation of our paths does not change how highly I regard you. You gave me two beautiful children and you are an incredible mother to them. Thank you for giving me the best gift a man could ask for.

I would like to thank Brenda Dempsey, my amazing mentor and coach, for showing me direction and helping me unveil and unleash my true motivational power. You are an absolutely amazing woman and friend to have in life.

Michael Khatkar. Apart from being the most amazing managing director, you are also an incredible mentor and motivator. You gave me guidance, direction, support and, more importantly, the big kick up the backside I needed to make this happen.

DEDICATION

I want to dedicate this book to my two amazing children. We've had some tough times together lately but no matter what, we will always be one, and together we will always ride those storms and come out on top.

I've achieved many things in life but no achievement will ever be bigger than being your Daddy and no matter what, remember that I will always love you both with all my heart and soul.

xxx

UNLEASH YOUR INNER POWER

AND BECOME A CONQUERING HERO

SATWINDER SAGOO

Filament Publishing

Published by
Filament Publishing Ltd
16 Croydon Road, Beddington, Croydon,
Surrey, CR0 4PA, United Kingdom
Telephone +44 (0)20 8688 2598
Fax +44 (0)20 7183 7186
info@filamentpublishing.com
www.filamentpublishing.com

ISBN 978-1-913192-12-9.

Printed by 4edge Ltd.

Unless stated otherwise, all quotes within the
book are by Satwinder Sagoo.

CONTENTS

OPTIMISTIC FIRE 29

NURTURED VISION. 39

EMPATHY-VALIANT COURAGE 49

SUPER WARRIOR MINDSET 59

A ★ RESILIENCE 69

TENACIOUS TROOPER. 79

TRIUMPHANT SOUL 89

INSPIRING DISCIPLE. 99

TRUSTED HOPE 109

ULTIMATE PARENT 119

DIVINE LOVER 131

ENERGETIC BRAVEHEART 145

EPILOGUE 158

FURTHER INTERACTION 163

"As a lifelong practitioner of martial arts, I'm trained to remain calm in the face of adversity and danger."

- Steven Seagal

CHAPTER 1
OPTIMISTIC FIRE

"Sometimes your inner calm is
your weapon,
and your biggest ally."

Life can really throw you off balance and can do so at the most important of times. One moment, you have your plans in place and achievement is inevitability, then all of a sudden... CRASH... it all comes down like a ton of bricks. In times like trouble, uncomfortable as it maybe, it is important that you keep a calm head. Our emotions rub off easy onto others so if we appear in a state of panic, like in a fire, others around you will panic too and may even collapse under pressure. Being calm enables you to make a more informed decision about the circumstances that lie in front of you and with consideration, you will always find a way to conquer and succeed.

"You become a peace master when you learn to control the volcano within yourself."

The first important thing here is your FOCUS. Sometimes, there can be a natural tendency to look at a whole situation as a huge obstacle with a series of sub-obstacles. It is always important to keep your eye on the end result as that is the only way you focus on solutions and make those obstacles invisible. Inn other words...

"Staying focused on the desired outcome steers you clear from the demons of calamity and interference."

It is also important to assert control over any challenge that throws its weight around with you. In Jujutsu, one of the first important rules we learn is that once we grab hold of an attacking arm or leg, it's 'Our Time' to neutralise the attack and take control of the assailant in our own way. Life's experiences are no different...when life attacks us with a challenge, we must stand up to that challenge, take control of our emotions, and focus on working hard to overcome it. The time you take to break down and curse the arrival of the challenge could be the same amount of time it takes to find the answers to it, which leads onto my next point...

Choices. Every situation we face in life, from the smallest occurrence, to the largest scenarios, gives us choice. In a job interview, we have the choice to either walk away, or be brave and have that interview. In a restaurant, we can either walk off after eating, or pay the bill. Whilst driving, we can choose to speed and be a risk to other people near the road, or we can drive sensibly and stay safe. Likewise, in facing a challenging situation, we have the choice to break down emotionally, give up and run away from that challenge, or face it head-on like a warrior.

I used to be an assistant store manager in a supermarket in Loughborough. On the Tuesday of one particular week, it was an important day. The directors and area managers were all going to assess the store for what was known as 'show and tell', meaning that all products were to be dressed and displayed as if the store was brand new...correction, the store had to be brand new. It was a key day for me as if anything went wrong – bearing in mind other stores had already done their show and tell, and were absolutely amazing, and we were one of the biggest stores in the company – my job would most likely be on the line, so the heat was well and truly on. A week's planning meant that I had my staff allocated and all my plans were in place. So, it was just a case of waiting for the delivery which would normally come at 1pm in the afternoon, so we could get stock out by 8pm as usual and dress the store down from

8pm to 10pm to perfection. It was all going to go smoothly as planned; I now had nothing to worry about and I was ready to rock…at least, I thought so anyway.

The day before their visit, my plans began to fall apart in front of me. Two staff had phoned in sick so I had serious staff shortages right from the start, which meant there was no one to break down the delivery from the cages onto the trolleys that would go out onto the shop floor. Despite this challenge, I knew that I had to find a solution to ensure that I was going to win this battle. Making a positive choice is something I can do. So I decided to amend my original plan to suit the situation I now faced. At the back door of the store, I waited eagerly for the delivery, my trolleys ready to be loaded. OOF! I get a phone call in the store…a third member, who was responsible for keeping the store tidy, phoned in sick…FANTASTIC! Surely the day could not get any worse? But it did… I received another phone call; this time from Head Office to inform me that my delivery was not turning up until 6pm, two hours before we would normally finish putting out new stock and making sure that the shop looks tidy and full. HOW INTERESTING THIS DAY WAS BECOMING!! However, it is times like this I apply what I have learned in my martial arts training. Remain calm and focused.

"Be the master and commander of your own mind; make your mind obey you for every result that you want."

I was down two members of staff from the output team, one member down tidying the store, and my delivery was going to arrive super late. This situation was exacerbated by the fact that I had members of staff who were to finish in an hour. I literally had no staff to complete my job, it felt like I was in ruins. I went into the office alone; I was shaking, I was sweating, I was having silent breakdowns, and all I could think about was the inevitability that I would lose my job. However, it was just me and my shift. If anyone was going to perform a miracle, it had to be ME. I had a glass of water and composed myself, put on my 'Me against the world' cape and said, 'LET'S GO, BROTHER'. I had to keep my thinking hat on as it was only me that could make everything happen. I had no time to panic so after I had composed myself, my focus swiftly switched to getting the job done and the urge of being the best in the entire company, always conscious of the fact that...

"The waters of your inner calm will always side with you against the flames of adversity."

It was 3pm, and the store manager, who had been in meetings all day, arrived to witness what was unfolding and became stressed. He took one look at me, and said, 'Your day is falling apart in front of your eyes, aren't you worried?' I replied, 'Yes, but we need to calm down and just stay focused; we can do this.' We had a meeting and I said the only way we can entice staff is by giving them double pay. Of course, the answer was a resounding NO as it would blow the budget. I had to lay it down. 'Look, Boss, needs must; it's either the budget, or the store and your reputation.' He was already recovering from an earlier spat with the area manager so was quite reluctant to speak to him. I took control. I simply picked up the phone in front of him and spoke to the area manager myself and explained the situation to him. After much debate and justification, I got the nod... I could call staff in on double pay... YES! I could sense victory. Belief is half the battle to winning.

How was I starting to win against all the odds? It is because I followed the golden rule that...

"If we persist in the doubt of darkness, we will eventually find the ray of hope."

BREAKTHROUGH. I spoke to my team supervisor, who was my subordinate, and asked if she could stay on until 12am for double pay – she agreed. At last, the tide was turning in my favour and I was starting to win. I asked hert hen to manage the shop floor whilst I searched around for additional staff. I spoke to all the staff who started at 2pm and asked if they could stay on until midnight on double pay and one agreed. Next, I grabbed the phone book and called staff to ask if they could work, but it just wasn't looking good; no one wanted to work. But on I kept, and eventually I managed to persuade another two members of staff to join us... I made a roll call on the tannoy asking that all available staff be deployed to my grocery department. On this occasion, I made a different decision. I decided to work reversely from normal. I would tidy the store before the delivery came.

Now I was starting to smile and things were looking great again… that is until I received an email saying the promotion change, which would normally take place on Thursday, needed to happen tonight, Tuesday… GREAT! I'd felt a premature sense of satisfaction by having the right number of staff, tidying up the store and getting out the delivery completed – now what was there left to do? As soon as I found a solution to one problem, it seemed that another would appear like magic to create more uncertainty within me. I knew the only resolve was to dig deeper. I had come this far, and giving up was not an option.

My only hope was to phone the next local store and ask for staff. I was told to wait for a phone call later. Two hours later, no phone call, my anxiety was growing. Out of the blue, three people entered the store, accompanied by their local store manager so I now had three extra staff to help complete this mammoth project, on double pay all out of the store's budget. They came as the delivery turned up. I even asked the store manager to stay behind and help with breaking down the delivery (being proactive and taking control felt cool). I was out on the shop floor and like a conquering hero with his soldiers, the delivery was soon complete. Would you believe it? At 8.45pm, the delivery was all out! Now we had over three hours to make the store look pretty. Parts of the store were already looking amazing from earlier work and just needed a general tidy. At 12am, one final inspection of the store and, oh my God, it looked spick and span – amazing!

On Wednesday morning, I received a call from the Area Manager. Oh my God, I was in trouble, surely? I nervously answered the phone and to my astonishment, I received amazing praise! The store was amongst the top three best-looking stores in the entire company. Wow, that hard work and calm attitude was so worth it!

THE KEY SATTITUDES: Composure, Determination, Focus, Conviction, Acceptance.

GROWTH FROM THIS EXPERIENCE

Every situation, no matter how stressful it may be, always requires a process of decision-making. It is important that we keep our focus on that process rather than the potential barriers in the situation, which can drive a huge sense of panic. We are all human and do indeed naturally experience emotions of panic and sometimes breakdown, as I did, but it is crucial at desperate times to compose ourselves. Time will always tick on, no matter what, so your most profitable solution is to keep exploring ways around the problem rather than surrender to it. It is the intended focus that will always determine your speed of process. If my focus had stayed on the late deliveries and panic about things not getting done in time for the big morning, I would have self-destructed and probably been given my marching orders from my position the following day. When you approach a problem in a calm manner, irrespective of size, your calmness steadies the rocking ship inside your head which means you can sail smoothly from one solution to the next and fix the problem far quicker.

By focusing on solutions only, it also enabled me to be self-motivated by seeing the potential reward and benefits of a successful operation.

SAT SIMPLY SAYS:

* Compose yourself after the alarm bells ring in your head
* Get to calmness and stay there
* Accept decision-making as a process in everything
* Act fast
* Focus on Solutions, not Problems
* Focus on the potential achievement and use that to motivate yourself

ALWAYS REMEMBER...

"Your calm is your strongest weapon against the storm."

"Most of what inspires us didn't come from a place of safety. Don't wait to feel safe. GO BE AUDACIOUS."

CHAPTER 2
NURTURED VISION

"And my mind uttered to me
'Stay here, you'll be safe.'....
But my heart whispered,
'Be brave, venture forth
and explore the magic.'

'Be careful, don't be daft or do anything stupid. Better to stay safe than take a risk.' This sound familiar? It's what my parents used to say to me all the time. You just have to love your parents for looking out for you. However, there comes a point in life where you recognise something that you just love so much and your heart dares you to make a sacrifice just to pursue that happiness. It forces you right out of your comfort zone as it realises that there is a great opportunity right in front of your eyes, but you have to sacrifice the standard form of action to grasp that opportunity. Yes, in life you have to be careful and avoid making rash, clumsy decisions, but when did life ever come with an instruction manual? You only live once, and one hallmark of living is the courage to take risks. The important thing here is not to focus on what you are losing, but what you are potentially gaining. I like to sum it up like this...

> "Opportunity is the woman that flirts with us endlessly, yet prefers to be chased and, if left alone for too long, will leave to seek pastures new."

Of course, arguably one of the biggest risks you take is walking a different path than what you have been used to for a sustained period of time. However, life is sometimes a game of trial and error, and we may have to go through that process many times to find the one passion that sets us burning alight with desire. This also involves many occasions of embracing change, feeling the fear and doing it anyway.

This leads onto my next point, the importance of decision-making...do you wait for the right time, or do you just dive into that pool of opportunity and adapt as you go along? Life is too short so we must be brave enough to make tough decisions and make them quick. Hesitation can often be an opportunity bubble-bursting needle if we hold onto it for too long. In time, that hesitation will turn into regret. So, you take a risk, walk a new path and you make big decisions. Where do you go from there? This is why it is important to have a vision. When you have that vision, it makes those tough decisions easier, and the risk associated with those decisions becomes less overwhelming because you now have a clear direction of where you want to go.

I was a department manager at Sainsbury's in the Produce department, which was bringing me a set salary each month. I was living a good normal life, I had a decent job and I was providing for my family. But deep down in my heart, I always wanted to be self-employed. I wanted to have my own customers and my own business, yet it was too risky as my income would always fluctuate up and down, and it was an expensive venture to start up my own business. That uncertainty led me to stay safe and comfortable as I didn't want to cause panic and unrest in my family. This was ultimately the problem; I was putting the feelings of others over what I thought was best and letting that hold me back. Yes, this is my family I have to look after, but I also had my heart screaming at me, 'This is not your place for success.' Why do we often get ourselves in this tense dilemma? It is because.....

"So many people find it hard to embrace change, placing too much focus on what they will lose in their current era rather than what they will gain in their new era."

However, life as a Produce Manager was starting to become quite cut-throat. As produce was a fast-moving department, I relied heavily on staff availability to constantly replenish stock, but I was always losing staff to other departments, which left me to complete every job on my own from replenishment to code-checking to wastage. As a result, I was regularly finding great difficulty in keeping up standards and I was always embarrassingly put on the spot at meetings. My managers, knowing the challenges I was facing, asked me outright in each meeting how I did in terms of sales, wastage, code-checking standards etc. I reluctantly gave my figures... low sales, unfinished code checking, high wastage... to the response of smirks, laughter, sarcastic applauses and even ridicule from the many standing in that meeting with me. I was experiencing this daily.

When I tried to explain the situation, I sometimes got responses such as, 'Because you can't do your job properly' or sarcastic 'Manager of the decade' comments. It was a bullying operation that I had to endure day in, day out. It was only getting worse when we regularly had stock availability checks from outside third parties, known as the MAC people. If stock was at the back instead of on the shelves, we would get a disciplinary for it. Oh boy, did I have to work hard to make sure everything was out, especially as my staff were always on checkouts... This is produce, for crying out loud, products literally fly out as soon as you put them on the shelves. On most occasions, stock was always on the shop floor but on a few occasions I had stock still sat at the back because staff were taken off my shop floor. I could be having lunch upstairs after a hard-working morning and still get reprimanded for it. Due to these challenges, I found myself from 'clean sheet' to 'second written warning' in no time. Two more and I would be out. I couldn't just sit here and allow this to happen so I found myself with a Big Decision to make about my future. My soul was yelling at me and telling me...

> "Don't be a prisoner to life through fear. Be a commander of life through courage."

One day, I was shopping in town on my day off, and I picked up a card from the cash point which said 'Earn Extra Income'. What was this all about, I wondered. I did more research and spoke to the person whose number was on the card. It was Kleeneze, a company that allowed you to find and develop a customer base and move as many products as possible through the use of catalogues. I could also earn a residual income through team-building. This was just too good to be true... ah wait, there was a joining fee of £165... Spam, I thought, so I took no notice and carried on shopping . However, this could also be my opportunity to not only walk a new path, but also take a direction I have wanted to take for a long time. I heard a voice in my heart say...

> "If you do not know the world
> you're stepping into,
> just keep the faith,
> compose yourself and
> make your presence felt so that
> the new world knows you."

That really got me excited about being my own boss and growing my own income.

Back at work, I was given more staff and was able to run my department smoothly again. As a result, my disciplinary record was starting to clear, but I was losing job satisfaction and beginning to feel depressed. I was going off sick, was feeling run down and ill, and wondering how much more I could take of this. One month after picking up that card, I rang up and decided to take that risk and part with £165 of my money to start up Kleeneze. This was a massive decision as I was parting with money I normally didn't have. I was paying out for bills and also clearing debts so this investment was quite audacious, given my circumstances, but I saw the value of it and decided to give it a go. I was working it around my full-time job so I was either working early morning before work or late after work.

Within two months, I was earning over £200 from Kleeneze and my customer base was growing. Within five months, I was earning £600, and this really convinced me I could make this work.

Back at work again, I was caught out again by the MAC stock-checker person…all my staff were on checkouts, and you guessed it… ANOTHER DISCIPLINARY. Once that was over and done with, I was then hit with yet another one, this time for absence. I had totally had enough of this; by this time, I had been in Kleeneze for eight and a half months.

Coincidentally, I had an accident which would funnily enough change my life. I was pulling a produce trolley and slipped and fell flat on my back, right in front of the supervisors who rushed over to help. After much examination, I was signed off sick. Luckily, I was still able to move and decided to ride the pain barrier to build my Kleeneze customer base. I was risking my health here because I could have injured myself further, but my vision was so strong, even an injured back could not stop me and I just wanted to leave Sainsbury's. I was off work for six weeks and this is when I decided that I had to make a very bold and brave move to pursue greater happiness… I decided that I was going to fire the boss and go full-time with Kleeneze just 10 months into the business. This was such a bold and risky move… I was only earning £700 from Kleeneze, and would lose nearly £1,300 regular pay. My wife panicked and my parents thought I was crazy, but I took the perspective that with more time, I could really build this business and replace my income quick.

It was hard work and for the first month I took a dip in pay but within two months, I had replaced my full-time job salary and just kept going with my business building mentality. My heart was singing away…

> "When the fire in your heart is burning bright, you must continue to add the coals of determination to keep it burning."

I became one of Kleeneze's top retailers, earning over double what my Sainsbury's pay cheque was! I now had the flexibility to spend time with kids when I wanted and also the motivation to pursue many goals and desires.

THE KEY SATTITUDES: Courage, Risk Taker, Embracing Change, Having a Vision, Excitement, Belief, Desire, Ambitious.

GROWTH FROM THIS EXPERIENCE

When people say to you 'play it safe' they are right...sometimes! But our heart is also right when it says 'be bold'. Your gut feeling will never deceive you. When we feel bad about not doing something, it is because we never listened to that voice in our heart...and 99% of the time, that voice is always right. Before I made the decision to quit my full-time job, I had many people push my focus on losing a set salary hence the income stability, and also there was no guaranteed chance of my business being a huge success. I withstood the pressure and focused more on the benefits of having those extra hours in Kleeneze and how fast I could build my business. Always take full ownership of your decisions, never let anyone else's opinions deter you from making the decision that suits them. If I focused on what others were telling me, I would still be a department manager and never have built the business that I had today. You have to be brave in life and take that step into that new path, with the faith that you know you will make the journey worth it. The only thing that will ever let you down is your lack of faith and effort. Life is too short, so if you have a dream with a strong vision, you want to pursue something that you know you are good at and have the confidence that you can make it work, then it is time to grasp that opportunity and make a success of it NOW. Doing it tomorrow, the next day, month or year will more likely become a 'not done'.

SAT SIMPLY SAYS...

* Do not put up with dissatisfaction; make that big decision NOW
* Listen to and follow your heart
* Be brave and take a risk
* Focus on the benefits of taking that new path, not the problems
* Help your decision-making by having a strong vision

ALWAYS REMEMBER...

'The bigger the vision, the smaller the risk, the easier the decision.'

"Love and compassion are necessities, not luxuries. Without them, humanity cannot survive."

- Dalai Lama

CHAPTER 3
EMPATHY-VALIANT COURAGE

> "Kindness is a type of magic that empowers the souls of the weak and the hurt."

There are just so many people out there who are hurting. Some are even in a situation of absolutely no hope and all they need is a bit of *compassion* to help and comfort them. We talk about working hard in life to achieve goals. Unfortunately, many people find themselves needing to work hard in life, just to find a bit of love. It's easy for us to give and, in most cases, it doesn't cost a penny to do so. Kindness isn't always about the value of money, it is also about the value of your heart. It is so true that…

> "We become mightier by feeding others with our tender love."

Sometimes, going out of your way to be compassionate can be right outside of your comfort zone, because you are dealing with a complete stranger and you have no idea how they will react, but going out of your comfort zone is also the opportunity to grow and become a better, wiser person. It is very easy to jump to conclusions about how people could react to you approaching them but this is where you stop for a minute and think in their shoes...how would you feel if a stranger came over to you to give words of encouragement when you are feeling down? These are rare gifts that, when found, give us a huge lift when we need it most.

I was in a convenience store buying a few snacks for myself on my lunch break, when I saw a woman and her children shopping. She looked distressed but I thought nothing of it and carried on. Then she raised her voice in annoyance at her kids getting in the way of others and I started to sense that maybe she was having a bad day. She then had a go at a member of staff because a particular brand of washing powder she always uses was out of stock. She spent ages rooted to one spot arguing and her anger was getting more heated by the minute…something was definitely not right with her. I tried to ignore the situation but my heart insisted that she needed help. I calmly bought my snacks and walked off; it was none of my business after all. Then as I was leaving the store, she broke down in tears. She needed comfort from surrounding customers and staff members; she was in a bad way. She told the staff that her husband had walked out on her last week and left her all alone to look after the household and her kids all by herself. Oh my goodness me, my heart was crying for her. This is exactly what happened to me (more on this later), and I felt so sorry for her. I just could not leave the store without giving her some sort of encouragement. Yes, I was going through my own troubles, but that should not stop me from helping anyone else in need, after all…

> "True nobleness is a tortured
> and wounded soul
> lending a warming heart and
> a listening ear to others in need
> without the need of a return."

So I walked back in, to the area where she was sitting down being comforted by staff and a few other customers. At this point, my heart was racing like mad and I was shaking...THIS WAS TOTALLY OUT OF MY COMFORT ZONE but I strongly felt this woman needed compassionate service and as there appeared to be no one else who could relate to her, I felt compelled to approach her with my words of wisdom. I could easily be told to get on my bike and mind my own business, but I shook off that anxiety in the knowledge that I was doing good for society on this occasion. So in I went, I knelt down, took her hand and said...'I feel your pain, I've been through this myself twice. I'm now happy as I realise the true value of myself, what I deserve and what I don't deserve. I know you're hurting, but please stop crying. Life is too short so as hard as it is, you just have to pick yourself off that floor, dust yourself off, and keep going like the awesome woman you are. Yes, it's hard, but the world doesn't stop for anyone and getting back up is the first step to awesomeness. Please do it for these beautiful children of yours; they are so worth it and YOU CAN DO IT!'

The whole store just went quiet and I was wondering whether this was a good idea. She then just got up, made plans to take her kids to the cinema followed by a McDonald's and booked a weekend away for them. I got a massive hug from her, with the words, 'Thank you, I needed that.' I also got a few hugs from staff members and a rapturous applause from the rest of the people in the store…

"Sometimes our willingness to reach out and help others is the only medication that will heal them."

Another experience I would like to talk about took place in an Asda car park. You are all familiar with the scenario of people approaching you in the car park asking for a bit of change as they are short to buy food. One lady approached me with her child and some cash for a bit of food. At first I thought, 'Get out of my way, I've just done my own shop. Why don't you get out there and earn some money, for crying out loud?' On the flip side, if it was me how would I feel being on the receiving end of that response? Yes, some people do play you for a fool and end up conning you, but not everyone does and there are people genuinely struggling out there…this could be one of those genuine strugglers. So, I pulled out a £10 note and gave it to her. How did I benefit from this… financially, I lost £10, but was that loss so severe as to prevent me from paying other bills? Was it going to put me in financial difficulty? OF COURSE NOT! I wouldn't think twice to spend £5 on a magazine if I really wanted it, or a McDonald's. When we go shopping, we often find we spend £5 to £10 on things we don't actually need so what's £10 to change someone's fortunes? The feeling makes you feel a lot richer too… I'd just helped a poor woman with £10. She can at least get food and drink to feed herself and her child.

> "Being a true hero is being there for people you have never met in your life as much as people you have known your entire life."

It's just so amazing what a golden heart can do for others. Had I not decided to walk back into the store, and talk to the distressed woman, how different would her attitude have been? She probably would have sunk deep into depression and perhaps even done something to herself. Had I not pulled out a £10 note for that woman in need, she would not have been able to feed her child for the night due to my selfishness. I cannot tell you how good it felt being there for a person in need. And the big thing here… IT DIDN'T COST ME A PENNY TO BE KIND…

> "Giving is one of those rare, unique gifts that doesn't require a shopping effort."

And speaking of things that don't cost a penny, I remember picking up orders from my customer base at Kleeneze. I picked up a catalogue from a regular ordering customer, but on this occasion she had not ordered. She had mentioned four weeks prior that her husband was in a very bad way. I didn't care that she did not place an order, I needed to know all was OK... It wasn't. Sadly, her husband had passed away a week earlier. I gave her a hug and stayed with her for 30 minutes just to talk to her, and I stayed and spoke to her each time I collected my catalogues from her...she needed someone to speak to and I was happy to be the listening ear each time.

To me...

> "Customers are not just business clients, they are your family and best friends for life."

THE KEY SATTITUDES: Kindness, Bravery, Empathy, Understanding, Caring

GROWTH FROM THIS EXPERIENCE

You know, each year we work hard to spend hundreds of pounds on birthdays, Christmas and other big occasions, yet for many of us it is difficult, for some reason, to spend a golden heart on the needy. Some people don't need money to make them happy, they just need a bit of love in their lives to lift them up and make them believe...you don't need a job to provide that.

When running my business, one of the biggest things for me is putting myself in my customers' shoes and understanding how they like to be treated, which is why I get so much repeat business. These scenarios I have given are no different. I put myself in the shoes of both women to understand what they were going through and what they needed to hear. If I was the woman in distress, how would the rest of my day have gone if I was not lifted up and told by another person, 'Head up, you can do this'? How would I have felt if, along with my child, I was in desperate need of cash, yet was rejected constantly and not able to feed my child at home? I didn't want anything in return, I just wanted to be the Superhero that saved the day and made people happy again. Seeing that happiness in others makes me feel like a millionaire.

SAT SIMPLY SAYS...

* Always be compassionate to people in need
* It doesn't cost a penny to have a golden heart, and it won't put you out of pocket
* Always take the opportunity to show a good side of yourself
* Put yourself in their shoes

"Always be the catalyst for positive change in others."

"The comeback is always stronger than the setback."

- Rabia Malik

CHAPTER 4
SUPER WARRIOR MINDSET

"A true warrior takes adversity
to the playground
and enjoys the fun of
a regular triumph."

We all know that life is never to be taken for granted. One moment you are riding on the crest of a wave, then the next minute we find ourselves at the lowest ebb of that wave. You can sometimes work so hard and achieve unprecedented success, but one moment of madness and it all comes crashing down. We can do two things here...we can give up, walk away into the wilderness and just leave the carnage, or we can rise up, take responsibility, clear all that carnage and build another world. The latter option is always the way to go, sadly, however there are many people who feel powerless and go for the former, hence why I was wrote this book...because I want to see you all comeback from a defeat. Giving up curbs your potential; it keeps you in the comfort of your misfortunes and everything just passes you by.

Sometimes destiny seizes your hands so tightly that you only have two choices...let it take you away and lock you in a prison cell, or drag it back your way and manhandle it so that it plays by your rules only. In other words, you must show your determination to win. Whatever happens to you, it is important to never let life's atrocities make you a victim...get up, fight back and move onwards! DEFEAT IS NOT AN OPTION! One of my big mottos in life is...

"To overcome any hardship,
you must always make sure that
you are bigger than
any big that is thrown at you."

When you get a huge knock-back in life, sometimes you can keep trying and trying with nothing to show for it, but you must be tenacious and keep going. Remember that knock-backs are actually pockets of growth and each of those pockets of growth give us a valuable lesson to prepare us better for the next attempt...NEVER GIVE UP!

At the very young age of 22, I became an Assistant Manager at a huge toy store. I did fantastically well in the interviews, passed the tests and was ready to step into the role of Store Assistant Manager. I moved stores within my local area, then I moved far south to Cambridge to run the Multimedia Department, which sold games consoles, TVs, music players, to name but a few. Things were looking fantastic, I gelled with the management team; I even got a call from the director congratulating me on some amazing sales. I was absolutely buzzing.

Then I got called up into the office by the manager for an investigation into my references. After a long interview, I discovered I had not disclosed the full information of my references and as a result, I was in breach of the terms of my contract. However unintentional this would have been, there was only going to be one outcome... DISMISSAL. I was dismissed from employment for gross misconduct. There I was, far away from home, with no job, the shame of what I had done hanging right above my head. If only I had phoned to make sure everything was accurate before delivering my application. Oh, how little errors and lack of judgements can come back to haunt you. However, as hard hit as we are, we must conjure enough power to wake up to the reality that...

> "It is only by falling that we become wiser."

So, no employment, and a dismissal to my name for gross misconduct. I was absolutely devastated! But I refused to accept that I had no chance of getting a job at the same level. It was time to start an incredible comeback! Sometimes you search and search hard in the darkness but if you are determined enough, you eventually either find some light or light up a torch yourself. I realised that I had to get up and fight on to get myself back up the level of retail store management. Yes, it was going to be mighty hard with a dismissal to my name, but who said there were set consequences that you had to accept? I went on the Internet back at home, applying away for jobs. I had to go back down the ranks of shop floor assistant and temping to keep money coming in. I was back at the job centre applying for job after job. I felt sick to my stomach…all that hard work to get to where I was, and then one silly thing undid all that and sent me crashing down again. I was getting rejected left, right and centre, no one was prepared to accept me... But was I about to let that stop me? NEVER! This was all on me and I was determined to get myself back to store management.

By this time, I had applied for about 50 jobs and not one was giving me any hope. I even had to claim Jobseekers' Allowance, having not got a job for three months...BUT I DIDN'T GIVE UP AND ON I FOUGHT! I had to take responsibility and make a change to get better results, so I sought professional CV help, explained my situation and how I wanted to improve my application form skills. I paid £30 for this service, money I didn't have, but it was starting to slowly make the difference. My mindset was changing for the better and I was starting to ride on the mentality that…

> "Achievements are far more worthwhile when they are born from trauma and fight."

After a further month of temping and applications, finally I had a response and I was getting interviews. At first it was tough telling them the truth about my last employment, and I was unsuccessful each time. The apprehension when telling them was just too much to take, but I just knew that there was a way around this and it was my responsibility to find that way. I spoke to a lady at the job temping department and explained the situation. Following the advice given, I applied for more jobs...I just didn't quit. My tenacity was paying off and I was getting more interviews. I was told by the temping jobs clerk to just be honest, with no fear, and put it forward as a learning experience, which is exactly what I did. This is where we need to become warriors, because...

"True warriorship is…
laughing when you want
to cry, being a 'yes' habitant
in a 'no' residence, having
courage when you feel fear,
marching forward when you are
wounded, achieving success
in the face of the impossible."

So, for my next three interviews, all for manager roles, one in a department store, another two for supermarket chains, I did exactly what the clerk had suggested and got to the final stage on all three applications… oh, I was feeling fantastic and the momentum was rolling. Just the last hurdle to conquer…which I knew I would!

Two weeks later, I found myself in store assessment role plays, where I had to imagine I was part of the management team and had to do a store assessment. I actually enjoyed this; who doesn't enjoy action! So I fed this back to the interviewers at the end on all three applications. Two days later, I got two job offers out of three for an assistant manager role, exactly the same position that I had been dismissed from...THE COMEBACK WAS COMPLETE! I was absolutely ecstatic! Six months of pure hurt and hell starting out right at the bottom and getting one job rejection after another, yet I believed that I could still become an assistant manager again and just kept on wielding my sword. Persistence pays, and boy did it pay off for me. It appears that I needed those challenges after all. In fact, it is true that...

> "To succeed, I fell in love with hardship. I loved her so much, I got down on one knee, proposed to her and made sure I wore the trousers."

THE KEY SATTITUDES: Taking Responsibility, Tenacity, Positivity, Determination, Defiance

GROWTH FROM THIS EXPERIENCE

The challenge of losing your job is one of the toughest scenarios to be in. Your first instinctive thought is how you will pay your bills, how you will keep your house, how you will be able to look after your family. Our focus on the potential losses is so strong that we totally forget about how we can actually grow from these losses.

Again, it boils down to the thing that I value so much in my life...'NEVER GIVE UP'. Yes, I was down and out for a day or so, I had my emotional breakdowns and feelings of shame. I had to start right back at the bottom and in addition had the weight of a dismissal to my name, but I was not prepared to put my life on hold. I had to take responsibility for my actions and success so I had to plan hard and fast. It was also important that I took this as a big learning experience and use it grow. It was important for me to show true grit and determination in the face of many knock-backs and maintain that tenacious spirit to achieve what appeared initially as an impossible goal. Remember...nothing is impossible, it's your attitude to challenges that defines how possible things are.

SAT SIMPLY SAYS...

* Don't stay down for long; work quickly on your comeback plan
* Accept that you will have to take a few steps back before moving forward
* Use your initiative to research and take the right action
* Always show the determination to win
* Believe in yourself, show tenacity and come back stronger

ALWAYS REMEMBER...

"Always be bigger than any
big thrown at you."

"Defeat is a state of mind; no one is ever defeated until defeat has been accepted as a reality."

- Bruce Lee

CHAPTER 5
A ★ RESILIENCE

I spoke in the last chapter about not taking life for granted, and how you can suddenly find yourself at the lowest ebb of your wave, but oh my goodness, can life do a number on you or what?! Life can seriously paralyse you and knock you right down to your knees. It can grab you by the throat, press you to the wall and choke you. This is where the true test of our character really comes into play. The true measure of a person is always what he/she does when his/her back is up against the wall. Of course, when the situation actually hits you, it is not the most pleasant feeling in the world as you are overcome by a number of negative feelings including sadness, stress, loss of hope, fear, anxiety, anger and revolt, to name a few of many. However, when we look into the distance and see ourselves at the other end of the tunnel, we realise the worth of what we go through and live to tell the tale to many of how we overcame it and became stronger than ever. After all...

"How do you discover your true strength and character without having yourself tested against the most elite of life's challenges?"

Of course, when life knocks you down, it puts your resilience to the test. Resilience is powerful. When we are resilient, we are such an unstoppable force that even when things appear to be going against us, we always find a way to win. There is one episode of resilience that has inspired me so much... the Champions League Final between Bayern Munich and Manchester United In Barcelona. Bayern Munich took the lead in the 6th minute. They were stubborn and did not let United through on goal. Two minutes to go to the end of the match and Man Utd finally, after so much persistence, scored the equaliser and then scored the winner in stoppage time. That is resilience for you! That is the true hallmark of never giving up. Life is the same...no matter how many things go against you, be resilient...BE A WINNER!

Another important factor to consider is this...NEVER FORGET HOW AWESOME YOU ARE! Sometimes, there can be a tendency to look at others who are deemed to be "happier" and "living a better life". As I have said before, life never came with a rulebook so there is no set rule for being happy. Happiness is what you make it but also remembering that you are awesome in your own way. For example, I used to hang out with friends who were big and muscular. I'm quite slim and don't have the physique that they do, yet I am faster and more flexible than they are. Also, when you are going through hardship, many 'friends' will try to advise you and insist you follow what they say. What they are actually doing is preying on your vulnerability. Remember, no one knows better than you; you know what is best for your situation and you are more than capable of taking your own steps to resolve your problems. To summarise this paragraph, always maintain your self-esteem, and never let anyone take that away from you.

It is important, whilst fighting hardship, to stay as motivated as you can. This is sometimes easier said than done but the beauty of life is that you can be very creative. Find unique ways that will keep your spirits high and ensure you remain focused on your goals.

I was to start 2016 in one of the most precarious situations that I could ever imagine. I was:

* 3 months behind on my mortgage
* 4 months behind on my council tax
* £750 in arrears on my water bill
* £1,200 in arrears on my gas and electric bill
* £950 in arrears on my phone bill

AND:
* My TV licence was cancelled as I could not keep up payments
* My car insurance was cancelled each month as I was always late with payments,
* My bank balance always on £0 and sometimes in my overdraft as I just had no money to cover it. On a few occasions, I went as far as £150 over my limit
* Direct Debits were being cancelled left, right and centre

I had inherited this from a marriage split-up and a crazy, brave decision to maintain the house alone. I had bailiffs come to my house on two occasions and was very close to losing my home, having received two separate letters from my mortgage company telling me repossession of my house was about to commence.

On top of that, I was also rejected by my then-girlfriend who had given me the love that I had missed for so long in my life. Family members gathered together to ridicule my decision to keep the house, told me that I would not be able to keep it for much longer, and insisted that I be wise and take their advice. When I rejected their advice, many stopped talking to me. I went deep into depression, crying myself to sleep each night, not getting enough sleep, growling at my family and just not acting myself...yet, deep down, I also felt a new urge of power, a power that made me realise that I could really turn this around and be happy again. Many celebrities have even committed suicide being in huge financial difficulty but for me, it wasn't just about finding that light bulb moment...IT WAS ABOUT LIGHTING A TORCH MYSELF! I was looking at everyone whilst out...holding hands with their partners, playing together with kids, going out and enjoying a lot of love and romance. I realised that should be me. This is the life I should be enjoying because I know I am so worth it. So, as broken, emotionally bruised and battered as I was, I picked myself up and really worked like a Trojan with my business. It was life and death; I simply had no choice but to make it happen. I set a plan for when I wanted to clear my debts and focused on my own personal development...

"It is not the consistency in your glories that set you out from the rest; you are truly created from the consistency in how you rise up following on from life knocking you down."

So out I went, working six days a week, constantly putting my catalogues out to existing customers and also working to find many new customers in the process. I started off fairly slow as the process was only just kicking in. I spoke to many of the top retailers and motivators in the Kleeneze network, as well as friends who had been in debt like I was experiencing.

I even did small, unique things. They say that phones are a huge distraction but I never could imagine how they could also become the biggest life motivators. I saw inspirational clips from my favourite *Transformers* movies. I then found an online YouTube to MP3 converter on Google so I downloaded my favourite clips onto my phone using this MP3 converter, then I used a ringtone converter to snip out the bit that I wanted and used that for my phone's ring and notification tones. I used a *Transformers* clip ringtone for notification for Facebook, Facebook Messenger, Instagram, Hotmail, Yahoo mail, Gmail, the weather, astandard texts, and so on, so each time my phone went off, it would always be to something truly inspiring that increased my drive to win. It was a very unusual form of motivation, but who cares, we must remember that…

"There are no set rules about how you live your life… After all, we were born with a creative mind from which we can set our own unique rules and make unique magic happen."

I also used images of my favourite *Transformers* character, Optimus Prime, as a screensaver to remind myself of who I see in the mirror each time I look into it...

Each time I looked at my phone and saw the image, it reminded me of the type of leader I really aspired to be. Optimus Prime symbolises warrior spirit, the ability to stand tall in the most stellar of adversities, the ability to stand by one's principles, be brave and stand out from the crowd. It also symbolises the ability to think with a wise mind, to educate the wrong whilst being humble to the right and, most importantly, TO NEVER, EVER GIVE UP.

This really sharpened up my vision and increased my drive to win and make a success from this challenge...

> "Vision is the ray of light that shines through the darkness of doubt."

Going on Facebook and speaking about my achievements also helped as I knew I could inspire a few others out there in a similar scenario. Eventually, around April time, I started to see a difference and I had already cleared two of my arrears. This freed up more cash to snowball other arrears...I was making progress, and I was feeling good about myself again. This was me at my creative best. I had found unique ways to stay motivated and my drive for success grew very quickly.

"Keep working at your goals, no matter how hard it may be, no matter how gloomy the situation you are in. It may hurt and feel uncomfortable at times, but it will hurt 10 times more if you look back with the regret of doing nothing."

In August 2016, my Kleeneze business really took off. I had my highest ever personal turnover and hit GOLD distributor level, with a pay cheque of nearly £3,000. Gold was the first milestone level to reach in Kleeneze and it meant we would walk the stage at a national showcase event, cheered by over 5,000 people. I repeated my income achievements month after month. By November 2016, I had cleared all my outstanding debts, and started ticking off one treat goal after another, which included:

* Buying a £300 laptop outright with cash
* Treating myself to new clothes and shoes, amongst other things
* Travelling to Newcastle, now I was able to afford the hefty train fare without worrying about money
* Treating my kids to more days out
* Spending £500 on Christmas presents, which included a brand new Xbox and five games

In five months, I had earned £15,000, cleared all my arrears, and had a healthy bank balance. I was feeling extremely proud of myself…

THE KEY SATTITUDES: Confidence, Self-trust, Productivity, Character, Resilience, Creativity, Self-Esteem

GROWTH FROM THIS EXPERIENCE

No matter how tough life is, never lose focus of your dreams and goals, and never ever give up on yourself. I was in a near huge loss situation; I could have ended up with no shelter. I could easily have just given up. I could have committed suicide so that no one could chase me, but I chose instead to stand tall and keep fighting…I WAS WORTH IT! I established my big reason WHY, which was my kids and the potential to really stick it to those doubters that laughed at me. I did unique things that kept me motivated and kept me smiling. No matter how hard a situation is, you must always, always believe that you can get out of it.

SAT SIMPLY SAYS...

* Never give up on yourself, even when you feel like it
* Show character and always be resilient
* Before you reflect on others' happiness, remember how awesome you are first,
* Set a plan and work it like crazy
* Be creative and do unique things that keep you motivated
* Don't let anyone bully you into following their lead. You can win on your own!

ALWAYS REMEMBER...

"Motivated resilience is the greatest form of invincibility."

"Endurance is not just the ability to bear a hard thing, but to turn it into glory."
- William Barclay

CHAPTER 6
TENACIOUS TROOPER

"Even with a wounded body, a pierced soul and battered emotions, the soldier still marches on."

PLEASE NOTE: I am not a medical professional so the information that I offer should NOT substitute medical advice. If you get seriously injured, please seek medical attention and advice immediately. It is important to understand your body and your limits.

Sometimes, achievement of your goals needs to happen through physical pain and endurance. You may have strict deadlines that you need to meet and out of nowhere, you get thwarted by an accident or injury that tries to slow your progress down. This is when you dig deep into your soul and remember your reason 'WHY' you are doing what you are doing, even when you are sick, tired or hurt. What is it about what you do that makes it worth going through the pain barrier? You must also reflect on the reason why we need to show that endurance...will going to hospital cause you a huge financial loss? How much does your family rely on you to provide for them? Is there a way you can work with the injury or discomfort?

Once you establish your reasons 'WHY' for needing to endure difficult situations to achieve your goals, you must stay focused on those goals. That focus must be so laser sharp that you even forget about the difficult situation you are in, YOU JUST MARCH ON! Life is a game, we play the game to win, right?

Once you establish that focus, along with your reason 'Why', you must be persistent in stubbornness... "No, I don't care how much it hurts, or how uncomfortable this is, I must follow through and complete my goals. I must win." The more persistent you are, the more comfortable your discomfort becomes, and bigger your will to win also becomes.

I am a crazy type of motivated guy, because the truth is…

"I love obstacles. I can show off my superhuman strength when I break through them."

It was a dry Tuesday morning and I went out to collect my catalogues. I started at 9am and had an order to put through by 1.15pm so as you can imagine, I was darting around like Lewis Hamilton in his Mercedes F1.

Everything was going great; my order levels were high, I was energised and my pulse was absolutely racing with excitement. I arrived at a set of flats where I had left two catalogues. I buzzed the trade button and got in. I picked the catalogue up from downstairs, BING! A £26 order. Then up to the top of the stairs, a huge £41 order. I was so excited and just could not contain myself…then a disaster struck. I missed my footing eight steps from the bottom and ended up falling to the ground awkwardly on my right foot…OMG the pain was excruciating! It seriously felt like my foot had come off inside my skin. I was writhing in pain for minutes on end and got my phone out ready to call the hospital. I just couldn't get up and walk…or so I thought. After much mental deliberation, I pulled myself up and slowly put my foot on the ground, but I just could not put any pressure on it… "No, sorry, I will not be beaten" I uttered to myself.

I still had a round to complete and 65 catalogues left to collect. I had stay focused and I was ready to do it through the pain barrier as my goals mattered to me far more than just resting. So I hopped into the car (yes I could still drive, but only just), got myself to the nearest pub and asked for an ice pack. After receiving one, I sat in my car for 10 minutes icing my foot. I had two hours to collect 65 catalogues – I was really going to do it! I didn't care about my injured foot; my love for my business and desire to finish the job was far greater. It is so easy in that situation to give up, however it is so true that...

> "The true strength of any character is when you are busted, sick, tired or hurt, yet you still march on with the determination to finish the job."

After 10 minutes of the ice pack, I finally found a way to move. Yes, I only had one foot but move on, I did. Using the heel of my now hugely swollen foot and loosening up my shoes, on I went. As painful as it was, I just had to get those orders in for 1.15pm. I didn't have time to feel sorry for myself, I had to simply just get on with it!!

After struggling along, it was 12.45pm, and I had 30 minutes to log £721 worth of orders, so t I tapped away in panic on my phone. I even had the signal die on me and had to wait a few minutes for the phone to reset. I was starting to have doubts, but type away I did and, hey presto, 1.14pm the order was through... JUST. I was so proud of this achievement, I took to my group chat and shared my experience. I received numerous texts and phone calls of how amazing a feat that was and how I inspired a few people in their team who had more permanent pains that restricted their movement....

> "The good thing about working through extreme hardship is that you live and inspire the world around you."

I would also like to tell you about another serious incident that happened. It was a Monday night at Jujitsu class at Penkridge Leisure Centre, and we were all training on the hip throw, known as O Goshi. I was the first in the circle of attackers. Bang, throw, bang, throw, one after the other, I was really enjoying this... Until I got to my final attacker, ALL 16 stone of him! But I was so buoyed by my progression at this point, I didn't put my hip through for the throw with this guy, so I ended up walking and carrying him a distance then click.... THERE GOES MY KNEE!

I was writhing in pain. My knee cap had popped out and was right on the other side of my knee socket! I had a 150-book blanket drop and 80-book customer base to collect the following day, so no, I couldn't afford to lay in hospital doing nothing. I grabbed my knee cap, weathered the pain and discomfort then CLICK, put it back in place! I was able to get up and walk again but, oh my goodness me, I had a knee swollen to the size of a mini football! Not to mention also that my knee cap was not properly fused to the socket. It was even painful to drive my car, but I had to get home so I took some painkillers, ice-packed for five minutes, then drove home. I wasn't even thinking about the severity of the injury, I was just uttering to myself that I had a big drop tomorrow to collect. I woke up the next morning and yes, my knee was absolutely causing me pain. There was a blanket of snow outside so the odds were really against me here...but I refused to surrender...

"The most debilitating and excruciating injury is staying down when you know in your heart you can keep going."

I ate my breakfast then got into my car and into my area. And no, I didn't get phased by walking on the snow, and the possibility of falling over and really breaking my knee. It was a long seven hours of slow walking but £612 orders later, I was back home and another big order went through.

That was to be one of a few nasty sports injuries I was to suffer. The next one, due to the same sport, was to be my shoulder. One Friday night, we started the class doing break falls and we started with forward rolls, but seniors were to do it over a chair. I went first so over I went, my usual confident self.... Then up I got to the most excruciating pain on my right shoulder. I had left my arm dangling down and instead of fully rolling over, I rolled downwards and popped my shoulder out of the collarbone. I had to hold my arm in position as it was just so painful. I couldn't even steer my car so had to leave it with my instructor. I was raced to the hospital, totally scared of moving my arm. I had an X-ray which showed the shoulder bone slightly out of place. I came out of hospital in a sling and was told to not do a thing for weeks and to go back for a check-up straight after those few weeks were up...oh wait, I had a 315-book blanket drop to collect in two days.

After a very uncomfortable night's sleep, I decided to sit downstairs and rest. I just couldn't take this anymore. I didn't just want to stay in and rest, I wanted to build my business. Off went the sling and I started moving my arm and shoulder slightly. It was hard at first but I kept at it and by midday I was able to put more movement onto it. I started doing half shoulder rotations forwards and backwards, and the movement was actually starting to ease up the pain a little. I then got into the car and I could actually drive. I no longer needed a sling, I could move my arm, rotate my shoulders a little, and drive. The following day I got up, still in pain, though it was better than the previous day, loaded up my car and collected my 315 catalogues, the shoulder bag pressing onto my bad shoulder to keep bones intact. Would you believe it, £326 orders came in, and I was just over the moon and relieved…

"The reason I am mad enough to carry on regardless, go through huge pains and discomfort, is because it would be 10 times more painful watching others achieve their goals before me."

In life, it's what we focus on that determines what happens to us. In all three scenarios, I could easily have given up and gone to hospital to just lie there and earn nothing. I would have missed out on many sales opportunities from my catalogues. My 'Why' on each occasion – to log those orders in time, to be a loyal and trusted distributor to my customers, and earn income to support my family – was so strong that nothing could offset my focus on my sales goal. My endurance, laser sharp focus and persistence, coupled with my reasons 'WHY', dissolved my distress and helped me over the line.

THE KEY SATTITUDES: Endurance, Persistence, Focus, Doggedness, Having a Strong Reason 'WHY'

GROWTH FROM THIS EXPERIENCE

Before I go on here, it is important for me to emphasise that I am not suggesting for one second everyone should keep going when they are seriously injured. Everyone is different… we all think differently, react differently, have different levels of strength, express emotions differently, and have different philosophies. This is not a 'one size fits all' world and you must at all times, even if you feel you can ride your injuries, seek medical advice at all times. However, I did learn the hard way that sometimes your best doctor and specialist is YOURSELF. I found regular movement a very quick healer. When I used to get up every single morning during my injury periods, boy did the pain scream out at me, but as I moved the muscles and joints throughout the day, the pain eased and movement was a little easier. It was the movement on all occasions that helped heal the injuries quicker. My ankle injury healed in four weeks and I was actually jogging after two weeks. My knee injury healed up in five weeks and I was jogging after three weeks. My shoulder injury eased up in just under three weeks. The endurance was developing me into a self medic. It helped me understand my body better and how I can best deal with physical challenges.

Having the focus helped me to see past those injuries and move forward, and being persistent in the pursuit of my goals kept me motivated with belief that I could collect plenty of orders and put in a big order before the deadline time of 1.15pm.

SAT SIMPLY SAYS...

* Find ways to work with any injury or discomfort you may have
* If it doesn't paralyse you and you can withstand a bit of pain, keep moving the affected limbs
* Don't let the hospital take you away from your dreams unless, of course, it is an emergency
* Stay focused at all times
* Stay motivated by being persistent

ALWAYS REMEMBER...

"A strong focus destroys all obstacles in sight."

"Every setback is a set-up for a comeback. God wants to bring you out better than you were before."

CHAPTER 7
TRIUMPHANT SOUL

"The true seal of unbreakability is gained when you take your brittle and vulnerable soul and hold yourself together as you travel through tormenting winds of adversity."

It's not just things that can break you up, it is also experiences with people, the most common being a marriage or relationship break-up, or a break-up with your best friend. This is where you truly have your eyes opened up as to the real people who will stand by you and those who want to drag you down. It also enables you to discover who you are and understand your true support circle.

At the time, it is painful having to let go of people who are either close to your heart or a huge part of your life, but in time you accept it and realise that this was in fact the biggest blessing you could ever have asked for. To achieve our goals in life, we only need people who will support our every movement, not people who will eventually reject us once we move out of their zone. It is always important to remember that...

"Our truest allies are always those that stand with us at our worst, not just at our best."

It is also important to take a different perspective...yes, an end to any close relationship is painful, but is it healthy to let go and move on, or hold onto it? When picking up a rose, do you pick out a wilted one and hold onto the thorns, or do you throw it away and pick up a nice, pretty rose? Losing a relationship can grow you as a person and set you up for even greater happiness later. We have to be willing to learn from the mistakes of your previous relationships and become a wiser person from those lessons.

In November 2013, right before our kids were due to have the most expensive Christmas ever, I learnt that our marriage of 10 years could no longer continue. Now, before I go on, I just want to say how amazing the mother of my kids is. She is a true, true legend and a testimony to how good mothers should be. She is an amazing mother to my two beautiful kids; she is sweet and adorable, which is why this was the most heartbreaking moment that I was to experience, for my kids were so excited about this Christmas. They were talking plenty about how they saw happy families, yet how could I bring myself to tell them that their amazing, loving mummy and daddy were no longer to be? These are things you never want to experience but sometimes you have to accept that things do have to come to an end, and it is through no fault of either of the parties. That is change for you; it can hit you so suddenly and most definitely very hard.

I took the tough decision to keep quiet over Christmas for the happiness of my kids and also for the sanity of my father-in-law who was blind and had also had a triple heart bypass two years before. What consequences would occur if he were to know? I didn't want to be responsible for anything serious. We agreed to stick it out together until I built my business large enough to take on the house myself. I thought at the time this was a hugely crazy idea but surprisingly we stuck it out, along with a few ups and downs, but the arguments were a lot smaller in both amounts and intensity than before. The kids were happy and it was actually going OK. We then sat down on Saturday 19th June discussing what the future would hold. There were a few disagreements but the conversation ended amicably and we carried on.

However, when I woke up the following morning, on 20th June 2014, on a wave of ecstasy as I was ready to take the kids to the Air Show that morning, which we had both agreed on, I woke up to the horror of discovering wardrobes and cupboards emptied out, the car gone and three letters left on my table. My then-wife had eloped with the kids to live with her new partner! It was easy for me to feel bitter about this, but she was never to blame. If anything, I felt really sorry for her…the fact that it took our marriage for her to realise who she truly was and she stuck it out for 10 years…that is why she is amazing. It takes big experiences to understand ourselves better and although this was heartbreaking for me, having lived with her for 10 years of my life, I had to let go and accept that this was a better way forward for both of us. The great thing about it was that she only moved a few minutes down the road so she had thought about me too. I actually felt lucky and thankful that she thought about me in this way as most exes will move as far away from their former partners as possible, restricting their access to their children. She did not and that is what made her a good mother to our kids.

However, despite the close proximity in distance, getting up on my own with no kids to cuddle was hard and painful. I had reached a huge low; I was depressed, angry; I was self-harming and giving myself concussion., I even knocked back neat shots of Bacardi now and then, this was not me at all...but then it finally dawned on me. This new life was my responsibility now and I had to live it, whether I liked it or not. I simply had no choice...

"They say you can choose your friends and your family, but the one thing you can never choose in life is the dawning on you of change. Friend, family or foe, it stays with you forever."

It was to get tougher. Four months later on 18th October, two days after what would have been our 11th anniversary, my brother got married. The emotions inside me were all over the place, watching happy families all around me with their partners and kids... I had no one. Although my kids were there with me, I had no partner to dance with on the few couples' dance songs. My 4-year-old daughter was angelic enough to take me by the hand and dance with me instead. I was broken, I was hurt, and I wanted to cry, especially when the vows were exchanged between my brother and his wife, but I dared not ruin the occasion for my brother so I decided to swallow my hurt and smile instead. I cancelled my original plan of going back home after the marriage ceremony, and decided to stay behind and party with the rest of the family. I was proud of myself as I showed amazing strength. No wife...but so what? I had my kids and the support of everyone there...it actually made me feel special. No matter what or who, as long as you are surrounded by positive and supportive people, that is all you need.

The following day, I woke up with a total change of heart and decided not to allow life to control how I felt. I wanted to control my own emotions and fate. I actually had many relatives and friends on that day commending me for my bravery and positive attitude, after all I had been through. No matter what strikes us in life, we must wield our sword and battle on, no matter how wounded we are. We must be brave to just accept change and walk our new paths, for if we stop walking we can never find those little golden treasures that create the new 'us'.

THE KEY SATTITUDES: Acceptance, Understanding Your Support Circle, Self-discovery, Perspective, Strength

GROWTH FROM THIS EXPERIENCE

Adversity is always waiting in the wings for you. It is something that you just cannot avoid. When it strikes, you will be down on our knees for a very long time. Even when you get up, you will be wounded for a long time, but having a positive perspective and being accepting of the situation does help to ease those wounds. Going back to the very first sentence in my introduction...Earth, our beautiful, galactic blue planet that never stops spinning. You have to either run along with it, or risk being left so far behind that you will never be able to catch up.

I was obviously in bits when my marriage break-up happened; however, the voice deep inside me was talking to me. 'Sat, whatever happens is for the best. You have done nothing wrong so it is time to let go and start over.' For me, this was another shot at life, to rejuvenate myself and take a different direction...it was time to discover a new 'me'. It was the harsh reality that I had forced myself into a relationship that I really shouldn't have in the first place. I was always more concerned about my ego of being a married man and how much a break-up would hurt my pride, and how would it make me look in front of my children. But to move forward, I just had to let go of that and find pastures new. I had to adopt a new attitude to help me here...

"Never be ashamed of a traumatic and stained past. Sometimes, walking those hard, rough paths is your only passport to true greatness."

94

I was nervous about having Christmas alone. Watching happy families having fun, watching films of happy families; it was breaking my heart. However, in time, being alone turned into a huge strength for me. It helped me find myself and enjoy life in my own unique ways. Christmas is about happiness, right? Why do we constantly attach Christmas happiness to just having a whole family? It is simply WHAT YOU MAKE IT, as long as you are happy. I had many friends and family whom I always communicated with, left inspiring posts for me, had many social media laughs with; had cakes and cookies; played all day on my Xbox – that was my Christmas and I loved it… It was because I created my own unique Christmas happiness, all thanks to being single and alone.

When I was left alone in my house and I had all those debts and arrears mounting up, the one thing I never lost was my focus. I knew what my business could do for me with effort so I set forth and really went for it all guns blazing. I set regular goals, spoke to my creditors on a regular basis, worked extra days, and kept myself motivated. It's that passion and energy that got me through and enabled me to miraculously keep a roof above my head, and clear all my arrears.

SAT SIMPLY SAYS...

* Following a hard experience, use the time to travel a road of self-discovery
* Accept that certain things happen for a reason and use them as a platform to grow a new lease of life
* Use the hurt as your strength to focus
* Take time to measure up your support circle; take negative people out of your life
* Always show the lion spirit and bounce back

"Every pain of life is a unique blessing for an even greater happiness later in life."

"Blood, sweat
and respect.
First two you give.
Last one you earn."

- Dwayne Johnson

CHAPTER 8
INSPIRING DISCIPLE

"Dedication is the binding of
your soul to your passion."

You discover within you an amazing talent and it becomes everything to you. It becomes the first thing you think of when you get up and the last thing you think of before you go to bed. During the day, you breathe it, eat it, see it, fantasise over it, dream it and everything associated with it. It is literally another organ inside your body. You practice it every minute of the day and you just cannot stop getting better at it. That is what you call true commitment.

Being a dedicated disciple is also about having a strong mindset. Some people will go out of their way to ridicule what you commit yourself to and even tell you to stop doing it... yes, of course they are only caring for us and have our best interests at heart, right??...WRONG! Get rid of these clowns. If they really cared for you, they would always encourage you to keep going and follow your heart's desires. You may also have physical restrictions. Having a strong mindset is about overlooking your physical restrictions yet still achieving the same greatness as others. Nicholas Vujicic suffers from tetra-amelia syndrome, which means he was born with no arms and legs, yet his main hobbies are fishing, painting and swimming. Jessica Cox, who is armless, flies a plane with her feet. If these guys can do it, why not you?

Whether it is singing, dancing, stunts or something more corporate such as customer service, if you feel you have a gift of something, get out there and manifest that gift to the world. This is a true personal expression of who you are and what you represent. Make it special for yourself and others, follow your heart, and embrace it as your own. When you do something that you fall in love with, it is not a chore, it is a passion, and following that passion is about using your initiative to make things happen and bring that magic out from within.

Since the age of 12, I have been dedicated to the life of martial arts. I started karate after being heavily bullied at school... I was always picked on, ridiculed, getting beaten up either in school or outside school. For me, martial arts was not just learning how to fight, it was also about building self-confidence, belief and self-esteem. It was about seeing the things I once thought were not possible and reaching for the stars to achieve them.

One of the big physical obstacles I had in training was that I have heavily inverted big toes which also causes the second toe to overlap the third toe. I couldn't run as fast as many other students and I couldn't properly connect any front kicks whatsoever, and yet front kicks were one of the first and most important techniques I had to execute for gradings. Also, my posture was not as taut as it should be and I could not do foot sweeps either as this would hurt my big toe bone. But I soldiered on and I trained twice a week without fail. I was extremely nervous when I took my first grading as I feared that my inverted toes were going to hold me back on a few techniques, yet despite those anxieties I took that grading and

I passed with flying colours. I found a different way to connect with my front kicks. In life, there is no such thing as 'no way', YOU FIND A WAY! After eight years of pure dedication and working around that challenge, I achieved my black belt at the age of 20.

However, things then hit a brick wall. The association I was training with was shrinking fast and I had no means to move forward with my training. The once mighty adults' class was now becoming a kids' class and I just could not continue like this. I decided I needed a new organisation to progress which I found and immediately I upped my training to three times a week, then five times a week. Now it was getting interesting. I had friends and family constantly telling me that I was overdoing it and that I was not leaving room for the most important things in life. A few even insisted that I quit but in spite of their criticisms, I carried on training to my desire. Why should I give these people the satisfaction of quitting? I was neither born to be told what to do nor heal the insecurities of others by joining them in their crowd. This is my life; I need to own it.

Having joined my new karate association, I was settling in well and learning many new things, both in terms of techniques, exercises and about myself as a person. However, I was to encounter a few challenges caused again by my inverted toes. We did a lot of bag work and to do a powerful reverse punch, I had to turn onto my big toe which I just could not do easily. I had to find a way to get onto that toe as this was a more dogged 'no mess' style class. Also, I had to now do jump kicks and jumping high was extremely difficult to nearly impossible, as I needed the flex in my toes in order to do so, which was impossible. My instructor told me, 'Sat, what would you do in a real fight? Would you have time to complain, or just fight?' That got me thinking and immediately I looked at finding ways around my challenges. I had personal training with my instructor who showed me a way to execute techniques around my physical challenges. When I first started executing them, they were way out of my comfort zone and they absolutely hurt. I nearly bowed down to the high physical demands and gave up, but I could not let this beat me. With much perseverance, training and encouragement from my amazing instructor, I prevailed and was starting to execute techniques like never before… I was finally prevailing against my limitations! Bearing in mind I could not even jump up an inch, I was now executing techniques like this…

I had always dreamt of doing high flying techniques like the ones you see in the movies, also known as extreme martial arts, and I had finally achieved that by learning to see beyond my physical limitations and realising that the only limitations are the limits you place on yourself. We must always remember that…

> "Dedication is pledging your soul
> to the order of your heart."

On the page opposite are some of my favourite moves I am doing at the age of 37, with heavily inverted toes. It shows that age is just a number; it is all about how you look after yourself and believing that you simply can. In other words...

> "Don't let your physical restrictions
> suppress your freedom of talent."

At age 23, I moved to London having just got a new job as an assistant manager... Oh my, how on earth was I going to keep up my training so far away? Again, people were questioning my choices. I was told that I should cancel training altogether as I'll never find another club that will teach the same type of karate. But I was already a black belt and one of the things I learned was to use my own initiative after all…

"Your best guide is always your experience and knowledge."

I got up every morning and trained. I also trained every evening after work and went to the gym regularly. However, I remained a member of the same karate organisation back in the Midlands. My instructor told me that at my level, I should push myself and as long as I had that drive in me, I wouldn't need to rely on having an instructor all the time. So I took the initiative and I trained the syllabus whilst in London. At the age of 24, I achieved 2nd Dan Black Belt status. From this, I moved into unique areas such as refereeing, coaching and instructing.

I am now doing Jujitsu, which is a self-defence martial art and I have been practising this for the last eight years. I took my black belt in Jujitsu on Monday 16th April 2018… another black belt! But who can't pass their black belt? Surely this is something that ANYONE can do, right? Sometimes in life, it's not what you achieve, but it's the journey you take to get there. I was extra nervous when I took this grading as I had, two years prior, failed my purple belt grading very badly. In fact, the grading was deemed 'Terrible' with a huge capital T, and I was extremely nervous, with this being a huge level up from normal grades, of history repeating itself. However, staying focused here was so important. In my 'Terrible' grading, I focused more on what would go wrong and that went to plan instead. On this occasion, along with brown belt gradings I took after purple belt, I changed my mentality to what I could physically do right, and one of the biggest factors was keeping a laser-sharp focus and trusting myself more. This new mindset got me successfully through my black belt grading and I am now the holder of two black belts in two different disciplines… a second Dan black belt in Karate and a 1st Dan in Jujitsu…

Martial arts was also my salvation in my most depressing times. As mentioned, and as you will also see in later chapters, I have had experiences which sent me into depression. Doing martial arts and training hard was not only a way to keep me out of my house, but to also imagine myself going to the dojo and literally beating the hell out of my demons. That imaginary trailer in my head – of grabbing every demon by the scruff of its neck and throwing it around like a ragged doll – gave me a positive buzz and the belief that I could really move on and overcome the biggest challenges of my life.

I have now done martial arts for a colossal 28 years and the one thing that got me through it was seeing past my hammer toe problems and just doing it. Yes, it was painful at the start but eventually my body settled into a new vibe of doing things and this, coupled with a positive change in mindset, is what helped me to grow as a true martial artist. I have also learnt to stand firm against negativity, stay focused and work hard.

I have said earlier it has not just been about learning to fight. It has become a way of life and helped me. Everything I have spoken about in this book has all built up from martial arts. It has helped me build the discipline to manage myself each day and do the things I need to do to build my business. It has enabled me to transfer my dedication abilities to build up a great network marketing business that pays for life. It has given me the tenacity to absorb life's most thunderous blows and carry on battling to achieve my goals. It has given me the energy to put into working crazy hard and achieving ambitious goals. To date, I dedicated 11 years to my Kleeneze business before Kleeneze sunk into administration. I had achieved a yearly turnover of over £83,000, became one of the network's top retailers, and also a great leader to the entire Kleeneze nation. It has also taught me to creatively pursue the sweet tastes of life and put my heart and soul into anything I believe in, hence why I was able to dedicate so much time to writing this book, not just in the HOPE but in the BELIEF that it can be a huge success.

Finally, it has taught me that it is not your situation, circumstances or physical problems that matter as much, but how you respond to them. If I had continued to use my hammer toe as an excuse and kept on cursing the problem, it would have been energy invested in the wrong area which would have dragged me away from achieving what I have done in martial arts today.

THE KEY SATTITUDES: Commitment, Focus, Self-Discipline, Initiative, Strong Mindset, Passion

GROWTH FROM THIS EXPERIENCE

Whatever you put your heart and soul into not only brings you much happiness and, in some cases, a very financially beautiful life, it also brings out the best in your character. We grow many traits that we can transfer to many aspects of our life.

Doing martial arts has instilled within me humility, discipline and respect whilst also showing that I can dedicate myself to anything that my heart and soul holds dear. Being a committed martial artist has enabled me to give full dedication to my businesses and grow a huge income that is paying me for life. It has also given me a hardcore work ethic which has enabled me to stretch my effort boundaries to incredible lengths to achieve huge goals whilst also developing the willpower to keep fighting when things get hard. Using my initiative and training on my own daily has also helped with self-motivation... I do not always need to rely on anyone to get me out of bed each day to get me going; I do that myself and I follow a set routine, without fail, in my business to ensure I achieve my daily, weekly and monthly targets.

SAT SIMPLY SAYS...

* Always follow your heart and pursue what you love in life
* Don't listen to negative people; cut them out of your life
* Use your initiative to train, learn and do what you love and allow it to grow you
* Always have a strong mindset to break past limitations and ridicule

ALWAYS REMEMBER...

"Commitment, passion and a strong mindset are your greatest allies to success."

"Grief is not the enemy. Grief can be one of our greatest teachers."
- Tom Zuba

CHAPTER 9
TRUSTED HOPE

"The soul fully heals from many damages, yet remains scarred in the loss of the closest people in your life."

We encounter many great challenges in life but none more painful than losing your nearest and dearest, the person whom you have known since childhood and who has become your family. It becomes even more painful when you see other best friends doing what you once did with yours, that whilst theirs is present and alive, yours is a chapter that has sadly come to an end. Sometimes the loss happens like a bolt out of the blue, so suddenly that it takes you what feels like a lifetime to get used to the notion that your best friend is no longer there and, for some strange reason, it is only after a long time it finally catches up with you and you realise, 'Oh my god, he/she is no longer here.' It is very easy for people to say, 'Time to move on, you can't bring him/her back,' but friendships like this are so deep-rooted and unique, it takes a similar loss to others for them to realise how it feels. It is important for people to realise that…

"Until you experience the pain of a person's loss, you have no right to tell them to 'get over' something that they never will."

In a situation such as losing your nearest and dearest – your best friends, your family and even your loved pets – it is important to first take acceptance of the loss and the fact that nothing can be done to bring that person back. This is always the first step in recovery. Remember…

"Though you may not get over a huge life loss,the one thing you can control is how easier you can make it for yourself."

Once you have accepted the loss, you can only start off slowly in the recovery process, moving with baby steps and taking one day at a time, but as slow as you need to go at the start, it is important to be resilient. As hard as the loss is, remember that at least YOU are still live and your family, especially your kids, still have you. They rely on you for support, encouragement and inspiration...YOU ARE STILL THERE FOR THEM! Be strong for them and hold them close to your heart. You have two choices...you can either let the loss reduce you on a declining escalator, or let it make you stronger.

A loss, as hard as it is, can also empower you. It can help you find new friendships with people who have been through similar losses, which eases the pain slightly as you now have people to share that with. It can also become a journey of self-discovery... what we must realise is that it is just the body that has gone, yet the souls of our loved ones live in our hearts forever. You sometimes feel that person speaking to you and encouraging you to do something great that you probably would never have thought of doing. You may find yourself being more productive, as staying in the house will more likely cause you to freeze in depression. Whatever it may be, use the loss to find purpose and reconnect your soul to the universe.

I had a best friend that I had known since school. We were in the same class, always hung out together, and occasionally attended each other's family functions. We were both avid football fans – he was a Liverpool FC fan while I, of course, am a Manchester United FC fan. He followed European football, so I decided to follow suit. In Italy, he followed Juventus, so I ended up following their direct rivals, AC Milan. He followed FC Barcelona in Spain, so I ended up following Real Madrid. The whole thing centred on the football arguing and banter; that is what truly made our friendship. Every afternoon in school at lunch break, we would play indoor football and have the occasional moan and groan at each other, whether in the same team or playing opposites but it was that footballing passion that made us. I attended his wedding, he attended mine, we attended each other's birthday celebrations and other family functions. In a nutshell, he was like my blood brother.

"Best friends are....
the light in your darkness,
the arm that pulls you out
of the quicksand,
your first aid in your time
of need and
the one that stands by you
when others turn on you."

In December 2009, my world came crashing down. I tried to phone my best friend a few times for a catch-up but there was no answer. I went to my mum's house in frustration and told her he wasn't answering his phone – what was up with him? She went silent and burst into tears. When I asked what was wrong, I was told that he had suddenly passed away. He was playing football with his family and a group of friends, and after a good game he had gone down to the floor in what many people thought was to take a breather. It turned out to be cardiac arrest as he never got back up. I was absolutely devastated. I had just lost half of my soul; how on earth was I going to cope with life knowing he was no longer there? This was going to be a huge challenge for me to deal with emotionally. However, deep down in my broken soul, I knew that...

"No matter how big life's challenges are, it is always important to be bigger than any big thrown at you."

This was, however, not the end of the devastation. At this time, my wife was six and a half months pregnant with our second child and she was not having an easy pregnancy, which meant my presence by her side was extremely important. Although she was six and a half months pregnant, she looked further along than this. She could not move around much – she was getting many cramps and pains meaning I had to be there most of the time for all the physical moving duties and to look after our son. Our son was only three and a half and there was no one, not even family, that could look after him. I was torn; I was hurt but I also had to be wise and put A before B. Taking everything into consideration, I made the extremely tough decision to not attend the funeral and say goodbye to my best friend. It was extremely heartbreaking and hurtful but it was a tough dilemma where I had to put my wife, my family and our unborn child first...

"In the alphabet of priorities, the first word is always family."

Many days passed of tears, hurt and loneliness, but eventually I had to get up and show resilience.

"Don't just look up; get up!!"

As painful as it all was, nothing I did or said could bring him back. I had to accept this and move on. Although his body was gone, his soul was still with me and I could still feel his power. We are not invincible and a loss can hit us at any time; that is the harsh reality but we can always move forward slowly, with positivity. I may have lost my best friend but no matter what, at least I was still standing, at least my kids still have their dad, at least my kids still have two parents. I have done so many great things in life but being a daddy to two amazing kids has to be the greatest triumph of all time. That alone was the starting point of my resilience.

Keeping myself as productive as possible also helped to keep my mind active. I attended more martial arts classes, put more Kleeneze catalogues out, played on my Xbox, spent time with my kids and set future goals – these were all things that helped reconnect my soul to life, rediscover my purpose and have gratitude that I am breathing and can make magic happen for myself and my family, but with the spirit of my best friend empowering my soul to make it happen. I was starting to feel more incredible than I thought I would. Martial arts helped me to channel that hurt into my training and have great sessions each week. It sharpened my attitude and my will to win. When playing on my Xbox, I often played on FIFA football as Man Utd against Liverpool and every time I beat them, I looked up and bantered with him, as I also did when real football was on. In setting goals, I set them in his honour to make him proud, as he himself was a passionate goal scorer and taught me much in this field.

I often look up to the skies and have a conversation with him, about football and my current achievements. It is probably the most insane and weird thing I've ever done but this also helped to make things easier as it felt like he was still around. It helped me to overcome the sadness of little things reminding me of him. Instead I look up to him and joke about the things he did.

Most important for me was a support circle. I always had my mum and wife around at the time, who were absolutely amazing, but I also joined online forums with people who had experienced the same. I made friends whom I eventually was able to contact personally so each time I felt low or hurt, I could let of steam, but at the same time listen to them and be just as supportive. This gave me the strength to move on and was another thing that helped me to reconnect with life. Having friendships would enable me to confide in people when I was down and also learn new approaches to overcome little pockets of grief that I would encounter.

THE KEY SATTITUDES: Resilience, Empowerment, Appreciation, Acceptance, Strength, Positive Grieving

GROWTH FROM THIS EXPERIENCE

Losing someone close to you is one of the hardest, if not the hardest, adversity to deal with. You simply feel empty and alone, like half of your world has crumbled down to nothing. Moving on from this isn't something that you can do straight away, but eventually you must accept the loss and take action as fast as you are mentally able to, before depression catches up with you. One of the biggest things I learned is that you must take each day one step at a time and keep as active as possible with as many things as possible, making each day easier to get through...but you must be resilient as the path of life goes one way...FORWARDS.

The importance of support groups is also a big help. Having many relate to you is one of the biggest positive pick-me-ups you can find, as you now have someone, or a few people, with whom you can let off steam with but also pick each other up, creating a unique set of friendships of people who can help you get through life better.

Let the loss empower you. The most important thing to remember, in spite of the fact that you have lost a loved one, is that YOU are still breathing and hence still live the life where you are able to achieve amazing things. Your kids and family still have YOU in the real world and you are still alive to be there for them.

SAT SIMPLY SAYS....

* Take time to grieve but be resilient
* Accept that you can't change what has happened but you can control your response
* Keep as occupied and as busy as possible
* Find a support circle and stay in touch with those who have experienced similar losses
* Appreciate that no matter how hard the loss, you are still here

ALWAYS REMEMBER...

"Sometimes our greatest losses become our biggest super powers."

"Parenthood involves massive sacrifice: money, attention, time and emotional energy."
- Jonathan Sacks

CHAPTER 10
ULTIMATE PARENT

"True fatherhood is acknowledging and respecting your kids' needs without ever compromising your love for them."

Fatherhood is one of the most rewarding experiences in life. Yes, it does indeed have its challenges but when you see your kids grow up in the process, it fills you with huge pride and honour at what you went through together to get them there. However, in the case of a marriage split, this can often prove difficult for children…the torn loyalties, the pain of seeing other families together whilst their own is apart, the different sides of the story they hear. It is hard enough being forced into a different way of living when you are older but to experience this at such a young age can be tormenting, hurtful and may even impact on academic achievements.

Regardless of marriage or relationship splits, where kids are involved, it is always important to put kids' feelings first. They may even feel that they don't want to see you for a while. While this may hurt, you must have an acceptance of these feelings because changing their mindset will not happen overnight. Loving our children is not just about showering them with gifts, taking them out and spending time together; it is also about demonstrating an understanding of their feelings and being patient. As they get older, they will mature and think independently.

One thing that nobody can ever take away is the fact that you are their parent. Yes, sometimes kids can be a challenge, particularly as they get older...BUT WHO SAID PARENTHOOD WAS EASY? Regardless of any challenge, we must show positivity in parenting. Wee must always find ways to love our children and connect from a distance... it doesn't matter what happens, deep down your kids will always love you.

In January 2017, I had my kids for the day. I ended up having a huge disagreement with my son over something really silly and petty. This led to a fallout between myself and my son. My daughter was distressed at this, and as a result, their mother insisted that contact was to be at her house, which I agreed to as I felt I was the one to blame; I could have dealt with the situation better. However, I was to have a nice conversation with my son a week later and all seemed forgotten. I continued to see my kids at their mother's house for a long period of time. Then suddenly I received a phone call from their mother asking if I would like to take the kids out and in an instant I said YES. This is what stood her out from many other exes... she still never stopped thinking of the importance of fatherly connection and she always worked hard to make the kids understand this. I took them out, we had fun and things were improving a lot. I had them on four occasions unsupervised so clearly the incident earlier in the year had been forgiven.

All of a sudden, I found access to the kids difficult. Attempts to get to the bottom of this were proving fruitless and the more

I tried, the more futile my attempts became. I made efforts to see my kids at school as a result, which had success until the school told me it was having a negative impact on their emotions and they were arriving to school each morning in tears. Many attempts to try and get contact with my kids went with no success at all, including mediation, so I took the tough decision to go down the legal route.

Unfortunately, whilst waiting for a date, it meant that I also did not see or manage any sort of contact with my kids for six months. I was heartbroken, bitter, angry, but I had to accept this and be strong for them. I had the fear that my kids would hate me because of this. I fell to my knees in tears in my house, wondering if things could possibly improve. However, that is when I rose up. I rose up and realised I needed to be strong and patient. I knew that…

> "Our most historic victories, and most incredible feats, are the battles we win from the brink of defeat."

I went on Facebook to speak of my experience as I was so tortured by all that was happening. However, little did I realise that this move was to make things easier for me. Support from many friends poured forward and some even personally messaged me to offer positivity and support. I eventually got the numbers of two good friends and continued to communicate regularly with them about what was happening, how I was feeling and how I could move forward. These friends had gone through similar circumstances so their advice and support through the legal processes, as well as emotional support, was the best thing I could ask for, as it grew my parenting positivity and changed my attitude towards what was going on. I found a new me and realised that I must let go of what I cannot control and focus on the things that I can control.

Eventually, the first hearing came and I had an order until the next hearing to see my kids every Saturday for four hours. I met them for the first time in six months and was overjoyed. Although their mother had to be there, she was brilliant as I was able to freely take my kids and enjoy their company full-on. As part of the order, I had to complete a Time Out for Parents and Anger Management courses which would then grant me proper, unsupervised contact with my kids. Things were going great; we were laughing and joking away, taking silly selfies together, and I was looking forward to building on this with them.

I found both courses very rewarding. The Time Out for Parents course was absolutely brilliant. It was highly engaging and I found myself helping other single parents out with their experiences. Such was my passion for it, I even got this email from the course coordinator...

Dear Premahark,

I run the Positive Parenting Group at Lowhill Hub. Satwinder has attended five sessions with us, coming early on the first to enable us to recap the previous week. During this time, Satwinder has been fully engaged, he is open to new ideas, asks appropriate questions, and discusses methods he uses at home. He has been an asset to the group with positive input and encouraged the other parents. His suggestions during question and answer sessions are well thought out and show how much he wants to be the best parent he can. When Satwinder talks about his children, it is with warmth and affection; when he discusses the children's mum, it is with respect. If Satwinder was from Area 7, we would have asked him to become a Parent Champion, to mentor other parents, something he did very well during group.

If you require any more information, please contact us.

Kind Regards

I could not believe it; the progress I was making was absolutely astonishing. I kept in touch with the coordinator so that I could touch base as regards to what was happening and the best way around child behavioural challenges.

The Anger Management course was also equally rewarding, also as a group discussion and sharing my ideas. I had a deadline with the Anger Management course which was originally referred by my GP but as there were many challenges and delays in that process, I took it upon myself to pay for a private one from my own pocket…I just wanted my kids. So, having completed the initial courses, I was set and ready for a potentially sweet conclusion to my child contact. I personally did not need to do these courses but that was not important; the important thing was putting my kids first, and personal development in parenting. After all…

"In the end, the biggest hazard is not what happens to us, but what we refuse to do afterwards."

However, days before our next hearing, I was hit with a bombshell. I was informed by my solicitor that my kids were feeling hugely distressed and as a result, an application to suspend contact was put in. Thankfully, the application was rejected;however, as contact then continued with my kids, my son became more distressed and hurt. Communication between the two of us broke down and the tension grew bigger each week. My son had also been referred to a Base 5 Child Counselling scheme, which was a scheme designed to support children with growing fears and anxieties. This meant that a further investigation by a social worker and more time without seeing my children. I was restricted merely to video calling. However, by this time I had grown positively with the experiences in the courses, spiritually reconnecting with the universe and my collaboration with my support circle that I had built. Because of this, I still had hope and was able to look at the situation from a different, more understanding angle.

After the social worker investigation, I was told that my daughter wanted to see me every two weeks, but my son did not want anything to do with me. When asked what could be done to make the situation better, he said that he wished his dad could vanish. This could have been heartbreaking and unbearable for me, but I had developed strength and confidence over the months to help me be truly understanding of this, and thanks to my amazing support circle, I found it easier to be strong and respect his wishes. On a video call, I spoke to him and told him that I accepted how he felt, I would give him his space and that I am always here if he needs me. Again, their mother was brilliant and playing her part, assuring me that she was doing all she can. She spoke to me one day and told me that as tough as this was, I had to be patient, as my son was growing and changing. As hard as she understood this was for me, I had to bear with it or I would risk pushing him further away. She was really good at explaining things to me and this helped me through the emotions. Whatever the situation, I always reminded myself that…

"Never resent your child for wanting time away from you. It may temporarily take away your time with them, but it will never take away your status to them as a parent."

A year or so on, I have spent quality time with my daughter each time I have met her. I have had a few nice conversations with my son but not pushed it too far to communicate with him. My perspective has changed and brought me greater hope. I am focusing my energy on my daughter, and the strong bond between us has also helped my son slowly come around. Over the Christmas period in 2018, we had three really good conversations and when I went over to their house to give them their presents, their mother opened the door and let me in… and there was my son. He hugged me and shook my hand and we talked about things in general. His voice had changed and I was really, really proud of him. Their mother was right; he just needed time and I just needed to be more patient. And she did an amazing job by talking him around.

THE KEY SATTITUDES: Understanding, Sensitivity, Willing to Grow and Learn, Loving, Patience, Accepting of Situations, Change of Attitude

GROWTH FROM THIS EXPERIENCE

It is challenging, and at times painful, when kids don't sing from the same hymn sheet as you, but being a true parent is allowing them to find their own two feet and never restricting their personal growth and potential. Whatever your kids feel, you must be accepting and understanding of their feelings. Building a strong support circle from the start is hugely important; this enabled me to keep better self-control of myself and my emotions. Being a true parent is also about maintaining respect and humbleness for the child-minding parent and appreciating the good that they give, not the bad that happened. This is about the kids and if you show a positive attitude towards your exes, we get a more co-operative and understanding relationship, which leads to better interaction with your kids.

From my own personal experience as a child, being given respect early in your life gives you the encouragement to discover yourself and leave your own unique trail from a young age. As painful as it has been, I have understood and accepted that my kids have wanted just that, without the family politics of what we feel is best for them. That is not to say completely let them loose; they need guidance and we as parents are always going to be there to guide and support them; however, as kids grow, there are only certain ways they understand to deal with life's challenges and as much as we may not like it, we must be supportive enough to let them have the space they need to work it all out for themselves and make sense of it. It is hard letting them go but it would be even harder trying to get your way and pushing them away even more.

My time with my daughter has brought me much happiness again and focusing on that has enabled me to enjoy time with her thoroughly. Although contact with my son is sparse, there is hope that in time the positivity in the contact with my daughter will swing him round positively in the future. In times like this, it may be hard, but calm is always the sensible path to take, no matter what. It is painful losing contact with your kids but even more painful if you lose control of yourself and end up pushing them away.

And always remember, try and be nice and respectful towards the other parent. It is easier said than done but remember, your attitude towards the parent they are living with is understood very quickly, so choose your feelings towards him/her wisely; always put your kids first. We are very quick to judge negatively about our ex-partners but always remember...if it wasn't for them, we wouldn't have such amazing kids to love, would we? Remember, you were both once in love with each other... cherish the better times you had and learn to be positive towards one another; this might just make child contact easier.

SAT SIMPLY SAYS...

* Always love your children unconditionally, no matter what
* Always maintain respect and humbleness to the other parent, no matter what
* Accept your children may not always think favourably of you but always take that as a sign of them growing up fast instead of hating you
* Never give up on your children
* Before you get frustrated, always understand that it is just as hard an experience for them

ALWAYS REMEMBER...

"Parenthood is not just a title, it's a journey."

"If you never tasted a
bad apple, you would never
appreciate a good apple.
You have to experience life
to understand life."

CHAPTER 11
DIVINE LOVER

"Never let your rough past
hold you back from the nicer
experiences of today."

Many of us are no strangers to relationships. Some of us are lucky enough to find that one special partner straight away and it works out for the rest of your life; others have the misfortune of being in a relationship and even a marriage that we are just not happy in; some of us experience this misfortune several times over before we finally mind Mr/Mrs Right. When you are in the right relationship, you are pretty much in heaven on earth…you have the right balance of support, understanding, freedom, love, friendships etc. Disagreements tend to be very minimal and when they arise, it does not often involve tempers flaring up. However, being in the wrong relationship can be quite the opposite…too much disagreements, drama, shouting, hurt, pain, tears, no freedom to be yourself, and at times control, manipulation and emotional bullying…by no means a pleasant experience. This can sometimes knock our confidence in having any relationship in the future, and draw us back into the comfort zone of being single. However, we must always remember…

"A bad experience is the only passport to growing wisdom within ourselves."

In any relationship break-up, it is important to accept the break-up and show respect for one another. Always be amicable, always be cooperative and always be understanding. Getting embroiled in a verbal battle will only develop a huge black cloud of negativity between both of you, and this is not healthy… especially where kids are involved. You just never know when you need each other so always establish that positive tune between you both and this may actually make the break-up a little more bearable.

As much as respect is important, it is also important to have self-respect. By that, I mean two things: firstly, always be humble and accept some responsibility in the breakdown. Remember, it takes two to tango so getting caught up in the 'blame game' loses you respect. If a relationship is to end, end it on a high and have positive closure. Remember, what I've touched on a few times in earlier chapters…it's not what happens to you but your attitude towards it! Secondly, when a relationship ends,

DON'T BE THE CHASER! Yes, I am a huge singer of being positive but that doesn't mean you forget about yourself. Never forget, you have value too, so as much as they need space, SO DO YOU. Don't look for a way back into their life unless you both genuinely feel something can work out. Why should you chase? Why should you have to get downhearted about them potentially being with someone else? Why should you have to be the only one mourning a breakdown of your future together? Remember, anything they can do, SO CAN YOU. You deserve just as much independence as they do, so if they are getting on with their life, oblige and do likewise...The only way in life is onwards; there is no turning back.

Finally, it is important to be dauntless. Have the courage to embrace new beginnings and discover a new you. Have the heart to adapt to change and do many things differently to what you normally would have done. And don't be daunted by meeting other people, dating and even going on to having a new relationship. Take each new journey nice and slow and use each experience as a learning curve to become a better, stronger person...you live life once, do exactly what it says on the tin; LIVE IT!

My 10-year marriage to my ex-wife was indeed a very turbulent experience. Once again, I am not going to come on here and say my ex-wife was bad, or vile... Never talk badly of, or run down, your ex-partners, as I have mentioned earlier in this chapter: it's about respect and self-respect. I am proud to say that my ex-wife was AMAZING. She always had the kids and my best interests at heart. When I was working hard to clear personal debts, she single-handedly managed the household to allow me to do that. She worked as a nurse and would at times miss sleep to ensure we were looked after. She was always very thoughtful, even on the smallest of occasions, she never forgot her traditions and was always very on the ball with things. She was a legend...however, time made us realise that sadly we were just not right for each other. What I felt was there at the start disappeared for some inexplicable reason and the arguments became more and more heated over the smallest of things. Whenever arguments happened, we found ourselves talking over each other and pushing each other over the edge. The arguments slowly became more regular, as did the shouting and bickering, and even the dish throwing, breaking and door slamming. We were both having mental breakdowns and it was just getting too much. Eventually, we had the biggest argument again over something stupid and that is when the penny finally dropped: she was seeing another woman and discovered she was not straight. We had an open, honest and very emotional conversation about this and we moved on from there. We both had to respect each other's feelings and both work together to find a new way forward for both ourselves and our kids.

Despite no one being in the wrong for this relationship breakdown, this whole experience had knocked my confidence on relationships and my own self-esteem. I was wondering to myself...

'... who would want a still legally married man who can't keep a marriage together? I'm in my mid-thirties, who will want me? My life is over; I have no chance of happiness ever. My kids are going to think I'm a rubbish father, my friends and family will laugh at me as they are happily married and keeping it going, and I didn't'...

These were thoughts that were continuously roaming in my head. I spent months and months in depression. I sometimes sat on a seat for half a day with no urge to do anything. I was often at my mum's house in tears and my mum often cried with me before wiping away my tears. Why did this happen to me, what did I do to deserve it? Then I stopped and my heart said to me...

> "Losing your marriage does not mean you have to lose your dignity and self-respect. Wipe away your tears, get up and walk on…there are better things for you out there if you have the courage to find them."

I had to stop feeling sorry for myself and have a little more self-respect. A soldier fighting in the army has little time to dwell over the enemy showing up and opening fire – they have to respond instinctively and fight back. It's no different in life. Yes, we need a bit of time to grieve but before life pelts us with its own bullets, we must get our own rifles and fight on…my common them in this book - NEVER GIVE UP! I knew that my life was going to change but instead of being apprehensive about it, I chose to be dauntless. Nothing was going to take the change away so my attitude was to embrace it and start a new era.

After two years of being alone, with my confidence in relationships a bit shaky, I met a lovely girl who I sponsored into my business. She was from the North of England, was very attractive and we just did not stop talking. In fact, our text conversation one day went from 1.30pm till 3am the following day. We had regular Skype calls and we really fell for each other so we agreed to take it slow and waited a few weeks before our first meet-up. I had my tyres done and was going to surprise her but ended up telling her I was planning on coming. She insisted on coming over to my house instead. I agreed and picked her up from the train station and she stayed at my house for a weekend. We had a great time and after a few weekends of staying over a few months, she wanted to move in, which I agreed to. We went together to her house in Mossley, Greater Manchester, collected her things and brought them over to my house. We were happy together; she even went out of her way to do bits of shopping and bought Christmas decorations so she was proactive in trying to make it work. We had a great Christmas together, my kids met her and her kids, and they all gelled well. Things were looking great and we were going to have a great future together. There was no way I was going to have a repeat of my previous rejection…at least, that is what I thought.

The first signs of a breakdown in the relationship showed from her insistence that she no longer wanted to live in my house. She insisted on letting the house go and looking for a place to rent. I disagreed with this. I had worked hard to keep this house above my head and I was not ready to put myself in bad debt with my property. She decided to go back to seeing me each weekend and moving back up North until we could get things sorted.

A few weeks later and she had completed her move back North, then out of nowhere came a piece of news…she was pregnant and expecting our baby! Although this was not confirmed, I was excited about this and wanted to get my car sorted before I could travel two and a half hours up to see her. However, our conversations appeared to be dwindling. I experienced difficulty in getting hold of her, and replies to my texts were not forthcoming. When my car was fixed and the time came for me to see her, she hesitated at the idea of it before saying no. I asked about doctor and scan appointments for our baby and there was no reply. Eventually ,I found out myself that there really was no baby involved! I felt used, yet I was still chasing her, begging fate not to repeat what had already happened to me. Out of nowhere, I then found myself blocked from her on social media and WhatsApp. Lightning had struck twice and for the second consecutive time, I had a partner that took off and ran away.

Again, I could not just put this all on her; I had to take responsibility too. There were things I surely could have done better and I took the time to reflect on this. I sank into depression...I was aggressive towards family, sat in one place for ages all day doing nothing, didn't sleep well or eat well; I was even using my cat as crying comfort. I was once again having breakdowns. Once was bad enough, twice was unbearable and it sent me into overdrive... But did I stay down for long? NO, I DIDN'T! I got up before, I was going to get back up again. Nothing stops the Man of Sattitude! My heart said to me...

"Why waste your precious emotions on those heartless people that would never shed an ounce of their emotions for you?"

The more I kept on reiterating this to myself, the more I rose from this, the less I was hit by depression and the more self-esteem I was starting to give to myself. I downloaded playlists of motivational songs from my favourite artists and listened to them each moment of the day...IT WAS TIME FOR A NEW ME.

A year had passed and I spoke to another lovely girl over the phone. Again, the same situation...we got close, started talking more and more, and dated. She seemed apprehensive at first then started talking about her past experiences and how it had greatly affected her confidence. I was only happy to help her through this and she eventually opened up and warmed to me. However, I was to find heavy involvement of alcohol and smoking which caused high tension, numerous arguments and fall-outs. I felt sorry for her. She was lovely and caring but her past demons appeared to be overcoming her and as much as I tried to help her out even as a friend, nothing was working. I decided to pull out of the relationship and stayed in touch as a friend, still determined to support her and be there for her. I didn't care how crazy things were; she needed someone to let her feelings out on and I was ready to be that person.

However, my confidence in relationships had now well and truly been destroyed...three major relationships, all very turbulent, a host of arguments, fall-outs and angry confrontations. I just could not do the love thing anymore so I closed the door on relationships altogether. I felt useless; my belief in happiness was well and truly shattered, and I planned a long-term future just for myself and my kids.

Going into Christmas in 2016, it was just about me and my kids. Relationships were thoroughly knocked on the head...or were they? Could there just be one more throw of the dice? Would I have the courage to roll that die? Of course I would, I'm the Man of Sattitude! Giving up is just not in my DNA!

"Sometimes it's that one final chance that gives you that one magical piece of happiness you have been looking for."

There was one lovely girl I had kept in touch with for five years. We were really good friends and we always spoke to each other about personal matters. In late 2017, we started having deeper conversations and hinted on a few occasions that we needed to get together for a drink. My anxieties started to rise from the bad experiences I had in the past so I held back. However ,I sat down and realised that I had to change my attitude towards this so instead of being anxious, it was time to accept my experiences as lessons that made me into a stronger person. Eventually, we decided to meet up and go out…I was quite excited and as nervous and shaking inside as I was, I was ready to carry on and do this. Yes, I did not want to risk going through the same hurtful experience again, and I actually looked for an excuse to not go out with her, but before I could deliver that excuse, I realised that the only way to defeat my demons was to face them. Everything has two sides to it…what if it didn't work out and I got hurt again, but then what if this actually did work out? We have to stay more focused on the positive side and make it happen. I had known her for ages and I needed to get out of my comfort zone so I eventually agreed to her just coming over and spending a day together.

The day arrived. I picked her up from the station...I was sweating and nervous but was determined to fight this. I waited and there she was! We drove back to my house and as soon as we arrived, we really hit it off. We got on like a house on fire but my anxieties about relationships kicked in again... NO, NO, NO, I was not going to let this beat me this time so I happily went with the flow and we had an amazing time.

We gave it six months before telling all our Facebook friends we were together. This is where I dealt with this relationship much better than in the past...took my time more. What was fascinating was that we literally had exactly the same experiences in relationships, marriage breakdowns, desires, likes; this was freaky but in a wonderful way...maybe I had finally found Mrs Right?

We were seeing each other on weekends and our love for each other kept on growing slowly but consistently. She was the most genuine woman I had ever met. I would like to share our happiness together...

Today, we run a new network marketing business together having grown a huge, huge team. We have set huge goals together, both personal and business related, and are determined as ever to achieve these. It has also helped me to become ruthless in identifying and taking out of my life fake people. It's always when you enter into relationships you see the true colours of many people close to you. Just remember....

> "Never hesitate to let those
> you once thought
> were your nearest and dearest go.....
> .....just watch your exhaust carefully as
> you drive off without them and you'll soon
> realise how much soot they intoxicated
> your life with."

THE KEY SATTITUDES: Courageous, Respect, Self-respect, Growth and Learning, Understanding, Acceptance.

GROWTH FROM THIS EXPERIENCE

Sometimes, experiences in life completely knock the wind out of you, shattering your confidence in the process, but experiences are also what make you understand yourself better. Remember, you only live life once so you can do two things with bad experiences...either let them take you to jail and torture you, or let them be your teachers and learn from them. By allowing them to help you grow, you open up amazing possibilities and greater happiness.

No matter how old you are, and what experiences you have had in past relationships, you must never, ever give up on future happiness. There is always happiness out there for everyone; some may take longer to attain theirs than others and some are destined to travel stormy channels to find theirs, but it is out there if only we have the courage to believe it and try, even when we feel we can't. That one last attempt, as emotionally drained as I was in relationship experiences, found me the woman of my dreams and we are really happy together, having the same dreams and long-terms aspirations... Never quit, even if you feel like you can't go on. The only way is onward; there is no turning back.

Remember to learn from your experiences...it always takes two to make a relationship, and two for it to fall by the wayside. Reflect on what you could have done better and use that in your next relationship, but at the same time also remember to show respect to your ex-partners to slightly ease the break-up but also respect yourself and not to be a pushover. Relationships are about compromise, not one having more than the other or being more important than the other, and also not moulding the other to your habits and way of thinking.

SAT SIMPLY SAYS...

* Always show respect to expartners to ease break-ups
* Be understanding and accepting of the situation
* Always take your experiences as a learning platform, not an anxiety
* Never jump in too quickly to happiness. Always give it time and play nice and steady
* Never give up. Be dauntless and pursue happiness

"Bad experiences are like the rain...without them, our growth cannot be nurtured."

"Just when the caterpillar thought the world was ending, she became a butterfly."
- Barbara Haines Howett

CHAPTER 12
ENERGETIC BRAVEHEART

"Sometimes it's that one thing
that we fear that creates
our destined path way."

Life can sometimes be really strange. We can sometimes have a mixture of overwhelming excitement and sheer nerves, and eventually it can get too much for you. You dream of so many things that you wish to do...and before you know it... BANG...an opportunity comes up for you to make one of those dreams a reality, but when you get closer to achieving that, there can be a tendency for anxieties and nerves to kick in. You instantly keep focus of the things that could go wrong and that can sometimes neutralise our excitement... 'What if I mess it up? What if I don't sleep the night before? What if people laugh and mock me?' You wait so long for great opportunities to showcase ourselves, and when they do arrive, you might hope that something drastic will happen to ensure that you don't need to do it at all!

On top of that, you can also have a situation where people will confront you and drag you down just before your showpiece, attempting to further dent your confidence.

In this situation, you have to be fearless..This is easier said than done, of course, and some experiences can be so overwhelming, they can literally break us…but whether they do or not is up to you so the rule is simple…DON'T LET THEM!!

It is also important, especially when anxiety kicks in, to change your perspective. These opportunities, as fear-generating as they may be, can also create you and move you forward in new exciting directions. That is where our focus should always be; the GAIN instead of the PROBLEM. You must show courage, and harness that positive spirit to enjoy these experiences. They only come once, so missing it now may well become your biggest regret, possibly for the rest of your life…

"The hardest thing in life is not stepping into the hardest limelight, but walking straight past it and spurring an opportunity to change your life."

What is also important is letting go of what you feel people might think of whatever you do. By doing that, you create yet another mental block that just doesn't need to be there. BE BOLD! It is always important to BE YOU and be you with a bold attitude, as it is through BEING YOU and stepping out of the crowd that you become a leader, create a huge following, and become powerful. For me...

"What defines me is my refusal
to cower down to
the shells of other people's
bullshit status quo
and stand up to be counted
for what I believe I am."

And for those people who do actually mock you, ridicule you and say you can't, DO NOT BE INTIMIDATED! Assert yourself, remember who you are, and be proud of it. Never be afraid to be assertive to the naysayers...that is how you win respect.

Having been in Kleeneze for a massive 10 years, I had always wanted to stand on the grandest stage at Birmingham ICC and speak in front of 7,000 distributors. The business had so many inspiring and incredible people that I was wondering if my time would ever come. However, looking at how nervous people got when they spoke in front of so many people appeared very daunting, and I was always wondering how I would cope, and if I would just fall apart when speaking. And then the moment came, on 13th October 2017, when I got a phone call from Head Office asking me to be a part of the 'Stronger Together' line-up of speakers and do a 10-minute testimonial! Oh wow, wow, wow, my moment had finally arrived and I was supremely excited and over the moon! Finally, after years and years of waiting, I was going to be speaking in front of 7,000 people. However, the anxieties also started breaking through... How was I going to cope for that week, getting all excited and not sleeping much as a result? What would people think about my participation in the line-up, considering I was mainly a huge retailer with barely any team and I had not ever qualified for one overseas destination in 11 years of being in the Kleeneze network? Would people take to me very well? How would I cope speaking out in front of so many people?? I had spoken in front of hundreds but thousands? This was all so exciting, yet also so nerve-racking. It was indeed taking my emotions to a whole new level, but this was also my opportunity to shine and show the world my power. I was determined to nail this!

In December, the whole speaker line-up for the New Year Showcase was being revealed in the official group one at a time and I was so eager for mine to happen as I wanted to see the excitement I was going to create. When I saw it, I looked at it with immense pride at how far my own personal brand had come...

New Year Showcase Testimonial Speaker
BOOOM, it's the Man of Sattitude! Gold Distributor Satwinder has built a fantastic retail business thanks to his boundless energy and positivity. Life and business may at times deliver blows, and Sat proves how important it is to build the strength to bounce back and gain from all your experiences to make the next chapter even better. Earning a substantial income from Kleeneze retail with energetic aplomb. Satwinder (in his own words) will be unforgettable.

The most liked Speaker Reveal had 279 'likes' and over 50 comments. I had 259 'likes' and 171 comments. I was humbled and honoured…this convinced me that I did not need a certain status or achievement to be so followed and respected; it's how you project your personal brand and image and how consistently and respectfully you do this that matters more than just status and position. So it was official…Sat Sagoo was going to be on stage, no walking away from this! It simply had to happen. I was being put up in a five-star hotel near the venue and I was anxious, as I do not sleep well in unfamiliar places…I prefer the comfort of my own bed. Yet the excitement just grew and grew…I was going to speak in front of 7,000 distributors… whoop whoop! All speakers were doing 10-minute testimonials about their life in Kleeneze. I started to realise that…

"Excitement brings much beauty and shine to your universe."

The week of January 2018 had finally arrived, A new year, new beginning and in the first week of that year, I was going to be a speaker! I was excited and calm for that week until the Thursday night...my excitement was so high, I could not sleep and come Friday morning, I had not slept a wink. I was upset, angry and even questioning whether I had made the right decision. I had worked in the morning then went straight to the hotel on Friday evening feeling a little low at my lack of sleep. I was due to rehearse at 5pm so I thought I could get a few hours' rest once I arrived there...it didn't happen and my anxieties were getting worse. I was sweating, my heart was racing, I would probably go another day without sleep and look like a zombie the next day...this was not looking good at all. This was a bad idea, I should really have said no...'Excuse me, what's your name again? 'It's Sat "Man of Sattitude" Sagoo and the crowd are waiting for you eagerly!' a voice in my heart uttered. I just needed to be fearless and embrace the occasion instead of feeling sorry for myself. Celebrities barely sleep at all and they find a way to cope and just enjoy the occasion. I needed that same mentality as I felt like a celebrity to many who followed me. I realised what I needed to do first...

"Don't forget to prohibit negativity from entering your positive premises."

I also spoke to another speaker who has sleep issues that made my problem smaller than I thought it was. I was finally starting to settle down and really look forward to this now. After I had rehearsed, I felt on top of the world knowing full well that I had got this.

As I mentioned earlier, all speakers were to do a 10-minute testimonial about their life in Kleeneze and what they had achieved in the business. Before the week of the showcase had arrived, I had received an email asking for my presentation slides which were well overdue. I had thought long and hard about how I was going to do this; I wanted to be different, I wanted to stand out, so I replied to the email explaining that I would not be using any slides. This was a shock to most at Head Office...never had anyone giving testimonials on stage ever spoke without the use of slides! I was going to try something really different here. I wanted it to be me and the audience, I wanted them to see me, not the TV. I was going to move around on stage and just be classy, uplifting Sat Sagoo... WITH NO SLIDES. I had rehearsed day, in day out and when hitting the rehearsals on Friday night, I spoke with confidence and everything flowed...I was ready to rock! This was my spotlight and I was going to grab it with both arms.

"Sometimes, bravery and courage are the safest acts of life."

I lay there after a busy night wondering if I would fall asleep... Behold, when I woke up the following day, I had slept! I could not believe it! I was ready to take on the world, I wanted my moment to come quickly. The first thing I did was put in my earphones and listen to music...Linkin Park and Epic Music... those are my favourite types of music as they inspire me to be a winner. I went downstairs to the ground floor where the other speakers were, shared my excitement with them and found they had not slept much either. The morning rehearsals took place and I walked up with one of the network's biggest and most inspiring millionaires. My nerves were slowly turning from sheer anxieties to sheer excitement. I was starting to feel like a sports car, ready to have my accelerator pressed...

"Excitement is the turbo power to our heart's engine, and the LED lighting to our soul."

The showcase arrived. We were allocated a special speakers' room and the wait was on. I encountered a confrontation that I didn't need...I had a confrontation with a few big leaders who approached me and told me I was not worthy of standing on the same stage as the other line-up of speakers...how would people be inspired by a guy who is just a big retailer and had not qualified for any overseas destinations? That is the thing about me...I am different. I didn't need overseas conferences or pin levels to become the 'Man of Sattitude'. I could easily have let this break me but I was so excited and pumped up I was not about to let it get to me. I simply got my phone out, pointed to my reveal for the showcase which was made in the official group back in October, and the number of 'likes' and comments, and uttered, 'I have proved my worth out there and that is why so many follow me. I have nothing more to say so unless you have something nice to say to me, move out of my way,' and then walked straight passed them! We have to remember...

"Proving your worth in the real world will always invalidate people's ridicule of you."

I was to come on after the break, after the recognition. I was pacing back and forth in the back in excitement, anticipation and nerves really kicking the hell out of me...I'm still human, right? But I was more determined than ever to master this. I was going to be different and produce a display that had never been seen on a big Kleencze stage before.

On I went to the soundtrack of Will Smith's *Boom! Shake The Room* and, with 100 butterflies fluttering in my stomach, and my body shaking like an earth tremor, I started off like this...

'ICC...Let me feel your energy, let me feel your passion and let me feel it loud and clear...ARE YOU READY TO ROCK 2018??'

That explosive beginning was received with cheers and applause. It was unlike anything they had ever seen at a Kleeneze showcase…that was the magic of stepping far out of my comfort zone. As I continued, my trembling nerves slowly turned into ecstasy and I was loving every minute of being me. People were out of their seats, cheering me a multitude of times and when finished, I received many hugs and messages for being so incredibly inspiring. Even after the showcase, I received many messages of thanks. The 'Man of Sattitude' had made his mark and made it in absolute style! Through all the challenges I had encountered, I had come out on top and conquered my emotions.

THE KEY SATTITUDES: Fearless, Bold, Perspective,Willing to be Different, Uplifting, Energetic, Inspiring, Assertive, Strongheaded, Calm, Defiance.

GROWTH FROM THIS EXPERIENCE

It may seem a normal experience to many being called to speak on stage in front of a huge crowd but for me this was covered in both positive and negative energy rolled into one…the sheer buzz from being invited to speak at one of the biggest Kleeneze stages, right down to the depression of not sleeping properly in the week. The anticipation of being unique, to being knocked back by unsupportive, discouraging remarks. The excitement of uplifting many, to the huge worry of how well the arena would take to me. But here is the important thing, guys…I took a different perspective on things as time got closer, which enabled me to follow through and get the job done to my hugest satisfaction. I was fearless towards being really far out of my comfort zone and I was bold in accepting how tough it was, but still going ahead with it in sheer excitement I did things to help calm my nerves and make me feel the excitement more, and as I have said many times, it is always your attitude to challenges in life that really make a difference.

If you have a big event coming up and it scares you, it is probably going to be the best thing you ever do, so grasp the opportunity. Even if it frightens the living daylights out of you, it must be completed as it is a one-off opportunity that may never come about in your life again.

Perspective is crucial here...it is always best to look at the situation from many different angles and this enables you to fish out the right attitude, through trial and error, to follow through and ensure you achieve success in the event in hand. Always try to be positive and excited about what you are about to do and where anxieties creep in. Remember there is always someone feeling worse than you, yet they still overcome all obstacles and succeed. Find those few little things, as I did, that warm your heart and make you feel excited.

NEVER let anyone make you feel you are not worthy for a particular cause...that is a huge reflection of their insecurities. Never let anyone reduce you to something that you are not; stand out and thrive in your new limelight because that is YOU and this is why you have been brought into this world...TO BE YOU.

SAT SIMPLY SAYS...

* Always take a different perspective to the situation when life gets you stressed
* If an event is scaring you or making you feel uneasy, it is probably worth doing and following through
* Find unique ways to help you calm your nerves and feel excited
* Always be bold and fearless
* Never let anyone tell you that you can't...be assertive

"Sometimes our gravest anxieties are the signposts to our biggest stardom."

EPILOGUE

> "Although we cannot determine the size of the war that comes our way, we can most certainly determine the size of our victory."

In the life that I have lived, I have…

*   Overseen and successfully completed an important work operation from the jaws of impossibility

*   Taken a leap of faith and sacrificed income from a full-time job, to a more uncertain self-employed income and made more money

*   Shown love, care and consideration for those in need where many would shy away

*   Got employed in a senior position, even with a gross-misconduct sacking reference to my name

* Walked successfully through the pain of a marriage break-up, becoming stronger

* Kept my house when I was on the verge of having it repossessed (twice), and clawing back from extortionate arrears that looked impossible to clear

* Worked with nasty, serious, hospital emergency injuries to still achieve my business goals and create momentum

* Shown true dedication to achieving unique goals, even with physical restrictions

* Found a way to move on positively after losing my best friend

* Remained loyal to my kids and stayed strong in the face of painful challenges in father-children relationships

* Remembered, regardless of past experiences, how still amazing the mother of my children is and how much of a positive influence she has brought to the kids' upbringing

* Overcome my anxieties from previous relationships to find the most amazing happiness

* Showed persistent attitude, patience and composure to achieve a long-term goal

The common denominator in all of this...I STAYED FOCUSED, MAINTAINED MY POSTURE AND NEVER GAVE UP!!

The ethos of this book is simple... It is not what happens to you but how you respond to it...how much courage you show, how tight you hold on when you feel like you are slipping, how much you are willing to fight for what you want. It is also about how much we value those in society, no matter how much of a stranger they are to us, and how far we are willing to go to reach out and lift them up. There is no such thing as a perfectly pure life; things are going to happen to us, we are going to make mistakes, both large and small, and people whom you once regarded as loved ones will betray and hurt you, but it's the perspective you take here that really matters... Do you accept it's over and give up, or do you get up, start over and power on forward? The choice is ultimately yours but remember, one choice bears a lot of fruit whilst the other is pretty fatal...

"I have had many exes in my life....
My worst one was the excuse
I made not to do something....
My best one was the exclamation
point I made when I got
out there and did my thing!"

As important as our attitude is to get us through life, what we say to ourselves motors the power of that attitude. Our words set our mood, our mentality, our drive and, eventually, our success. If we persist in negative self-talk, we will forever remain shrouded in our clouds of darkness and our fortunes will disintegrate perilously. Persistent positive self-talk will always set the tone for productive, profitable and achievement-filling days, topped up nicely with pride, happiness and success. When you are engaged in negative self-talk, obstacles are present in their masses, but positive self-talk firmly eradicates these obstacles.

Challenges are a huge inconvenience when they happen but without them, how do we grow? How do we write our amazing story? How do we become warriors? If everything in life was rosy and perfect, we would remain the same people throughout our lives. We would get bored from not having a means to learn or grow. It is these tough experiences in life that have made living worthwhile and created the most magnificent platforms to tell our tales. It is important that we embrace them and tackle them head on to become real-life legends.

Remember, and please never forget this, there will be people that will try to defy your motivation through ridicule, belittlement and constantly saying that you won't get through it or achieve it. You have a choice…you can either accept their claims and let them set the tone for how your life turns out, or you can break free from their shells of expectations and become your own true leader and master of life. There is NO status quo in life…you were born to sing your own song and dance your own moves; stay true to your own philosophies and way of life. It is important you impose upon yourself YOUR STYLE OF PLAY, not anyone else's.

Another important ethos this book brings out is the importance of giving to society in their time of need. No matter what we go through, there are people out there who are always far worse off than we are and when they come to us in their time of need, or we can see that they are distressed, we should always be there for them. A huge heart can make a huge difference to many people's lives. And one last point...never let your past experiences come back and haunt you; never let them place a ceiling and barriers in today's world. Always remember this...

"The only time you look back
in life is with pride to see
how far you've come."

I sincerely hope this book has truly inspired you to rise, shine and be the true warrior that you were brought into this planet to be. Keep pumping, keep fighting and Never Ever Give Up...

BOOOOOOOOOOOOOOM!!

FURTHER INTERACTION

I have always been passionate about reaching out to others and inspiring positivity in attitude and action, and have always wanted to take up motivational speaking, not just locally but internationally. Having undertaken motivational speaking already within my network marketing business, I have found this a rewarding and fascinating experience. I have enjoyed passionately encouraging and supporting many people who have been through the same challenges as myself, so I would be delighted to take up an opportunity to speak in front of a huge group of people and inspire confidence, positivity and a determination to win and achieve, even the most seemingly impossible of goals.

To get hold of me, please email me on: Sat_h@msn.com
Mobile +44 07500833283

Satwinder

D^UNAMY S

*A*DRIFT

By Carlos Moreno

Edited by D'Ann Mateer
Cover art by Wesley Goulart

www.wonderlightproductions.com

ISBN: 979-8-3303-9792-1

Table of contents

PROLOGUE. SUN 3

1. MERCURY 15

2. VENUS... 39

3. MARS.. 67

4. CYDONIA... 85

5. JUPITER.. 105

6. GANYMEDE 129

7. CASSINI... 151

8. TITAN.. 171

9. SATURN 191

10. URANUS 209

11. MIRANDA 231

12. NEPTUNE 253

13. TRITON 275

14. PLUTO 297

15. KUIPER 317

EPILOGUE 335

ABOUT THE AUTHOR 339

Table of contents

PROLOGUE. SUN 3

1. MERCURY 15

2. VENUS...39

3. MARS 67

4. CYDONIA..85

5. JUPITER..105

6. GANYMEDE 129

7. CASSINI..151

8. TITAN 171

9. SATURN 191

10. URANUS 209

11. MIRANDA 231

12. NEPTUNE 253

13. TRITON 275

14. PLUTO 297

15. KUIPER 317

EPILOGUE 335

ABOUT THE AUTHOR 339

PROLOGUE
SUN

JEN

The countdown continued almost as loud as Jen's heart.

"10, 9, 8 ..."

Will is out there ready to battle real fighter jets!

"Jen!" Commander Partridge called her name. "Status report!"

"Something is happening, sir. Systems have activated on their own. And there is a fog or a cloud forming all around us. But systems are normal and we still have communications at 100%"

"Good! Continue with the countdown."

"7, 6, 5, 4 ..."

"Commander, a huge army of tanks and fighter jets are coming our way sir!" Major shouted.

"Tell our fighters to not engage. Our jets are faster and more maneuverable than theirs, just order them to guard our ship. Don't let the enemy to get close."

"3, 2, 1"

The spaceship moved, giving Jen the feeling of being on a fast elevator. She tried every camera angle, but she could only see a layer of fog everywhere, like they were engulfed in a huge transparent cloud allowing her to see how they were ascending slowly towards the sky. The sensation of elevating continued for several minutes, then a noise like a hail hitting metal.

"They are firing on us!" Star screamed.

"Steady, as she goes!" Commander Partridge ordered.

A lightning bolt flashed, followed by a strong shock wave. The spaceship shook for a few seconds and then stopped. The fog surrounding the spaceship began to shine with orange, red and yellow hues before thick gray and black clouds surrounded them. Several minutes later, the colors disappeared and the cloud surrounding the spaceship turned to normal. Then the sensation of elevating continued.

Over an hour later, the cloud disappeared, revealing the blue sky. Then the sound of hail beating against the ship resumed.

"We're under attack again, sir," one of the pilots radioed in.

"Disregard! Continue ascension as normal."

"Yes, sir!"

"And order the squadrons to return to base."

As Jen listened to the conversation between the pilot and Commander Partridge, a weight lifted. Her brother was coming back inside the spaceship.

"What was that bright orange thing, sir?" Star asked.

Commander Partridge remained silent for a moment.

"Every fighter jet is on board Commander!" A voice said through the radio.

"Good!" Commander Partridge turned to address the crew. "Ladies and Gentleman, I think it is fair to say this ship is worth what we paid for."

Almost everyone looked as clueless as Jen felt, except Major Rogers and Doctor Mendel.

"What you heard earlier," the commander continued, "the hail-like sound, was an intense missile attack. The bright hue and shake were the result of a small nuclear explosion directed at us. But I am happy to say our spaceship is intact."

"And it absorbed all the radiation of the blast," Doctor Mendel added.

While everyone cheered and clapped! Jen noticed her brother, Will, entering the bridge. She rushed to hug him as the blue sky turned to black then the stars began to shine.

"Will, Daddy and Mom—" Jen choked.

"What is it, Jen? Are they ok?"

She nodded. "I saw them come to the ship, but the doors were already closed. They left before the most intense attack began."

Jen held tight to her brother trying not to cry in front of the rest of the crew.

"Navigational systems are set in automatic, sir!" Star said.

"Excellent."

Will sat next to Jen.

"This is indeed an extraordinary craft," Star said.

Others around the bridge nodded.

"Yeah, big explosions but not a scratch." Major Rogers chuckled from his post.

"Dynamite!" exclaimed Star.

"*Dunamys,*" said Dr. Mendel.

"That's a Greek word, isn't it?" Major Rogers asked.

"Yes," the doctor responded. "It means power."

"Well, a mighty power certainly saved us."

Commander Partridge looked thoughtful. "*Dunamys,*"

Doctor Mendel grinned. "I think that's a good name for the spaceship."

Will leaned close to Jen. "Mom and dad were taken away a long time before the detonation, and according to Doctor Mendel, the fall out didn't spread because the shields of the spaceship– I mean the *Dunamys*– absorbed all the radiation.

"Yeah, and Joshua told me they will be ok," Jen said, as much for herself as for Will.

"Jen, please tell everyone to take the seat belts off," Major Rogers instructs her.

Jen flipped on the intercom system. "Attention, passengers, we have reached outer space. Feel free to take your seat belts off and relax and enjoy this beautiful view."

"Let me welcome them." Commander Partridge came to her station and spoke into the microphone.

"Ladies and gentlemen, this is Commander Ian Partridge speaking. Welcome to the *Dunamys*, the name we assigned to this vessel. It means 'power'. Our personnel will guide you into the rest of the ship. There is a common area in the center where you can hang out and enjoy the view. We are still in the process of building more facilities for our accommodations here, and as you already know by now, your living quarters are similar to a decent hotel room, so you can live comfortably during our trip. But please stand by for further instructions. And again, welcome to the *Dunamys!*" Commander Ian finished and asked Jen to turn off the transmitter.

"Hey look!" From Jen's screen they saw people getting out of their chairs moving closer to the windows. Most of the people were speechless. Everyone—children, parents, old and young people—seemed to be in awe.

"Wow! So, this is what Earth looks like from space! We are so small!" Jen wiped her tears.

"It's amazing, Jen!" Star approached Will, who was staring at a window.

"Yes, quite a view, Star!" Jen finally had a feeling that everything would work for good. Leaving their parents had been hard. At least they were taken with Elizabeth's parents and would have some company.

"Look at this, Will." Jen pointed to her monitor which showed people gathering in the main areas of the spaceship. They stood in small groups admiring the Earth and the stars. From the youngest to the oldest, everyone seemed happy.

At least until a new voice came out of the speakers of the bridge. Jen tried hard to make a sense of the transmission, but it was impossible. It sounded like muffled speech. Or distorted speech. Or maybe a different language she'd never heard before. Before she could ask someone else, there came a series of sounds that reminded her of an alarm warning. Then the transmission stopped.

Commander Partridge looked extremely worried, white as a paper sheet.

"Right there!" He suddenly shouted.

"Maximum zoom!"

The screen showed a little corner in space near the Earth's horizon. They zoomed in the screens to reveal a small group of flashing red lights moving quickly in their direction.

"Jacobs, Will, Jen, Dr. Mendel. Come with me." Commander Partridge strode into a private briefing room and shut the door once the four were assembled.

"Dr. Mendel, give us the translation," Commander Partridge barked.

"Translation?" Jen looked at Dr. Mendel. "Do you know that language?"

Dr. Mendel appeared completely calm. He polished his glasses on his shirt as he spoke. "I do, Miss Morant.

This transmission is from the *Daiminion*. Enemy aliens. You don't want to mess with them."

"What?" Jen scooted closer to Will and reached for his arm.

"Don't worry." Will patted Jen's hand. "The *Dunamys* is invincible!"

Commander Partridge shook his head. "You have no idea who we are dealing with. Many years ago, there was an international agreement with the aliens that no human would ever leave the earth with the intention of going beyond the solar system. This agreement allowed us to launch spacecraft without human pilots or crew. In exchange, they said they would give us technology and protection."

He looked at each person in the room for a long minute. "We have broken the treaty."

Jen. felt suddenly anxious. And afraid. Two things she'd never felt before about their mission.

"It was classified information," Dr. Mendel explained, his glasses perched on his nose once more. "It's a secret that's been kept even from our government for the last seventy years. Maybe longer. I am one of the few people who knows the alien language and can interpret it."

"And the message said ...?" Commander Partridge put his hands on the table and leaned toward Dr. Mendel.

"It said that we have violated the treaty, and if we don't surrender, they will haunt us down and destroy us. No mercy."

Will and Jen locked eyes.

What have we done? Jen thought. *Maybe, mom and dad were right. Maybe we didn't know Joshua well enough. Maybe he wasn't trustworthy.*

All of a sudden, Joshua appeared in the middle of the room. He stretched out his arms as if to gather them all in a hug. "Don't be afraid."

"Thank you for the encouragement, but we need to do something." Commander Partridge turned to a computer in the room, effectively dismissing Joshua.

"Follow my instructions, and you will live."

Will stepped forward. "Sir, respectfully, I think we should listen to what Joshua has to say."

Commander Partridge ignored Will and continued looking at the computer.

Joshua disappeared.

"Commander," came a squawk from the box on the table. "The red lights are approaching,"

Commander Partridge rushed back into the bridge. Senator Jacobs, Will, Jen, and Dr. Mendel followed.

"Activate the hyperspace engine, now!" Commander Partridge ordered the navigator as he entered the bridge.

"Sir, we need to turn off the shields to calculate—" Dr. Mendel suggested Commander Partridge, while the navigator started the procedure.

The navigator stood looking at Dr. Mendel, who was overseeing the engineering of the ship, waiting for confirmation to resume.

"Ok, turn off the shields and do the calculations as quickly as you can, but we need to leave now. That is an order," Commander Partridge instructed with anxiety in his voice. Then he gestured Dr. Mendel to return to his station.

Protection shields off, the computerized voice announced.

"Jen, notify all passengers to go back to their seats," Senator Jacobs instructed.

"Right away, sir!"

"One more thing, sir," Dr. Mendel interrupted. "The FTL Hyperspace system hasn't been tested yet."

Before the commander could reply, Joshua appeared again, this time in the very back, by the door. "Don't be afraid. Follow my instructions, and you will live."

"We don't have time to figure out what Joshua's hologram is saying," Commander Partridge insisted. "He can't know our current situation. It's just a hologram."

"Please, sir, let's wait to hear what Joshua has to say," Major Rogers insisted.

Commander Partridge didn't respond. Jen had never seen him in such a panic, his fist closed as he walked to each station and looked at every monitor closely. He looked terrified.

Then she noticed Senator Jacobs, his face was pale as a sheet of paper, with eyes wide open.

"I'm afraid the commander is right," he said. "We will listen to Joshua's hologram after we outrun the aliens."

"Activate the FTL Hyperspace module," Commander Partridge told Dr. Mendel.

"Sir." Dr Mendel stood. "As I was trying to say earlier, we need time to calculate the distance in order to follow the route indicated. If not, we might end up in an unknown region of space and we don't even know how to properly use hyperspace yet."

"It doesn't matter. This is an emergency. You don't realize how powerful these aliens are. We don't have a chance against them."

Dr. Mendel looked nervous. His finger lingered over the button to operate the navigation system.

"Proceed with my orders! Now!" Commander Partridge crossed the bridge to the navigation system and pressed the buttons himself.

Hyperspace initiated.

In a flash of light that was so bright that it was hard to see anything, a huge wormhole became visible. The *Dunamys* whirled through it at great speed. A noise increasing in pitch, tone, and volume sounded from all sides. Jen sat next to Will, who gripped the arms of his chair more tightly. Finally, the space outside the window began to clarify. A great spherical object appeared on the screens. It grew bigger and bigger, emanating radiation and high temperatures. This object triggered the alarms, warning of impending danger.

"It is bigger than the Earth!" Star screamed.

Jen turned toward the door. But Joshua had vanished. And she seemed to be the only one who'd noticed.

Jen looked at her monitors, making sure everyone on board was okay. Most of the people stood looking out the windows. Jen switched cameras. David and Elizabeth stood together, gazing out the window.

I don't understand those guys.

"Would you look at that!" Star whispered.

"What is it?" Jen turned to the main screen on the bridge. A bright multitude of colors appeared from the bottom, like a rainbow. It moved around like Aurora Borealis coming out from the bottom of the ship.

"It's so beautiful," Jen said, mesmerized. "What do you think it is, Will?"

"Maybe it is from the wormhole. Or maybe not. Maybe it came from that huge object the systems detected."

"How come the systems won't tell us more details?" Commander Partridge asked Doctor Mendel.

"I think many of the systems are not working properly."

Suddenly, the spaceship shook violently. The temperature rose rapidly. The sound of several explosions seemed to come from inside the spaceship. Then a vibrant orange light filled the windows, like a summer sunset in a clear sky but much, much brighter.

"Damage report!" Commander Partridge yelled.

"I'm afraid we have a huge problem, sir," Major Rogers answered.

"The FTL engine is not responding," Dr. Mendel reported. "We just have basic thrust. Many of the systems are out of commission. We have alarms going off all over the *Dunamys*, reporting several systems are down across the ship, including basic lighting in the living quarters. The cargo hall has been damaged, there is a hole there where the water tanks are. And many other areas of our ship also have been bridged, and−"

"Sir!" Jen shot to her feet; her eyes still focused on the view from an interior camera. "Most of the reserves of water are gone!"

"Multiple breaches on the outer hall!" someone yelled.

"Dr. Mendel, what's actually working?" The commander's voice sounded tight.

"Basic ship systems, artificial gravity, life support, basic thrust and fifty percent of the shields."

"Ok. Activate the shields."

Immediately, the protection shields activated. Then the lights went off.

"Sir, we lost power in other areas of the ship," Doctor Mendel noted. "And the temperature of the ship is increasing very quickly. But it seems the shields are holding."

"What does that mean?" Commander Partridge asked.

The main screen showing the view outside the ship filled with bright orange and red colors, like a lake made of lava or fire. Even went still.

"The good news, commander," Dr. Mendel said, "is that we are not lost. But the bad news? That big object the system alerted us about earlier is the Sun, and we are headed directly towards it!"

I
MERCURY

JEN

Star gaped at the vision on the screen. "Wow! I have never seen the sun so close!"

"Star, please keep your thoughts to yourself!" Commander Partridge snapped.

"Yes, sir."

"We are too close! This is very dangerous!" Dr. Mendel pushed buttons and pulled levers. "Right now, the temperature inside the *Dunamys* is around one hundred degrees Fahrenheit, thirty-eight Celsius. It might increase to about one hundred and twenty degrees in the next few minutes, even with our shields protecting us. The instruments indicate that the temperature outside of the spaceship is of about thirty-three hundred degrees Fahrenheit, eighteen hundred Celsius, and rising rapidly."

"How close are we?"

"About 29 million miles from the sun." Dr. Mendel's voice sounded worried. "We are near Mercury's orbit, sir. According to my calculations, we will crash into the sun in about seven hours at our current trajectory."

"Are you sure?"

"Positive."

"What should we expect?" The commander asked.

His question perplexed Jen. Yes, she was scared and nervous, but at the same time, a feeling of wonder and amazement flowed over her.

"As we get closer to the sun we can expect stronger turbulence from the solar wind, far worse than what we experienced earlier. Also, intense heat and strong G forces which will ultimately tear the *Dunamys* apart." Dr. Mendel stopped manipulating the controls in front of him.

"How long?" asked Commander Partridge.

"Seven hours." Dr. Mendel leaned back in his chair as if defeated.

"Get to engineering. See what they can figure out."

Dr. Mendel left the bridge while people in his team confirmed the calculations.

"Put it on the screen, Star," Commander Partridge ordered.

"Yes, sir." Star, who was in charge of the missions, exploration and logistics station on the bridge, turned on the screen. It revealed a surface similar to the moon. Around it floated a set of shiny, multicolored particles, like Aurora Borealis.

Dr. Mendel returned to the bridge. "Sir, I have good news and bad news."

"What did you find out?"

"The multicolor lights we saw earlier are the result of the magnetic field and the exosphere surrounding Mercury, which means we are very close to the planet. The good news is if we get closer to Mercury, the gravitational pull of the planet will keep us from crashing into the sun. Therefore, we will be okay. For now.

"The bad news is that if the temperatures continue to increase at this rate, we will lose more water and then the air within a few hours. We don't know how long the shield will protect us."

"Take us to shadow side of Mercury, we will stay in orbit there, for now." Commander Partridge ordered the navigator as he walked closer to the window, sweat dripping down the side of his face. "Will was right. We should have listened to Joshua. Dr. Mendel, can you make the necessary calculations to get us back to our original destination?"

"Yes, sir, but also I will need time to troubleshoot the problem with the hyperspace engine and—"

"How long?"

"At least an hour. I don't know how long it will take and we need to do repairs. We are still assessing the damages."

"Start immediately."

"Yes, sir."

Commander Partridge turned to Jen and asked her to prepare to broadcast to the entire ship.

"All ready, sir."

He stepped to the microphone. "Attention everyone. This is Commander Ian Partridge. We are in the orbit of planet Mercury. We apologize for the inconvenience of the heat. We are taking the necessary precautions to supply you with water and necessary fresh air. Please be patient as we restore power all over the ship. And sit tight where you are. Remember, the name of this vessel is *Dunamys*. It is a powerful ship, so you are in a safe place and all will be well."

As the Commander spoke, Jen watched as the *Dunamys* circled Mercury's orbit, thankful the passengers didn't have the worries of the crew or know the danger they were really in. Instead, they could simply enjoy the awe and wonder of space, the close up view of another planet, and a sun bigger and brighter than they'd ever imagined.

WILL

Will listened to orders from Commander Partridge and Major Rogers as the others checked every system and evaluated the damage on the *Dunamys*. Will remained seated not knowing what to do.

"Sergeant Morant, you are dismissed," Major Rogers finally said to Will.

"But, sir—"

"There is nothing you can do for now. Go to your living quarters, get some rest. Our engineering team and the crew will take care of this. I will call you if I need you."

"Yes, sir." Will left unwillingly, wanting to do something to fix the situation, but Major Rogers was right, there was nothing he could do.

Will went directly to his living quarters, guided by the emergency lights flickering. On his way, he couldn't avoid thinking about Elizabeth's words hours earlier. *You know, sometimes you get so busy that you forget to look at the little details around you.* Elizabeth's words, from their last brief talk.

He shook the words from his head, returning to the present. He activated the light on his communicator to illuminate his way. Once he reached his room, he laid down on his bed, turned off the small light of his communicator and tried to rest, as ordered by Major Rogers. But thoughts of the imminently approaching sun made it impossible. After a while he turned on the light on his communicator and walked out of his living quarters. He rode the elevator to the big common area. There he noticed some of the passengers wandering around holding emergency glow sticks, including David, Elizabeth, and David's parents. They were heading toward the elevator and had already had seen him.

Elizabeth was trying to cool herself with a small battery fan.

Will decided it was best to acknowledge them.

"Hey guys!"

"Hi, Will, how are you?" Elizabeth smiled.

David greeted him politely.

"Good, quite a ride, isn't it?"

"No kidding! Although why did the Commander order us to stay put? This heat is unbearable!" David said.

"It is just protocol. You knew this wouldn't be an easy ride," Will answered, trying to avoid revealing more details.

Going to rest?" Elizabeth asked. "I would love to, but I fear this stressful day is not over yet. It has been a long day, for all of us."

You guys have no idea! Will tried to keep the thought from showing on his face, unable to tell them how bad the situation was for the entire ship.

"See you guys later." Elizabeth gestured David's parents toward the elevators. Then she hugged David and then Will. "Good to see you."

Will tried not to make eye contact with her. "Good to see you all!" He addressed David's parents as they waved goodbye, leaving Will alone with David.

"Can I ask you a question, Will?"

"Sure, what is it?"

"How bad is the situation really? I mean, we all heard Commander Partridge's announcement, but it seems to me this is very bad, especially with the intense weather inside."

"Sorry, David, I can't tell you more."

"I totally understand."

"Anyway, I guess I'll go try to get some rest before the bridge calls me for action." Will turned to the elevator again. He stepped on, then wondered why David was following him. The doors closed leaving both of them inside.

"By the way, I heard there are many areas still in development."

Dude, we are in the middle of an emergency and all you want is to chit chat?

"Yeah, they are building more out sections. They are just finishing a botanical garden," Will told David.

"How is the ship able to accommodate over eight thousand people plus all the extra areas?"

"The *Dunamys* is much bigger than the largest cruise ship on earth, plus the living quarters are occupied by families or by groups of two or three single people."

The elevator doors opened and they stepped into the hall and continued their walk.

Ok since you are here let's just get it over with.

"Hey David, I noticed Elizabeth was very serious today, is she okay?"

"Not really. She has a lot of mixed feelings since her parents decided to stay behind."

"I can relate. My parents are with them."

"I have been trying to encourage her, trying to tell her she's not alone. She needs her friends more than ever. By the way, I never had a chance to ask you—why have you become so distant from us lately?"

Why is he asking this now, we are in the middle of this stressful situation? Oh civilians!

Will paused for a second and wanted to evade the question.

"It is just the pilot's life; they are keeping very busy."

"So, you are on the same floor as us."

"Us?"

"Yeah, Elizabeth is also on this floor."

"I guess it makes sense. This floor is for the crew and staff." Will stopped at his living quarters.

"She went with my parents to their room. They wanted to talk to her."

Will wanted to tell David to leave him alone. He was already stressed out. Now he was frustrated with having David and Elizabeth living on the same floor as he was.

"Okay, this is it." He hoped David would take the hint and leave.

David pointed to Will's room. "Really? This is mine, too. Cool, we are roommates! I guess it is because they consider me a consultant staff."

Will nodded. He'd thought the day couldn't get any worse.

JEN

"Close all window blinds." Commander Partridge barked. "Repair progress, Dr. Mendel?"

"Nothing yet, sir."

"I want a status report asap, is that understood?"

"Yes sir."

"Jen, remind the passengers to stay in their living quarters."

"Yes, sir." Jen tried to follow the orders addressed to her, but Commander Partridge was talking to several people so quickly that she had a hard time trying to keep up.

"Sir, the repairs on the cargo area had begun sealing the bridge over our water supplies." Dr. Mendel reported. "But, temperatures are now over one hundred and rising, at this rate our remining water supplies will evaporate in a few hours and people won't be able to handle the heat."

Commander Partridge remained quiet for a moment, then he called Jen into the briefing room.

"Yes, sir?"

"Jen, I apologize for ignoring your advice on the situation before. We need to do something now." Commander Partridge kept his voice low.

"What do you want me to do, sir?" Jen frowned, her frustration with Commander Partridge rising.

"We need to access the holographic interface."

"Do you mean reach out to Joshua again?"

"Do not patronize me, Jen!" He frowned.

"I'm so sorry, sir. I stepped out of line."

"It's ok, Jen." The commander ran a shaking hand through his hair. "We are all stressed out."

"I think we can talk with Joshua any time."

Before she'd finished speaking, Joshua appeared in the room.

Commander Partridge stepped away from Joshua, obviously surprised to see him appear almost at the mention of his name. He glanced at Jen, then back at Joshua. "I'm sorry I didn't listen to you the first time. Please help us. People will perish on this trip with the heat and without water."

"Lower to the surface of the planet and look for the edge of the shadows at the one of the poles," said Joshua patiently. "There's a crater where you will find an abundance of water."

"Water on Mercury? That's impossible."

Joshua didn't respond to Commander Partridge's disbelief. Instead, he walked out onto the bridge and continued on, they followed after him. "I am leaving you instructions on how to repair the ship and replenish what you have lost, but it won't be easy."

"I got it sir. It is a very deep list of items and locations." Star reported as she continued researching Mercury. "Water deposits are found on Mercury's poles.

"Despite the high surface temperature, the poles are not heated by the direct rays of the sun," Joshua explained. "You will also need to get different resources from each of the planets. Each planet, and some of their moons, have unique things you will need to survive and to repair the ship. Follow my instructions and you will live." With that, Joshua disappeared.

A scavenger hunt in the neighborhood of the Solar System! Jen felt a bit giddy at the prospect.

Commander Partridge remained quiet for several minutes.

"Let's do what Joshua advised this time," Jacobs urged. Commander Partridge ignored him and walked towards the navigator. "Can you still maneuver the ship?" He addressed the navigator.

"Yes sir, thrusters are working fine. We are going to our destination slowly but surely," answered the navigator.

"Good, then locate the edge of the shadow side near the pole, find the biggest crater, and take us there," Commander Partridge ordered. "Jen, take a few hours of break. You will need your strength when we begin the exploration of Mercury's surface."

"But, sir, I'm fine."

"It is an order, Miss. Morant!"

Jen reluctantly went to her room to get some sleep. When she arrived, Elizabeth was there, wiping away tears.

"Jen! It is so good to see you!" Elizabeth hugged Jen, then explained that her parents decided not to join the voyage. Jen shared she saw Elizabeth's parents leaving safely with her own parents.

"You know, David's parents told me I'm not alone. They called me their daughter. I know I can count on them for anything I need. They are so sweet! But I wish my actual family was with me," she said, her eyes still wet.

"I understand my friend, I know the feeling." Jen hugged her again, then both girls set about silently organizing their belongings while streams of tears rolled out from their eyes.

WILL

After a few hours of sleep, Will's communicator woke him with a message from Major Rogers.

Report to the briefing room for your mission on Mercury.

Will pumped his fist in the air. Yes! *They have something for me to do!*

He rushed to put on his white uniform and report for duty. For the first time, he paid attention to the uniform's design. On its right side, it had a gold stripe above a red stripe. Underneath that, his rank and name.

Sergeant William C Morant

He walked fast to the elevator and rode until he reached the floor where both the bridge and briefing room were located. A sign on the wall read *Authorized personnel only.*

Down the hallway, he arrived at a private briefing room close to the bridge. He took his seat among the rest of the gathered crew. Doctor Mendel led the meeting. He projected a three-dimensional image of Mercury as he explained what Joshua had revealed and the need to retrieve water from a crater.

"As soon as Joshua gave us this information, we began studying the planet from orbit. It might look similar to the moon but don't be deceived by its appearance. It is very different."

"We found the crater, sir, just as Joshua's hologram said." Star pointed to a spot in a valley darkened by a big shadow. "See the sparkles? The reflections of light? That's a big piece of ice. Definitely much cooler there. This could be our solution to the water issue."

Commander Partridge studied the image for a moment, then turned to Dr. Mendel. "How we can retrieve the ice from the crater?"

"One of our small spacecrafts can laser cut the ice and warm it. And on board the craft we have some vacuum with hoses which will pull up gas, minerals, and liquids. We can use one of them to acquire the ice."

"Sergeant Morant," Major Rogers turned to Will. "This is where you come in. You will pilot the shuttle and collect the resources."

Will snapped to attention and saluted. "Yes, sir."

Commander Partridge took over the meeting, and Major Rogers and Dr. Mendel pulled Will into the corner of the room and explained procedures, preparations, and security measures.

"Are you up to the task, son?" Major Rogers said.

"It is doable, sir."

"How long do you anticipate it will take?" The major asked.

"Three to four hours, sir."

"I guess we are stuck on Mercury for a while then." Major Rogers nodded at Dr. Mendel. The two of them returned to the bridge as the commander dismissed the meeting.

Will was not the only one selected to do the flight. Two other pilots were also assigned to use the experimental shuttles equipped with protective shields.

Dispatched to the vessels, Will and his fellow pilots flew in circles descending onto the planet slowly, like a commercial airplane landing in a huge airport.

This time Will allowed himself to enjoy the ride and pay attention to every detail of the experience, his first glimpse of an alien world. Even though it was just rocky, he was excited to know he was one of the first humans to get close to the planet, which certainly looked like the moon.

After several minutes, the shuttles slowed, then gently touched the surface of the planet. Will and the other two pilots exited wearing special suits to protect them from radiation and extreme temperatures. The suits were also equipped with very strong lights, allowing them to see clearly. They walked in the middle of the crater and started to cut the ice.

JEN

Jen tried to sleep. And she did manage a brief nap. She was happy civilians were spared from that uncertainty of day and night cycles. The information booklet explained that an accurate clock ruling the day and night routine was installed on the bridge and another, with the exact same time, at the center of the spaceship for every civilian to see. Everyone synced their communicators, clocks, watches and other devices with that time. This helped everyone to have a more normal life as they move in the wilderness of space inside of a spaceship.

Jen knew life wouldn't be the same anymore. She missed her parents and her emotions started to catch up with the whole situation: the invasion of the base, her parents left behind, the other agents who captured them, the nuclear explosion. It had all happened too fast. She rose from her bed and put on another one of her uniforms and prepared to report to the bridge.

As she rode the elevator, she checked her timer and realized she had time to stop at the common area. It was hard not to compare it to the center of a cruise ship, with multiple seating areas, the tables and chairs attached to the floor, and windows all around.

Suddenly, she noticed David and Elizabeth seated together. She greeted them from a distance and approached their table.

"Hey, Jen!" Elizabeth invited her to take a seat. "I didn't want to wake you when I left the room earlier."

"You didn't, Elizabeth. I still have about 45 minutes before I have to report back to the bridge. Actually, I need some friend time right now."

"You have a lot on your mind, don't you, Jen?"

"Yeah, I guess all of us do to one degree or another."

"Ladies, why don't we explore the spaceship? I mean many of the areas are still in development but we can see what they have now."

"Great idea, David!" Jen smiled.

All three of them walked around what looked like a brand new mall, then they stopped at a space that looked familiar.

"A coffee shop?" David said as all three of them looked through the thick window, revealing chairs and tables attached to the floor and a small counter on the right side.

"This brings up so many memories." Elizabeth pointed to an open area in the corner left which seemed to have a small stage.

"The vintage proverb!" Jen said, breathing deeply.

"It is hard to believe it all began in that little coffee shop!" David laughed, then urged them to continue on.

They finally reached the botanical garden with its canopy projecting outside of the spaceship.

"Wow. This is so beautiful and unexpected. Mercury really looks like the moon with all those craters." Elizabeth pointed to Mercury's surface hovering just outside of the canopy. Then Elizabeth burst into song, one Jen had never heard before.

"You are God of the skies, of creation.
God of the Universe.
The whole cosmos is from God,
and everything in it.
Your mercy is without end,
without limits is your power.
Your Kingdom is powerful,
without end is your dominion.
With justice you will reign."

She turned to them. "Singing keeps me joyful, especially in the middle of hard situations, and it reminds me to enjoy the beautiful things we have all around us. I'm so glad we decided to come, David! But I wish..."

"Your family was here. I know."

"I want them to see all of this. And I miss them so much. I don't know why my dad is so stubborn!"

"We will come back for them, I promise. We will find a way to rescue the rest of the people we left behind. I'm sure that's part of the plan."

"I know, David, but still, I'm worried."

"Don't be Elizabeth. Joshua promised us they will be safe," Jen reminded her friend.

"At least we have each other!" David gave Elizabeth a side hug.

"Wow, what is that?" Elizabeth walking away from David while wiping sweat from her forehead.

"Yeah, this is weird. All of the sudden the humidity in this area is intense," Jen noticed.

"Maybe they are using some kind of water vapor to keep the garden fresh. Why don't they use the gardening water supply for this?" David added, looking around for the source of water.

"Oh, maybe you didn't know—and please don't tell anyone— but we lost most of our water supply when we arrived in Mercury's orbit," Jen whispered. "We don't want to say more because we don't want the passengers to panic."

David blinked hard, as if trying to keep his cool.

"What are they going to do?"

"They found a crater with ice on it. They are working on a way to extract it while the repair team fixes the damaged areas of the ship, one of which is by the main water tanks."

"So, the damage is extensive then?" Elizabeth frowned.

"I won't lie to you, Elizabeth. We lost power, water supplies, the FTL Hyperspace engine is damaged, and other things. The repair team is fixing some of them as we speak, like the power in some areas, but they still have much work to do."

"Thank God no lives were lost," Elizabeth responded. "I'm trying to remind myself to be thankful and believe that we are now on our way to paradise with our dear friends."

"Yes, we all need to keep reminding ourselves of the good things. By the way, I need to report to the bridge in a few minutes. Thank you for letting me hang out with you both." Jen waved goodbye and started toward the bridge.

WILL

A hose from the shuttle now reached the crater, where Will and other pilots were cutting pieces of ice. As the two other pilots returned to their crafts, Will remained on the surface of Mercury to watch over the hose sucking up the ice to be like a large vacuum cleaner.

Will's communicator lit up. An incoming message from the bridge. "Will, we see two objects on the radar. They seem to be the same kind we encountered before the wormhole. Can you confirm visually?"

Will squinted into the stars above him. "Yes, I see two moving objects. They have something... it looks like... wings, and they are very reflective, as if made of shiny metal."

The two objects moved closer, suddenly appearing like metallic dragons with a sparkly tail. Will rushed into his shuttle and checked the instruments.

The dragon ships moved very fast. So fast that the instruments on Will's spacecraft couldn't read them consistently. *What are those things?*

"Sir, they are headed toward you," Will warned the bridge.

"They are firing at us!" came the transmission from the bridge. Then, "Squadron leaders, leaders, prepare to intercept!"

Immediately, a squadron of fighter jets whizzed out of the *Dunamys* ready to engage the two red metallic dragon spaceships that seemed to appear and disappear because of their tremendous speed.

How do they do those crazy maneuvers?

Will listened to the pilot's chatter.

"I got it! No, I don't—now, it's behind me!"

A jet suddenly disappeared into an explosion.

"Sir, this is Sergeant Morant," Will said to the bridge." Please let me help."

"Negative, focus on finishing your mission."

Suddenly, giant flames flew out of the dragon ships, destroying several of the jets.

Will made fist, frustrated that he was unable to do anything to help them. He waited until the his shuttle's containers were totally filled with the ice. He wanted to do something else, but he knew how important it was to take care of his mission. When the process finally finished, he waited for the hose to retract and quickly returned to the *Dunamys*, with the rest of the shuttles and delivered their precious cargo. Will landed the shuttle and indicated allowed the crew to take over the delivery while he rushed into the launching area where his jet was and without hesitation asked his team to prepare his jet for departure right way. Then he joined the battle.

His jet rose from the surface. He tried to follow the enemy ships, but they whizzed past him. They were on his tail.

"These ships are too powerful for us!" he cried out. "Too advanced... we don't have a chance."

"Fear not, William." Joshua's voice. Although he didn't know where it came from, he felt comforted. "Reach out for the light."

Immediately, Will flew towards the sunny side of Mercury as fast as he could. Still his pursuers followed him.

Then Will dipped very close to the surface. The temperature elevated, but the protective shield of the shuttle activated. The dragon ships reached him, but as he looked behind, the dragon's shape began to blur, then the ships began to glow. They morphed from chiseled beast to misshapen blob.

They are melting!

One of the ships tried to pull out of Mercury's atmosphere, but it was too late. A big ball of fire ignited, releasing a wave of energy that briefly shook the *Dunamys*.

"Sergeant Morant to *Dunamys*, please respond."

Silence. Had the ship taken a hit before the dragons exploded? He feared the worst. Throwing his jet into overdrive, he circled back to the *Dunamys*. The solar brightness blinded him momentarily. His heart beat fast. Then his view cleared. The *Dunamys* hovered intact, with no enemy ships around.

"This is the *Dunamys*. Are you ok, Will?"

"Yes, sir"

Once back on board, Will reported the details of his mission in the briefing room.

"We lost reception from your spacecraft for several minutes."

"That explains the silence. I was expecting the worst," Will explained.

"Apparently, the electromagnetic field of the planet had interrupted the communications for a brief moment, but thanks to Doctor Mendel and Miss Morant, the communications were restored."

"What about the water supply?" Commander Partridge asked.

"We got enough, but less than our goal. We are fine for now," Doctor Mendel responded.

"I still don't understand how the *Dunamys* can handle such high temperatures this close to the sun," Star said.

Doctor Mendel turned to her. "The truth is, we don't know. We do not even understand how the fighter jets weren't affected by the high temperatures."

"Ladies and gentlemen. "Commander Partridge stood up. "We will continue on the route that Joshua asked us to follow, using only the basic thrusters."

"Yes, sir," Major Rogers responded. "At our current speed we will reach the next planet, Venus, in about thirty-seven hours. There we will collect the resources from the list given by Joshua."

Will left the briefing in silence, and in shock.

"Are you ok, Will?" Jen asked him on the way to their living quarters.

"Honestly, no." Will looked down.

"What happened out there?"

"More than I expected. People died in front of our eyes, facing enemies more powerful than I could imagine. This is too much!" He stopped and faced his sister. "Jen, this journey is going to be way harder than I initially thought. We have a long way to go before we can fully repair the ship and initiate the actual interstellar trip."

Jen's mouth dropped open in shock and her eyes filled with tears. Will led her to her room then went to his own quarters, where he fell into a long sleep.

2
VENUS

JEN

The journey continued at slower than full speed, but they finally reached the orbit of Venus.

"Such a beautiful planet. It looks so serene!" Jen nudged Star to look up from her monitor at the bridge.

"Nice! Too cloudy, though," Star responded.

"Don't be deceived by its looks." Doctor Mendel turned his chair to look at both ladies. "That place is the closest thing to hell in the Solar System!"

"Crew meeting in five minutes." Commander Partridge's voice carried through the bridge.

Everyone gathered nearby. Various crew members gave reports on the conditions of the planet, including the high temperatures—about 863.6 Fahrenheit or 462 Celsius on the surface. They planned continue the trip after their brief stop in its orbit.

"We detected a high content of carbon dioxide in the atmosphere, plus a good amount of sulfur dioxide. The clouds are mostly composed of sulfuric acid droplets." Dr. Mendel frowned as he delivered his report.

"Not exactly paradise, is it?" Star looked at Jen

Suddenly Joshua appeared in the middle of the meeting. "You must go to the planet's surface."

"What??" Commander Partridge positioned himself in front of Joshua, as if preparing for battle. "You're joking, right? Didn't you hear the report? The atmosphere is poisonous as well as scalding hot!"

"It is a light tribulation. You must go. I will be with you," Joshua insisted. "Trust me."

Dr. Mendel approached Commander Partridge, as if to support Joshua's argument. "The atmospheric pressure of the surface will crush us. It's 92 times greater than Earth's," Commander Partridge addressed Joshua

Instead of answering back, Joshua vanished.

"Such a patronizing hologram!" Commander Partridge complained.

Dr. Mendel shrugged. "On the other hand, he's been right about everything so far."

Still, Commander Partridge and the crew worried about the high temperatures and the pressure on Venus. But for some reason Dr. Mendel stayed calm. Jen knew, as Doctor Mendel mentioned, that Joshua had been right all along. That he had protected and cared for them. She wanted to say something, to support that doctor Mendel in following Joshua's instructions even though it sounded scary and dangerous.

"What is your decision, Commander?" Doctor Mendel asked.

"What do you think, Doctor Mendel?" Commander Partridge asked after walking back and forth across the bridge quietly.

"Regardless of the risks, I think we will survive. The protective shield is active and Joshua knows the full capabilities of the *Dunamys* so..." Dr. Mendel seemed to be processing his thoughts while talking.

"Fine. We go to the planet's surface." Commander Partridge said firmly, still looking at Dr. Mendel. "Please activate the protective shield. Jen, proceed with the announcement," The commander said.

Jen pressed the button to send her voice to all the speakers on the ship. "Attention all passengers: We are in orbit around the planet Venus. We will dive into the surface for a little while. Please be advised that the planet contains high temperatures and strong pressure. We will be fine, but please make your way to the shelter area of the spaceship located in the middle deck and follow all crew members' and announced instructions. Please stay there until we advise otherwise. Thank you."

Jen switched off the microphone, then turned to the commander. "May I join my friends in the shelter area?"

The commander nodded. "You are dismissed. But be ready to return Immediately when you receive notice."

Jen assured him she would do so, then she exited the bridge. She took the elevator down, then passed through the common area. Some passengers lingered for a last look at Venus before heading to the shelter.

Jen considered the planet again. Surrounded by brown, yellow and beige clouds, it looked peaceful and tranquil, slow and warm in a romantic kind of way. Then she proceeded to the shelter. Before arriving at them, she stumbled into David and Elizabeth.

"Hey, guys! I was just enjoying the view."

"Those clouds over there look just like the ones on earth," Elizabeth said, pointing out a bank of fluffy white ones.

"Yeah, they do. I know you miss home, Elizabeth. I'm sorry this has been so hard on you."

"Thank you, Jen. It has been hard on all of us. But I know we did the right thing. Even though it is painful, I really wanted to be on this trip."

"Me, too," David responded. "I know this isn't easy, but I really believe we will be able to come back for the rest of them."

"You know, Jen, we were just talking, sharing past memories, and in my heart, I concluded it was all worthwhile. And it is so good to be in this long journey among friends." Elizabeth leaned against David, who frowned after Elizabeth's words. "And special people!" Elizabeth added, gazing at David.

WILL

Will and other officers were sent to make sure that every passenger had made it to the shelter. When he saw Jen talking with David and Elizabeth, he hurried towards them.

"Sorry to interrupt, but we need you to get to the shelter immediately." Will spoke directly to Jen, trying not to glance at Elizabeth or David.

"It's okay, Will. No worries. What's going on?" Elizabeth moved slightly away from David.

"You heard Jen's announcement, right?" Will asked.

"We did," David said. "We were on our way to the shelter, but I guess we got distracted. Is something wrong?"

Will frowned. *Even if David and Elizabeth hadn't paid full attention to the announcement, why hadn't Jen urged them to hurry and obey?*

"We must be in the shelter area of the spaceship while we land," Will explained. "The surface of Venus has very high temperatures and pressure, so it might be bumpy."

"Why are we going there then?" David's tone turned serious.

"Believe it or not, it was Joshua's idea," said Jen, trying to ease the growing tension between the guys.

"Please be on your way. I need to check for any

others." Will dismissed them as quickly as he could and left with another officer to continue checking for wandering passengers.

After finishing his rounds, he reported to the bridge. When he arrived, the crew was making the necessary adjustments before entering the planet's atmosphere. Although the crew only knew the basic functions of the spaceship, they knew how to follow Joshua's instructions.

"Shields activated and functioning at one hundred percent, sir!" Doctor Mendel reported. "Commander, it is worth mentioning that this is a great opportunity to study the planet and the spaceship's capabilities."

"As long as it does not interfere with the mission and normal duties, that's fine. Do what you need to do. It will help to improve our chances of survival."

Star approached Will. "Can you believe that foggy thing is the shield? It wasn't what we were expecting, nothing like a science fiction movie."

"Have you actually seen the shields from the outside?"

Will asked her.

"Not really. We haven't had the time with everything that happened. We only followed its activation with the instruments.

"Star, do you see anything?" Commander Partridge asked.

"No, sir. Only a semi-translucent cloud surrounding the spaceship. I mean, besides the foggy aspect of our shields."

"Are you sure it's not part of the shield protecting the Dunamys?"

"No, sir, the yellow cloud is definitely part of the atmosphere," Dr. Mendel said after checking the monitors. "We haven't even breached the second layer of clouds from the planet yet."

Each crew member attentively concentrated in their own station checking every detail. Silence reigned in the bridge for several minutes until, finally, the craft hovered closer to the surface.

"Steady as she goes!" Commander Partridge said.

"I think this is it." Dr. Mendel pointed something on his screen. mirroring it in everyone else's.

Commander Partridge nodded. "Let's go in."

JEN

Jen, David and Elizabeth hopped on a cart driven by military personnel and rode towards the shelter.

"I heard you are doing great in your new position, Jen," said Elizabeth, trying to start a normal conversation.

"Well... I'm trying to do my best. How about you?"

"We are still adjusting. We really just want to be regular passengers and remain available as consultants."

The military guy interrupted. "I'm parking the vehicle for a moment. Please remain seated."

David assured him they would.

"Do you guys have plans to continue performing?" Jen asked.

"We haven't had a chance to talk about it since we got on board, but we are still writing songs. You know, songs about the Creator, about peace and love, some vintage style and some more contemporary."

"She's already composed a couple of complete songs so far," David smiled at Elizabeth.

"Awesome! I would love to hear them sometime. You know, you guys, you should record your songs so people on the whole spaceship can enjoy your music and—"

An automated announcement, programmed by Jen, said they were entering the Venusian atmosphere.

"Wow!" cried David & Elizabeth together, as the military guy returned to the vehicle to continue driving to the shelter.

Through a small window, they could see the orange, yellow and beige clouds moving at immense speed and lightning flashing in different places. The *Dunamys* shook. The driver stopped. Elizabeth clung to David while Jen clung to Elizabeth.

While the *Dunamys* slowly crossed the last thick layer of clouds, Jen, Elizabeth, and David wanted to look out the window for a moment since the ship had stopped shaking. But the military guy rushed them to - the shelter.

"I think we are okay now," Jen assured them.

But then some clouds grew with a bright light,

shining between them like the reflection of the sun into a mirror.

"That lighting came very close to hitting us" David looked concerned as they passed the window that reflected the lights in the orange, white, and yellow clouds.

"Are you sure we're safe, Jen?" Elizabeth shook while trying to peer out the window.

"By now the shield has been activated. Besides, Joshua promised us that even if we walked in a valley of death, we would have nothing to fear."

A military officer approached the window and called his superiors to confirm the safety of the spaceship, then immediately called told all the people in the shelter that it was safe to come out.

"Well, I guess there is no shelter for us." David turned the back towards the living quarters.

Jen watched, astonished, as the *Dunamys* crossed a bank of clouds, before the view opened to the surface. She knew this was the place especially selected for having the lowest temperature and pressure on the planet.

*****

About two hours later, Jen returned to the bridge. The *Dunamys* had come to a mountain with bright white reflections on its top, almost like snow. Immediately Commander Partridge decided to land near it.

The instruments activated themselves, making several noises and lights like sparkles.

"We are detecting high levels of sulfuric acid and carbon dioxide," Dr. Mendel said after reading the reports. "Also, the instruments indicate high temperatures and pressure, even though this is the lowest we could find." He squinted at the screen in front of him. "But inside *Dunamys* the oxygen and atmosphere are ... perfect."

The spaceship passed by other small hills, and Jen she was filled with wonder and fear at the same time. The place was desolated, and everything there had orange and yellow colors, like someone had put a filter into a camera lens.

"Steady as she goes!" Commander Partridge repeated.

Finally, the spaceship touched the surface of the planet. The instruments immediately began gathering data.

Regardless of the harsh conditions, Jen felt peaceful, as if lying in a hammock on a summer vacation.

"What is it, Jen?"

"I just feel . . . relaxed!" Jen breathed deeply. Then she noticed the rest of the crew looking at her.

Jen rose from her chair and walked to the hall to take a break and call Elizabeth.

"We still don't know why Joshua's brought us here, but knowing him, I'm sure it's a good reason," Jen heard

David say in a confident tone near Elizabeth. "And we are safe, as he always promised."

"Yes, you guys are right, and the journey so far has been good."

"I know, Jen, and I think I'm beginning to understand what you meant earlier. This morning, I turned on my tea brewer, sat in my recliner, and put on some music, Minutes later, as I was drinking my tea, I got a spark of inspiration based on the experience we've had so far. Then I began to write another song. Do you guys want to hear it?"

"Yes, that would be great!"

Jen remembered to put some items into her to-do list and at the same time she tried to listen.

> "When you show up
> the desert turns fertile
> and all green bloom
> Like a campfire in the snow
> Like refined gold everything is
> When you show up."

The song affirmed her peaceful feelings she had earlier.

"You know, Elizabeth," she said. "I'm totally sure everything is going to be all right."

"How do you know, Jen?" Elizabeth asked.

"I just know." Jen gazed through the window. "You guys enjoy the beautiful and interesting view."

The commander poked his head into the hall. "I

still recommend everyone to go back to their living quarters. Please make the announcement, Miss. Morant."

"Did you hear that, Elizabeth?" Jen said as the commander vanished back inside the bridge.

"No problem, Jen. We're going to our quarters now."

"Good. We are still on alert just in case something goes wrong."

"I understand. Talk to you later." Elizabeth hung up. Jen returned to the bridge and immediately made the announcement as ordered.

"Whoa! That looks scary!" Star said.

"What is it, Star?" Jen started towards Star's station, which was closer to the window. Although the view was beautiful, it was also weird and distorted, like driving through a very high-temperature desert.

"The instruments are acting crazy reading all the information from the atmosphere and surroundings, Dr. Mendel said. "They seem to be detecting some kind of radiation or heat."

Suddenly geysers expelled liquids and gas on the surface of the planet.

"That is not good!" Major Roger's said.

"And that's not all!" Jen looked at the monitors attentively.

"What is it?" Star asked.

"Some of the passengers look very scared."

"What do you mean?" Commander Partridge inquired

"I will put it on the main screen, sir"

Some passengers were in the hallways, out of the living quarters, their faces frantic as they appeared to be trying desperately to find an exit.

WILL

Will was trying to relax in his bed before his next assignment making his best effort to adapt to sharing the room with the guy who was hanging out the girl he had loved for so long, but at the same time, they were friends and shared the same common experience of knowing Joshua. So, he had mixed feelings about David. He'd thought he had a chance with Elizabeth after his short one on one conversation with her a while ago.

His thoughts were interrupted by his roommate's communicator.

"Hey, Elizabeth! Do you like the view?" Will heard David say.

"Yeah, I can see it too. An interesting mountain. So shiny."

Will was curious and got closer to the small window shaped like a commercial airplane window. He saw several hills, but also the mountain they landed by.

"It's wonderful." Will heard Elizabeth's voice through David's communicator. "I've never seen something so beautiful. I'm more encouraged now, thankful and joyful..."

"I'm glad."

Will began to walk towards the door to avoid hearing the rest of the unpleasant conversation between David and Elizabeth.

"Elizabeth? Elizabeth...!?"

Will stopped.

"Elizabeth, talk to me!!" David jumped up and crossed the room to Will.

"What is it?"

"She complained about an intense headache. Then she stopped responding. Let's go!"

They both ran down the hallway toward Elizabeth and Jen's room. As they went, several people around them passed out.

Maybe that's what had happened to Elizabeth, too.

They needed to get to her. And fast.

JEN

On the bridge, Star put her head down on her control board. "Sir, I need to be relieved of duty, I don't feel well."

"Me, too, sir." Dr. Mendel turned to face Commander Partridge. "I suggest we all get out of here!"

"No," Commander Partridge ordered firmly. "We are going to wait."

At that moment, Jen received a report from Doctor Hackett, the chief of the medical bay.

"Sir, we got a report from Doctor Hackett.

Passengers are passing out all over the place and many others have severe headaches."

"Miss Morant, put Doctor Hackett on the screen."

Jen switched the board and called Doctor Hackett. He appeared instantly on the main monitor.

"What is the situation?" Commander Partridge asked.

"It is the change in atmospheric pressure. Some people can't handle it. I'm sure it is temporary. Once they adjust, they will be okay."

Jen immediately reached for the intercom to try to calm the passengers.

"Attention everyone, please remain calm. We are all adjusting to a different atmospheric pressure, but we will be okay. Please remain calm and–" Suddenly Jen saw a group of passengers heading towards one of the bay doors and forcing a guard to open the security area for them.

"Sir, a small group of civilians are trying to exit the *Dunamys*."

"What?"

"They are in panic mode, and they are about to open a bay door," Jen reported.

"Put it on the main screen, Miss Morant."

"Yes, sir."

"I just dispatched some military guards to stop them," Major Rogers announced.

Jen continued speaking on the intercom trying to calm the passengers, but it was pointless. Instead, she activated the microphone near the secure area so they could hear the conversation between the guards and the civilians.

"This is a restricted area," one of the guards said.

"We don't care," said a civilian. "We need to get out of here or we are going to die!"

"Please, go back to your rooms!" One of the guards insisted. "We will be safe."

"No!" They shouted as a group. Then the civilians attacked the guards, leaving them unconscious. They found another gate, one which led to the hangar where shuttles and escape pods were kept. There, they found an small shuttle and immediately got inside

"Sir, they already the ship on a shuttle. It seems they are aiming to go into space."

"They are trying to break outside of Venus' atmosphere."

"Attention, shuttle craft." Jen spoke calmly but sternly into her microphone. "For your own sake, come back to the *Dunamys*, it is not safe out there."

The bridge went silent, waiting for a response. But none came.

Commander Partridge turned to Major Rogers. "Send some jets out there. Bring them back immediately."

But as Rogers moved to obey, the commander held up his hand to indicate for him to wait. A voice crackled over the speaker.

"*Dunamys*, please help this is shuttlecraft. Someone is firing at us. It seems to be a massive spaceship from afar, probably six times bigger than the *Dunamys*. We are sorry we left. We need−"

The communication ended. Jen tried desperately to reach them again.

"Call me crazy, but I'm looking at . . . dragons." Star motioned the commander over. "Am I hallucinating?"

Commander Partridge breathed deeply and nodded. "I'm afraid it is not a hallucination. They look like dragons, but they are small battleships from the *Daiminion*. The same ones Sergeant Morant saw around Mercury."

"They are firing at the shuttle without mercy. Shall we call out the pilots, sir?"

The crew on the bridge followed the movements of the shuttle on the large, main screen unable to do anything. The small craft tried to return to the surface of Venus and evade the attack, but it couldn't even get move away from the dragon ships. Then the shuttle fell to the surface close to a canyon.

"Call the main squadron! We need to rescue our people," Commander Partridge ordered.

Dr. Mendel turned to the commander. "But, sir, it is very dangerous outside!"

"Disregard that, Rogers. Do what I said. That's an order. We must rescue them, whatever it takes!"

"Aye, aye, Commander Partridge."

Immediately Major Rogers ordered Will to get ready for a rescue mission.

WILL

Will and David arrived at Elizabeth's living quarters within a few seconds, as it was just a few steps from theirs. But everything seemed to occur in slow motion.

"Elizabeth!" Will yelled, but she didn't open the door. "It's me. Will and David!"

She didn't answer. Will's head started to ache and he felt sleepy. Then his intercom interrupted. Major Rogers explained that a shuttle had crashed on the surface of Venus.

"I've got to go." The words felt thick in Will's mouth. "There are civilians in danger."

David turned around; eyes wide. "Are you ok, Will?"

"Just a headache, nothing to worry about. Take care of Elizabeth." He shut his eyes tight then opened them again, hoping to make the pain and fuzziness go away. It didn't help. He used all his strength to hop on a golf car and drive to the defense area. By the time he arrived, both his body and his mind were moving even more slowly.

He went to the lockers and somehow knew which suit to take, as if a faint voice were telling him what to do. The bulky astronaut suit, designed to withstand high pressures and heat, was like an armor. As soon as he put it on, the headache stopped. He advised members of his squadron to wear the same ones. Then they all boarded their jets and headed toward the site where the shuttle crashed.

The initial report indicated the passengers survived the impact eighty miles from the *Dunamys*, but also that the little ship was damaged beyond repair. Their final act had been to send a weak transmission asking for help.

"We have several survivors here.... People are panicking and some have already passed out, but they are still alive..."

After listening to the transmission and locating the shuttle, Will called the bridge.

"Sergeant Morant reporting. We just landed but we have low visibility due to distortions from the heat."

"Proceed with caution." Rogers responded.

The suit weighed Will down as he stepped from his ship. The landscape shimmered with heat waves, but he appeared to be protected from the extreme temperature. He couldn't see the sun in the sky, only yellowish clouds. The surface beneath his feet seemed to be made out of black volcanic rocks. From afar, he saw a volcano erupting. In the opposite direction, a lightning storm. No wonder the civilians were panicked.

According to the plan, Will and his squadron carried several of the same kind of spacesuits they were wearing for the civilians. It would take far too long trying to repair the shuttle, so the best course of action was to rescue civilians one at the time.

The suit made it hard to walk. Slowly, he climbed over the mound of rocks, then down to the shuttle crash. He approached a small window. He could see about ten people inside, most lying on the floor, a few seated, holding their heads.

Will took a step back. How would they give them the spacesuits?

Using his intercom, he tried to make contact with the shuttle. "This is Sergeant Morant from the *Dunamys*. We are here to assist you. Please stay calm. Is anyone injured?"

"Thank you! Most of us are okay, but there are several minor injuries, and a few are unconscious."

Will switched buttons on his device. "*Dunamys*, this is Sergeant Morant. The civilians are mostly okay, but the damage to the spaceship is beyond repair, as expected."

"Can you get the spacesuits to them?"

"Negative. At least not without exposing them to the toxic atmosphere."

"Sergeant Morant, this is Dr. Mendel. There is a small compartment on the top of the pod which can connect to another spaceship. Your fighter jets are equipped with bottom doors capable of docking with the pods."

"Roger, that."

Will inspected the shuttle and found the docking area and signaled the rest of the pilots to bring their jets as close as possible.

Will returned to his communication with the shuttle. "This is what we're going to do. I will connect my fighter jet to the top of your pod and send you one spacesuit. We have ten fighter jets here, each with an extra seat and a spacesuit, so every fighter jet will connect and receive one passenger at the time, please be patient. Please stay calm. We will help you each step of the way on this process. I repeat, stay calm."

"Thank you." The voice that answered breathed heavily.

Will had enough room in his jet to hold one of the suits and a sit. Immediately he returned to his ship and docked into the shuttle. Then he proceeded to pass them one spacesuit and waited until one of the passengers put it on one of the civilians who was on the floor unconscious. Carefully, the passengers help her to reach the top to the shuttle and Will picked her up and carefully placed her on the passenger seat on the back of his jet. Will disconnected from the shuttle and sent his men to rescue one civilian at the time, starting with the rest who were unconscious.

Half of the civilians had boarded when Will heard a faint voice on the communicator.

"Help us quickly, we cannot..."

"Sergeant Morant to the civilian shuttle. Please respond."

No answer.

A few minutes passed. Still nothing. Had the last five passengers passed out?

Will spoke to his pilots. "We might need to carry out the rest of the passengers. I think they are all unconscious."

Each pilot took care of a civilian. One of the pilots whistled a melody, trying to keep the woman in his arms calm and alert. Will and the rest of the pilots followed his example. Finally, all of the passengers had been rescued.

JEN

Meanwhile, at the bridge, alert systems detected extra signals, the four spaceships with the form of dragons that fired at the shuttle earlier were entering the atmosphere.

Commander Partridge clenched his fists. "What was the point of coming here? Now lives are in greater danger!"

Dr. Mendel turned to Jen. "Try to get an answer from Joshua."

Before Jen could think or speak a word, Joshua appeared.

"Don't be afraid," he said. "You are not alone."

"You're only a hologram. But what can you do to help us?" Commander Partridge's voice rose in volume, and Joshua disappeared.

"Bridge to Sergeant Morant. Four enemy ships approaching. Be careful with your cargo. We need to get them safely back on board," Jen said.

"Roger, that."

"Major Rogers, prepare full defense systems," Commander Partridge bellowed.

An overwhelming peace bathed Jen, in spite of the situation. The same peace she felt before. It was a resting tranquility she couldn't understand. She pressed the communication button that connected her with Will's headset. "Will, do you feel—"

"A serene peace?"

Jen exhaled. "Yes. But I don't understand it."

"Is everyone okay on board the *Dunamys*?"

"I think so. Here on the bridge our headaches aren't that strong anymore. And we've had reports from all over the ship that people are getting better. Was the rescue mission successful?"

"It was a little difficult, but we managed. All—wait a minute!"

"Will, is everything ok?"

"Put me on the speaker."

Jen did as he asked. Suddenly her brother's voice filled the control room.

"Enemy ships are on the way to intercept us! Waiting for instructions."

"Do not engage." Major Rogers suddenly stood over Jen's shoulder, speaking into her microphone. "I repeat do not engage. Get here as quickly as you can. We will send another squadron to cover you."

Jen glanced to the spot where she'd last seen Joshua and wished he hadn't left them again.

WILL

Will hoped the second squadron would keep the enemy ships busy until the civilians were safe. But like Jen, Will experienced the same presence and peace he had felt when he was on Mercury.

"Guys, follow me," he told the rest of his squadron.

"What about our orders?"

"Let me contact the *Dunamys*."

Will informed the bridge of his plan, although Major Rogers didn't sound too happy about it. Still, he authorized Will to proceed. Immediately, all the fighter jets approached the bottom of a canyon. There they found a giant cave located inside of a crater, and immediately they all flew inside. The four enemy ships passed by, looking for them. They waited a few minutes and then they tried to escape, but Will saw them again and told everyone to remain where they were.

The dragon ships seemed to be flying in circles looking for the survivors of the spacecraft. After a long time, they appeared to give up and left.

Finally, the ten jets rose out of the crater. But when they approached the area where the *Dunamys* had been, they couldn't find it. It was gone.

As Will was trying to figure out what to tell his men, the ship emerged from the other side of the shiny mountain. As they got closer, Will saw another shuttle taking several pieces of rock from the mountain with a hose in the same way he did in Mercury.

"Sergeant Morant reporting, sir. Mission accomplished. Permission to come on board."

"Good job, Sergeant Morant., proceed."

"Please notify Dr. Hackett that we have some people injured and unconscious."

Inside the spaceship, the medical team treated the passengers in the medical bay.

The headaches and the fainting symptoms began to disappear after the system for regulating the pressure was fixed.

Once back aboard, Will found out that the *Dunamys* had been hiding behind the mountain and that its reflective material had hidden their signal from the enemy ships. Now they knew why they had to go to Venus – to hide from a massive enemy ship and to retrieve the minerals found on the mountain. According to Dr. Mendel, the metal was a key necessity to repair many of the components of the *Dunamys* that had been damaged earlier.

JEN

Jen obtained a leave to return to her living quarters. She was exhausted but relieved that everything had worked out for good. When she arrived, she saw David on the floor by her door. He looked like he'd just woken up. He groaned, holding his head in his hands, while Jen cautiously entered. Elizabeth was lying on her bed. Slowly, she opened her eyes, and Jen immediately helped her to sit up.

"How are you feeling, Elizabeth?"

"A little tired, but otherwise I'm fine." She looked toward the window. "Are we still on Venus?"

"Yes. The atmospheric pressure caused some issues until *Dunamys* adjusted the environment inside. Do you want to go for a walk?"

63

"That is a great idea. I feel like I've been in this bed for a while."

"David?" Elizabeth said as she saw him trying to stand up at the door. "I thought Will was with you."

"He was called to a mission," Jen told Elizabeth as she approached David to see how he was.

"Is he okay?" Elizabeth asked.

"He is. He saved some civilians, too. Long story. We should go out for a little bit. You will feel better.

Together, they all walked to the big common area. As soon as they got there, Jen noticed the speakers playing soft strings music in the background. They continued their walk, trying to find a place to sit.

David's dad found them and led them to David's Mom. "This is a good place."

The area looked like a mall under construction.

"For what?" asked David.

Before his dad could respond, an announcement came across the main speakers.

"Ladies and gentlemen, we are going into space again. Feel free to enjoy your view of Venus for the last time. Next destination, Mars."

Elizabeth turned to Jen. "Was that you?"

Jen laughed. "Yes. I programmed it to come out as soon as the *Dunamys* reached a certain altitude. That way I can enjoy hanging out with you guys!"

"Fancy!" Elizabeth said, but a garbled transmission over the speakers drew all of their attention. It sounded like someone trying to tune an old shortwave radio. Then the noise grew increasingly metallic. The volume rose. People covered their ears. Suddenly the background music returned, as normal.

The passengers seemed to dismiss the strange occurrence, but Jen wondered what was coming next.

3
MARS

JEN

The stars were bright, and the view from the window was majestic, but after days of traveling, the absence of day and night was starting to feel weird for all of them. David, Elizabeth and Jen talked about it during dinner time one evening on the way to Mars.

By this time, the tables and chairs in the common area had been fixed to the floor, so people could bring food and eat there.

"Do you get tired of seeing just stars for so long?" Elizabeth asked Jen

"Not really. It reminds me of my childhood. I used to go out in the country with my family where we could see a clear sky full of them. I'll never get tired of looking at stars, finding the constellations, planets, galaxies, nebulas, and other amazing things."

"I remember hearing how you and Will both loved astronomy back then."

Jen stared out the window and wondered what her parents were doing now.

"You miss them, don't you?"

"My parents? Yes, just as you do."

"You are so fortunate to have your parents with you." Elizabeth turned to David.

"I know, but I wish both of your families were here as well."

"Thank you, David." Jen gazed into David's eyes for a moment and then turned to Elizabeth. "What keeps me encouraged is that Joshua assured me that I will see them again. I have his promise and that is enough for me."

Jen noticed David trying to hold Elizabeth's hand while she talked to her. *I thought they were not official yet I wonder*

"Anyway, changing the subject, you guys never told me your story. How did everything between you start?"

"You really don't know?" Elizabeth looked surprised.

"It's a long story," David began. "As you know, we met at the first open mic of the Vintage Proverb. We became best friends. But after graduation, we separated. I decided to study meteorology and... "

"He became more passionate about cars and music," Elizabeth continued, "so he didn't have time to hang out like we used to. One day I saw him singing at the Vintage Proverb, and I knew it was something special that I didn't want to lose. So, I went there and..."

"And that was when I saw you... again," David went on, staring into Elizabeth's eyes now. "You were smiling whit that special smile of yours. I couldn't stop staring at you even when I was trying so hard to focus on my music. After I finished playing, we started to chat again. But I forgot to unplug my guitar, so when I got up, I tripped on the cord and almost fell. She laughed at me."

"Ha! That prevented you from seeing that I spilled some coffee on my blouse earlier. I took advantage of the moment and cleaned it."

"Ha ha ha!" He laughed. "Yeah, I remember,"

"I didn't know what to say. It was an awkward situation," Elizabeth smiled.

"That's right. I broke the awkwardness by singing one of my songs. And that was the first time you joined me. remember?"

"Yes, I do."

"Then we started seeing each other. But this time it was quite different than before." David held Elizabeth's hand while Elizabeth remained frozen, like she didn't know what to do.

"Wow! What a great way to meet someone special!" Jen smiled at David and then turned away quickly thinking she might blush. Inside she wished she was in Elizabeth's shoes.

WILL

Will thought about reaching out to Elizabeth to see how she was doing, if her headaches had gotten better. He picked up his communicator and called Jen.

"Hey, I have a quick question. Do you know where Elizabeth is?"

"Here with me... and David. We are in the common area."

"Cool, I'll come by to say hi."

"Sure, come join us!"

Immediately Will made his way to the common area. Jen, David and Elizabeth seemed to be having a deep conversation.

Was David there for Elizabeth all the time after I left? Did he faint like the other passengers?

He stopped overthinking, gathered all his courage and joined them. But it was harder when he overheard Jen commenting on how David and Elizabeth got together.

Never mind that! Let's just do this!

He started walking forward, but his bold step was interrupted by his communicator. Major Rogers requested his presence.

"Right, sir. I will be there immediately." *Woosh!* *Saved by the bell*, he thought.

But then Jen waved. She had seen him, so he approached to say hi.

"What is it, Will?" Jen sounded concerned. She could always tell when he had something on his mind. The twin connection, he imagined.

"Major Rogers wants us to initiate a more intense training program based on what we learned about the enemy who have been harassing us. Sooner or later, we will have to fight back. I have to go to a meeting about it now. I'll talk to you later."

"Sure, Will," David replied in a friendly tone.

"Good to see you, man," Will fist bumped his roommate.

"Elizabeth, how are you feeling?" Will gently put his hand on her shoulder.

"Much better, thanks. I ended up lying on my bed. I was unconscious for a while I guess, until Jen opened the door. Thank you for checking on me, Will. I heard you went on an important mission."

"I'm so glad you are doing better. And yes, I was just doing my job!" Will smiled at her. "Speaking of duty, I got to go! Good to see you guys!"

Minutes later, Will joined Major Rogers and the rest of the military crew in the briefing room.

"Sergeant Morant reporting, sir."

"At ease, sergeant. We're starting new required training, effective immediately. We need to be ready to face this new enemy. I want you and your whole unit to present yourselves tomorrow at 0600 hours. We will start with tactical study and virtual training before we initiate real dogfight exercises."

"Yes, sir. I will tell my men to be ready."

The troops started flight simulations later that day, which consisted of several hours of study followed by intense combat exercises. Finally, they received a series of briefings analyzing the new enemy and its tactics.

The same kind of meeting and exercises became a routine over the next few weeks, before they arrived in Mars' orbit. By that time, Major Rogers had presented videos of the enemy alongside the results of the simulated battles to Commander Partridge and the rest of the crew.

"We still have much to do," he told them. "This enemy is extremely fast and powerful. But we trust in the word that Joshua told us – that he will instruct us on how to face the enemy."

Right after that meeting Will found Jen by herself in the common area.

"How's the training going?" She asked.

"Honestly, it has been very tough. This enemy is too much for us!"

"But Joshua knows that. It's why he asked us to hide on Venus. I think by this time we should totally trust him to protect us."

"You are right, Jen. But I still can't help but worry a little bit."

JEN

Jen returned to her living quarters after her shift on the bridge. She slid her key card to unlock her door and quietly opened it. It was late, and she didn't want to wake Elizabeth, who had been ready for bed when Jen left earlier.

"Hey, girl. How are you doing?" Elizabeth said.

"Oh, good. You're awake!" Jen sat on Elizabeth's bed with a sigh. "I just talked to Will. He says war is imminent."

"Maybe. But Joshua sent this spaceship and taught us all these wonderful things—and he said he will help us, so I'm sure he will. After all, he has been correct so far, right? He has never let us down."

"Yeah, that's true. And every time I talk to him, I have such peace."

"I haven't seen his hologram in a while. Have you?"

"No." Jen flopped on her own bed and crossed her arms behind her head. "But I think I will if I believe. Besides, I have been telling everyone that he's not just a hologram. He's real and alive!"

Elizabeth sighed. "I hope to see Joshua again – the real Joshua, not just a hologram. If it wasn't for him, David and I wouldn't be the duet we are today. You know, Jen, lately I have been thinking about how privileged we are to be on the adventure of a lifetime, traveling across the stars, seeking a new home beyond our most unbelievable dreams. So, I've decided to be thankful for what we have. I don't regret going on this journey at all, even if my parents aren't here."

"I'm glad, friend. I feel the same."

Jen opened one of her bags and picked up the book she had started to read back on Earth.

"What are you reading, Jen?"

"This is one of the books my mom used to read me when I was very little, so I wanted to read it again." Jen tipped the cover toward Elizabeth.

"*The Voyage of the Dawn Treader*. That's one of the Chronicles of Narnia, right?"

"Yes, it reminds me of happy times."

"I'm sure."

"You can borrow it when I finish, if you like."

"Thanks Jen! By the way, do you mind if I play my keyboard for a little bit?

"Yes, please do, it is relaxing, and it helps me concentrate when I read."

Elizabeth began playing her synthesizer while staring out the window. Jen read for a few minutes, but then she fell asleep.

WILL

Later that evening, Major Rogers called Will to a meeting with Commander Partridge, Dr. Mendel and Star. After the analysis of previous encounters, it was evident they needed to avoid a direct confrontation at all cost.

"Dr. Mendel" Commander Partridge, began to speak in a more serious tone than usual. "Do you think we are doing the right thing, trusting in this hologram, when we don't even know if it's actually Joshua, as Jen claims it is?"

"Sometimes, I have some of those concerns too. But he has been right so far." Dr. Mendel answered

Will leaned forward. "We need to trust, to have faith that it will work out. And even when we know so little about him, the information we learn through the fruit of the seeds has been helping us on this journey."

"I know, Will. But regardless, it seems like we're taking a leap of faith."

"Yes, Dr. Mendel." Star responded. "Faith. That's what it is, and so far, he never has failed us."

"I understand but we need to be wise in how we proceed. Honestly, I would rather skip navigating through the whole solar system, but we still can't figure out the hyperspace engines and many of the repairs are not even close to being done. Besides, we are still researching the proper way to use the materials found on Venus. I need time to continue with my research on the spaceship and study its manual carefully. So even though it is a leap of faith, in a way we have no other choice but to follow the instructions, hologram or not." Dr. Mendel continued.

An alarm clanged loudly, bringing the crew to the bridge.

"Sir, we've reached the orbit of Mars, according to the planned route."

"Finally," the commander said taking his position on the bridge. "Major Rogers, dispatch a squadron to do the survey."

"Yes, sir." Major Rogers turned to Will. "Sergeant Morant, prepare your men and remain on standby close to the surface of the planet.".

Will immediately departed, leaving the crew to assess the details of the next mission.

Minutes later, Will's fighter jet passed in front of the bridge window. "Ready and standing by for your orders, Major."

Will received specific instructions and proceeded to survey the orbit of the red planet.

He switched his communicator to speak to the pilots in his squadron. "Okay guys, get ready. This is why we were trained for, so I expect the best of all of you. We are going to the surface of the planet. First, we will do a quick observation."

As the squadron got closer to the surface, Will and his team saw the sunrise from Olympus Mons, the tallest elevation on the planet, a giant volcano unbelievably wide and high. They kept watch for signs of enemy ships or other danger as they flew over the area and made closer surveys. Then Will reported their observations back to the Commander.

"Morant's squadron," Commander Partridge's voice came over the intercom, "begin descent to Mars."

JEN

Jen woke up from her nap to see Elizabeth still staring out the window, but now at the planet Mars.

"Oh, Elizabeth. You didn't have to stop playing the keyboard for me."

"It's ok, Jen. I was just processing all my mixed emotions. You know I'm happy to have such good friends, but at the same time I miss my family." Elizabeth stood up and walked towards the suitcase she still hadn't unpacked.

"Do you mind if I get settled while we talk, Jen?"

"Not at all Elizabeth, I'm all ears."

"Thanks. You are an awesome friend. Anyway, even though my family decided to stay behind they let us go graciously and..."

As Elizabeth began putting away some of the items she had brought along, she found the music box given to her by her grandma. Jen remembered she never had the chance to listen to its music the day before their departure.

Elizabeth's tears started to flow as she opened it, remembering her family and her hometown.

"Sorry I'm so emotional. It has been many years since I've heard that sound."

The melody sounded familiar to Jen but she couldn't remember why. It was sweet and calm, and at the same time kind of epic.

Elizabeth played it over and over, her eyes wet. "It is like I'm relieving good childhood memories."

"Aw, it's ok friend."

Suddenly a strange transmission from the intercom speaker interrupted her trip down memory lane., The sound was like an atmospheric music of some kind. Elizabeth closed the music box and both of them listened attentively without saying a word. The ambient music had a humming quality, and it grew louder and louder. Then it stopped abruptly. Immediately, the power went out, leaving only the red emergency lights glowing.

Now the speakers emitted a sound like old shortwave radio interference, the same kind that Jen had heard earlier. Then unintelligible words, like an alien language, burst into the room.

"Aaaah!" Elizabeth jumped and screamed. Jen rushed to her friend and hugged her.

Another voice joined in. It seemed to be a dialog between two individuals, one sounding as if begging.

All of the sudden, one of the voices began to imitate the melody of Elizabeth's music box.

Jen's heart beat faster and goosebumps sprouted all over her body. The second voice joined in the singing.

Elizabeth was in shock, so Jen decided to stay with her before reporting to the bridge.

How could they possibly have heard the music box inside the spaceship? How did those strange voices get into the speakers?

Then the singing stopped. Jen turned her gaze towards the window. An alien spaceship appeared. She began to shake, even more frightened than before.

The voice returned, but this time the muffled voice in the strange language began to say short words in certain intervals, like a pattern.

It sounds like a countdown.

Behind the odd words hummed a sound like an engine but with the tone of a strong electric trumpet. The noise grew louder and louder.

Suddenly, all went quiet, still with the power off, only illuminated with the red emergency lights, Jen and Elizabeth rushed into the hall and began to walk carefully to avoid tripping. They found the stairs and made their way down to the common area. It was crowded with civilians. Some stood looking at the window. Others walked around, looking distressed.

Jen turned to Elizabeth. "I need to report to the bridge. Will you be all right?"

"Yes. Go. I will find David."

They hugged, then Jen hurried to the bridge.

"So creepy," Jen heard Star whispering as she entered the bridge. "Like a whistle!"

"What is going on, Star?" Jen took her seat next to her friend.

"As we got closer to the atmosphere of Mars, this weird sound and voices came out of the speakers."

"Yes, we heard it in our living quarters, too. I think it was all over the ship,"

"We immediately began trying to find the source

of the sounds. All of a sudden, there was silence. Everyone seems to be puzzled, even Dr. Mendel." Star stopped talking as another crew member passed by them. Then she leaned closer to Jen. "The alien language was unrecognizable by the commander – and even by Dr. Mendel and his team. But we are determined to find the source."

A long series of beeps turned Star's attention back to her monitor. "Commander!" cried Star, looking pale and scared.

The spaceship Jen had seen earlier now hovered in front of the bridge's window. "I was about to tell you about that, Star," Jen said as she stared.

The ship looked like a helmet. A red light shone from underneath it. In the light, a humanoid form appeared– a figure with reddish skin and light brown hair in the shape of an afro. He peered arrogantly towards the *Dunamys*.

Suddenly, several other spaceships appeared, surrounding the *Dunamys*. Jen immediately went to her post at the communications board. On her monitor, she could see passengers gathered around windows, their expressions full of fear and anxiety.

But the alien ships didn't attack. Instead, they seemed to be analyzing them. The mysterious image projected by the main craft waved them on and then disappeared. At that moment, full power returned all over the ship, and the red emergency lights turned off. Immediately, the rest of the ships turned back to face them.

Star stood up. "Commander Partridge, I think I know what they want, sir. They want us to follow them to the surface of Mars."

"How do you know that?"

"Well, sir, they appear to be waiting for us."

"It could be a trap."

"Yes, sir, but they look like different aliens than the ones we encountered when we left Earth, sir."

The commander turned to Dr. Mendel. "What is your opinion?"

"This is strange. I think we should continue on course with caution."

"Maybe we should follow them," Commander Partridge mused. "Perhaps we've found allies. If they intended to harm us, they would have done it already."

Commander Partridge made the announcement to descend to the planet Mars and meet the aliens. He assured them that there was a very low possibility of suffering any harm, but they all wondered how it was possible, since Mars was such a hostile environment for any complex life form. It contained no oxygen and no protection against solar radiation.

By the time the *Dunamys* descended, it was sunset. The alien spaceship hovered above the ground. Then a red beam of light, like the one earlier, appeared. As before, the beam illuminated an alien. But this time it wasn't a projection – it was the actual being. Then the beam of light disappeared, leaving the alien alone on the surface.

The unknown language transmission returned. After a moment came a translation with a strong accent. The aliens indeed wanted to make contact with them. Commander Partridge immediately dispatched an embassy committee headed by Dr. Mendel and Jen.

WILL

Will and his squadron were briefed about the strange invitation. Then they were ordered to escort the committee and watch over them closely. Will kept an especially close eye on his sister and Dr. Mendel. Their shuttle landed close to the alien ship. They came out wearing spacesuits. Will zoomed in on his monitor, and stared at the alien. To his surprise he looked human, though a little taller and with orange or reddish skin.

The alien started to speak. His accent was strange, but apparently, he'd managed to learn their language. "We come from the planet Omma, 14.2 light years from here, from a star system you call Wulf 424. We call ourselves the Ommites. This barren planet once was populated by our civilization, but it became a desert, and we were forced to leave. But we had help from another civilization. They... that is a long story. We saw your spaceship after monitoring a hyperspace window activated not long ago. It is rare to discover one of those in this solar system, so we wanted to meet you and invite you both inside of my ship so we can talk on the way."

"On the way to where?" Dr. Mendel inquired.

"To the place where our civilization started, now we only have a small outpost. Please meet me at this same time tomorrow, in this place, and I will take you there. And I have one more request. I heard certain sounds from your spaceship when we made contact."

"Sounds?" Jen asked.

"Yes. Beautiful sounds I want to hear again." The alien seemed to be in a hurry.

"What sounds?" Jen repeated.

He repeated the sound that they'd heard in the original transmission, like singing.

Jen muted her voice transmission to everyone but Dr. Mendel. "I recognize that melody."

"What is it, Jen?"

"I heard it in my room. It came from Elizabeth's music box."

Dr. Mendel was quiet for a moment. "You know, this reminds me of the experiments Dr. Hackett conducted on the effect of David and Elizabeth's music on the *logos* trees when they were together, singing to the Creator. I wonder if they might be able to help us."

"David and Elizabeth?"

"Yes. It's worth trying!"

Immediately Jen activated her external mic and called the alien who was getting inside his spaceship.

"Please, wait!"

"Yes?" The alien turned around.

"We think we know the sound you mentioned. If you give me time, I can show you."

"I don't have time now, but tomorrow you can show me." Then he entered the spaceship and was gone.

Jen and Dr. Mendel returned to the shuttle. Will followed them back, still wondering if the aliens had true friendly intentions. He didn't like the fact the alien asked them to follow him and then he was in a hurry to leave. It didn't make any sense, but he was open to the possibility that they might have come in peace.

4
CYDONIA

JEN

Jen and Dr. Mendel returned to the *Dunamys* and debriefed with Commander Partridge.

"He didn't even give us a chance to introduce ourselves," Jen said.

Commander Partridge nodded. "And it is curious that they have so much interest in this music box. I mean, a culture as advanced as theirs? It doesn't make any sense."

"Sir, I think we need to bring them with us."

"You mean David and Elizabeth?"

"Yes sir. They may be able to help us connect with the Ommites."

"Okay. Get some rest and return with them in the morning, Jen."

She left for her living quarters, all the while trying to figure out a way to tell Elizabeth her plan. The room was dark when she entered. Thinking Elizabeth was asleep, Jen tried to be quiet. But her roommate rose and turned the lights on.

"Sorry," Jen said.

Elizabeth shook her head. "You didn't wake me up. I couldn't sleep thinking of the strange sounds and the alien voices."

"I understand."

"I talked to David earlier, but to be honest, Jen, I'm really in a hurry to leave Mars."

"Well, about that. . ."

Elizabeth gasped. "What is it?" Elizabeth sat on her bed.

Jen shared about her mission to Meet the alien, then asked Elizabeth if she could go to the bridge for an early meeting in the morning–and bring her music box. She shared her idea of performing a song in front of the aliens, but she didn't want to pressure her friend, so she asked Elizabeth just to go to the meeting with David.

Elizabeth remined silent wide eyes opened.

"Well, I–I, eh–let me think about this."

Elizabeth let herself fall on her bed laying down for a moment.

"I understand if you don't want to do this, I get it."

Elizabeth grabbed her communicator called David. She raised up and went into the small bathroom and closed the door behind her. After a few minutes she came out. She said yes, but with hesitation.

WILL

The next morning, Will reported to the briefing room for a special meeting about the alien encounter. Jen and Elizabeth arrived soon after. He greeted them but tried to limit himself to mission related conversation. Elizabeth seemed to be more uncomfortable than any other time in the past. David joined the meeting shortly after they started.

They explained that the aliens had asked about Elizabeth's music box. The big question was how the aliens were able to listen to the music from outside the spaceship. It was very strange indeed. Will shared his suspicions about the alien, because he was in a hurry, and he suggested caution. They all agreed.

Will could tell David felt uneasy about the mission, just as Elizabeth did, but both agreed—although a little reluctantly—to help out with the diplomatic mission.

At the end of the meeting, Will crossed the room to talk to Dr. Mendel about some ideas he had for the mission. As he waited for Doctor Mendel to finish talking with Commander Partridge, Elizabeth moved closer to him.

"Hi, Will," she said.

"Hi." He stood awkwardly for a moment. Then he looked her in the eyes. "Is everything okay?"

Elizbeth frowned. "Just a little distressed. But something tells me this is what I am supposed to do."

"I know what you mean, Elizabeth. You will be ok, all of us will be ok."

"I need to do a little research first," Dr. Mendel commented while he walked towards one of the working stations to sit down in front on the computer.

"I think Dr. Mendel activated a databank within the *Dunamys* systems, so he definitely can set you up." Will assured Elizabeth.

"I will talk to him. Thank you, Will. Good to see you."

"Same,"

Will decided his idea for Dr. Mendel could wait. Instead, he went to meet with his squadron to prepare for the encounter with the Ommites.

A few hours later, Dr. Mendel, Jen, David, and Elizabeth wearing the space suits boarded a shuttle. Then Will escorted them with half of the squadron. Will was determined to keep an eye on them the whole time. This was not easy for him, but he tried to be strong and carry on with his orders.

They approached a region called Cydonia where they saw a unbelievable features, small hills that look like pyramids and north from there Will saw what it look like a giant face with a helmet on looking at them. By the time they landed it was clear that the face was just a hill over a mile wide. The coordinates given by the aliens instructed them to land at the bottom of that hill; and when the appointed time came, Jen, Dr. Mendel, Elizabeth and David went out and encountered the alien, just as he told them.

JEN

Jen examined the terrain of Mars carefully as they moved across the surface until something interesting gabbed her attention, a hilly area ahead, and a very small mound that looked like a big disfigured face with a helmet.

The famous face of Cydonia.

Jen was inpatient to get out and see by herself what many in the past though was a giant alien sculpture, that ended out being just a hill. They landed there

Jen, Dr. Mendel, David and Elizabeth exited the shuttle. As they approached the alien, Jen signaled David and Elizabeth to come closer. Elizabeth clutched her music box, ready to show the alien, but the alien seemed hurried again. This time he asked them to follow him. Dr. Mendel and Jen consulted with Commander Partridge and Major Rogers on the bridge. They were authorized, so they agreed to go after him.

Jen listened as David and Elizabeth talked about Mars. They were amazed at the dunes and the dusty, red, yellow, and orange rocky vista in view as they walked. It was like looking at Devon Island in Canada, a place they'd only seen in a documentary they had watched together.

But Jen had a strange feeling inside, like something was out of place. Even when the alien was smiling at them, his eyes had an arrogant look, and his head was always a little bit tilted up, the same countenance she had seen in the hologram they projected in the orbit of Mars.

They walked for a few minutes around the mound that seemed to be about three quarters of a mile wide. Just as they came the other side of the mound, another group of aliens met them, all with the same height, skin color and unusual tilt of the head and eyes as the first one.

The alien, who at this point didn't say anything, pointed to his spaceship that landed close to an entrance on the mound.

I don't like this.

Jen tough while the alien invited them to go inside their spaceship to take a look. Jen studied the alien craft, noticing the complex engineering system, much too advanced for her to understand. The vertical pilot's seat rotated on its own axis. The alien that now began to behave like a fast passed tour guide, showed them every corner of his spaceship and then lead them outside. And instructed them to follow him to the entrance of the mound.

"I don't think this is a mountain after all," David observed as they got closer.

The alien shook his head. "No, not a mountain. Our civilization built this outpost a long, long time ago. It has been deserted for quite some time. Please come inside."

The alien spoke a few words in his strange language and suddenly the sand covering part of the wall spread away until it revealed a door with a ramp leading up to it. The whole group went inside.

WILL

Will and the other pilots who landed their fighter jets near the mound hill, followed them behind trying not to interfere.

"I think it is ok sir, they are not saying anything to us. I think they understand we are here to escort them." Will reported. "They are getting inside their spaceship sir. Should I get after them?"

"Negative, wait."

A few moments later the alien came out of the spaceship followed by everyone else.

Will was already stressed out so he decided to join the group and asked the rest of his squadron to go back to their jets.

The alien welcomed him with a smile and all together entered through the door reveled in the entrance of the mound.

An outpost!

Inside it looked like a huge cavern with polished rock walls lit by orange lights. As they went deeper into the structure, they found ruins of machines alongside various artifacts, including a papyrus that looked like blueprints for some kind of device. Finally, they arrived in a small room with a door on the opposite side.

"Our leader wishes to hear your sounds again," the alien informed them.

Elizabeth nodded and presented her music box. The alien pointed her toward the door. The group from the *Dunamys* advanced with her.

"No," the alien protested. "She must go alone."

"No." David stepped forward, but Dr. Mendel drew him back.

"I think she'll be okay. Trust me on this one, David."

After a tense moment, David nodded his consent.

The alien gave an order and another door deeper within the monument opened. Elizabeth followed the alien inside.

Will put his hand on David's shoulder. "I will guard the entrance. Call me on the communicator if you need me."

"Thanks, Will." But even as he spoke, David continued staring at the door where Elizabeth had left with the alien.

JEN

Jen crossed her arms and shivered as Will went back outside. Then another alien in the room picked up a box and held it toward Jen.

"I have a gift for you and your people." He opened the box. Inside, a rock like a diamond seemed to be made out of what looked like pink sapphire. It rested on a velvet pillow. Sparkles of light emerged from within the rock and illuminated the room.

Jen couldn't pull her gaze from the hypnotic light.

WILL

Will checked out the alien spaceship while he waited outside. It really looked like a helmet. The basic structure was spheric inside. He thought again about the alien being in a hurry, but then he took his time with Elizabeth. Something wasn't right. He looked carefully around the giant monument carved in the mound. It really looked like an ordinary mound, a little smaller than the *Dunamys*, but from the air it looked like a disfigured face with a helmet.

Why did they bring us here? What do they want?

As time passed, Will started to worry. Maybe he should check on Jen and his friends. He slid his gun from its holster and went back inside. He looked everywhere, but he couldn't find them. At least, not in the room where they had been earlier.

Perhaps they had been summoned through the door Elizabeth entered?

"Commander, this is Sergeant Morant reporting."

He received no response. *Perhaps there is some kind of interference inside the mound? I don't like this!*

Will hurried outside and tried again, reporting everyone missing. He was ordered to go back inside and look for them. As soon as he entered, the door closed behind him. He tried to open it but couldn't find the way to do it. He had no other choice but to go to the other door where Elizabeth had left with the alien.

Again, he couldn't find a way to open the door.

"Please, God, help me!" He kept inspecting the door. When it finally opened, he heard a girl scream. Elizabeth.

"Oh, Will." Elizabeth trembled before him. "I thought you were one of them."

"Are you okay?" Will hugged her.

"I'm fine." She began sobbing. "But I don't know about them."

"Where are the others?" Will asked.

"They're gone, Will. Rather, they have been taken away. We need to rescue them. And the *Dunamys* is in danger, too."

Footsteps approached. Fearing the worst, Will pulled his weapon and pointed it in the direction of the steps.

"Please don't hurt me!" The alien with orange skin approached him, bowing his head.

"He is with us, Will," Elizabeth put her hand on his arm.

"What is going on?"

"Your friends have been taken to become slaves of our masters, the Sarkos."

"No, no no no no." Will worked to contact the

Dunamys again. After a long time, he got a response.

"Will!" Star said. "Finally. We've been trying to reach you. We all are very concerned."

"Same here, Star. Let me talk to Major Rogers, we have a huge problem."

"Sergeant Morant, what is happening down there?" Major Rogers sounded upset.

Will explained the situation. Major Rogers instructed them to get back to the *Dunamys* for an emergency debriefing and ordered him to bring the alien with them to question him.

On the way to the *Dunamys*, Elizabeth shared everything that happened.

"As soon as I entered with my escort, all these glyphs of the stars were surrounded by blue lights. I was so distracted that I didn't see there was another alien there. He asked me to approach, then he requested the other to leave us."

"When we were alone, I asked who they were. At this point I was very frightened. He didn't respond. Instead, he asked to listen to the sound I was carrying."

"Your music box!"

"Yes. I asked him how he was able to listen to it. Apparently, their spaceships are capable of capturing certain low frequencies. Especially those we are unfamiliar with. Then he asked me to play the music one more time. When I opened the box, a smile spread over the face of the alien and he contemplated the box like it was a monumental wonder. I couldn't remember the song but then suddenly it came back to me. It was weird. It was like a movie of a lost memory playing in my mind with vivid details. The music is from an old song, based on a poem called 'Urbs Dei', the city of God. The poem talks about God's Kingdom, a place where there is no sorrow, or hunger, or pain."

"What? That's the final destination for all of us on board the *Dunamys!*"

"Yes, that is what I told him. Then he asked me about God, and I told him he is the Creator of the universe and of all we see."

"Freedom!" The alien with them exclaimed.

"Yes, freedom for all of us, Desperado," Elizabeth responded in a serious tone.

"His name is Desperado?"

"That is me," the alien responded.

Will pressed the button to communicate with the bridge. "Approaching the *Dunamys*, permission to board."

"Granted."

After docking, Will escorted Elizabeth and Desperado to the briefing room. Will could barely focus. Jen, David and Dr. Mendel were still missing.

Will was instructed to leave the alien outside with two security guards. Immediately Will and Elizabeth were urged to deliver their report.

Inside was Commander Partridge, Major Rogers, Star, and Doctor Hackett. Elizabeth shared what she told Will.

"Explain again what is so special about this song, Miss Carrington," the commander said.

"The song is an old hymn written in the 1920s called 'I Vow to Thee, My Country.' When I told him the music had lyrics, I started to sing with passion, the way that I used to, remembering the promises of Joshua and how everything he said so far was true."

"Go to the point, Miss Carrington. We are wasting time. We have people in danger." Commander Partridge interrupted.

"Sir, please listen to her. This is relevant," Will said, defending Elizabeth.

"Wait, I have the recording." Elizabeth touched her recording device that looked like a diadem on her head. "I will forward it to the important part, I think is here." She connected the audio to the speakers and immediately the recording began to play. Will listened attentively.

"God?" Desperado's voice.

"Yes, the Creator of the universe and of all we see. This music has lyrics. I can sing them for you."

"Yes, please."

And there's another country,
I've heard of long ago,
Most dear to them that love her,
most great to them that know.
We may not count her armies,
we may not see her King.
Her fortress is a faithful heart,
her pride is suffering.
And soul by soul and silently

her shining bounds increase,
And her ways are ways of gentleness,
and all her paths are peaceful."*

The recording was silent, then Desperado spoke. "What is this?"

"I'm hugging you. The Creator loves his creatures, so he loves you. We left our planet, leaving behind people and things in the search for a new, better land, the land this song talks about. We are strangers and exiles from our world in search of a new homeland, a world far away called Zion, His Kingdom. It is a place of true freedom, joy, fun, and peace, a place we can call our true home. Maybe you guys can come with us."

Then the alien produced strange sounds, like he was in pain or crying. "We shouldn't do this. To you and your friends. You are good people, and perhaps our last hope."

"What do you mean?"

"We prepared an ambush for all of you. So, you will become slaves of our masters."

"What?!"

"Our race is dying on this desert planet. One day a group of powerful beings called the Sarkos offered us the pink light, an addictive jewel. They also gave us technology and a different planet to live on. All in exchange for our freedom. We are now forced to do their bidding."

---

* I vow to thee my country. Public Domain Hymn. Music composed by Gustav Holst and Lyrics by Sir Cecil Spring Rice.

"What, exactly, are your people planning to do with my friends?"

"Take them to our home planet, Omma. That is the name these beings gave to our planet. They call us Epithymia Ommites."

"So, these beings have been ruling over you for a long time?"

"Yes!"

"I don't want the same thing to happen to my friends. Please help me to rescue them. I promise I will try to do as much as I can to help your people as well. As I said, you can come with us to this place of freedom, joy and health! So please help us!"

"I will try."

"Thank you so much! By the way, what is your name?"

"My name in your language means Desperado."

"Desperado. Wow, why that name?"

"One of our masters gave to me."

"I'm sure you can get a new name. Do you think there is any chance your people will let my friends go?"

"I don't think so. The Sarkos will kill them if they get a chance to rescue them."

"I was afraid of that." Then Elizabeth screamed.

"I've heard enough. Turn it off." Commander Partridge struck the table with his hands open. "Major Rogers, tell the navigator to take the Dunamys to the high orbit of Mars."

"Sir," Will said. "I just realized that we didn't ask Joshua about any of this."

"You're right," Commander Partridge said. "We

were so focused on this mission that we forgot about him. Can we contact him now?"

Joshua appeared immediately, his peaceful smile in place, and asked them to let Desperado in. Will found the alien sitting on the floor, still with the two guards. He looked deep in thought.

"Desperado, do you want to meet him?"

"Who?"

"Joshua, the one who showed us the way."

"It would be an honor!"

As the two of them returned to the briefing room, Joshua said to Desperado, "Don't be afraid. You will know the truth, and the truth will set you free."

Desperado looked at Joshua and listened attentively. As Joshua spoke, Desperado's skin began changing, slowly turning more human-looking. Joshua came closer to Desperado.

"I want to be free," Desperado said, "but also, I want freedom for my people. I want to go to that land that Elizabeth told me about."

"You will." Joshua looked him in the eyes. "I sent these people to help you. Go with them."

"Joshua, what are we going to do?" Will asked, still worried. "They have our friends."

The conversation was interrupted as they all turned to the window. The rest of the alien spaceships shot up from the surface of Mars. They flew straight toward the *Dunamys*, attacking without mercy. Commander Partridge ordered all of the fighter jets to depart and start the counteroffensive while he activated the shield to protect the *Dunamys*.

"Please don't hurt them," Desperado begged. "They are being forced to do what they do."

"We will try," Commander Partridge assured him. "But I can't guarantee anything."

Will ran to his jet and joined the battle. Soon, he spied the bigger alien ship behind the rest of the others. The main ship, he assumed. He elevated his jet as fast as he could and descended in an arc pattern right above the bigger ship, getting so close that he was able to see through one of the windows. Jen and the rest were there.

But one of the other ships started to attack him. While battling the enemy, Will asked permission to rescue Jen, David, and Dr. Mendel from the main spaceship that was now descending on the surface of Mars. Permission was granted, and he was ordered to take a squadron with him to pursue the main ship.

His fighter jet descended close to the surface of the planet. The other jets joined him. He led them through the *Valles Marineris* canyon in pursuit of the Ommite spaceship.

At the same time, a smaller spaceship attacked him from behind. Will advised his squadron to avoid the dangerous rocks falling from the hills, all while dodging the enemy, who was now attacking from both sides, the front, and behind.

The chase continued. A big rock fell right behind his vessel, but he proceeded onward. He, shut off a vital part of the spaceship. Still, he continued on, evading the dangers, until the large enemy spaceship began to lose altitude and fell to the ground. Will ordered the rest of the squadron to land with him.

He exited his fighter jet and ran to the crashed spaceship.

"Jen? Dr. Mendel? David?"

"We're here, Will." Jen ran into his arms as the two men followed behind her.

Will held Jen tightly. "Thank God you're okay How did you...?"

"Joshua appeared. He helped us to resist the power of the pink light."

"Oh yes, Elizabeth told me about it."

She whispered something else in his ear, something that made him freak out for a moment, but he tried to keep his composure.

David approached and extended his hand. "Thank you for rescuing us, Will. And thank you for taking care of Elizabeth."

"Any time, my man!" Will shook his hand quickly.

Will ordered his men to capture the enemy aliens who hadn't run away.

"Forget about them, Will," Dr. Mendel said. "Let's just get out of here,"

They boarded the jets and headed back to the *Dunamys*. On their way, they picked up a signal of Elizabeth singing. The rest of the enemy ships immediately fled.

JEN

Jen tried to enjoy the celebration of victory once back on board the *Dunamys*, but she was exhausted. She just wanted to return to her living quarters and calm herself down a bit after the creepy time on the alien spaceship. She was safe now, but it had been quite an ordeal.

Elizabeth arrived soon after. "Are you okay, Jen?"

"I'm fine. I just need time to process everything."

"I understand. I glad you guys are safe and sound."

"Thank you, friend" Jen hugged her. "I heard one of the aliens was captured."

"Not exactly captured. Desperado, that is his name, came willingly. He had an amazing encounter with Joshua and genuinely helped by giving us some intel. Still, he is being treated as a prisoner under strict vigilance. What happened to you guys? I was so worried!"

"We were under some kind of hypnotic influence. It was freaky. I don't remember much until we were inside the alien vessel. Then Joshua delivered us. But before Joshua saved us, I heard music, the same melody from your music box."

"Interesting! Remember what Dr. Hackett told us? How he concluded that certain kinds of songs had a powerful effect on the trees from Joshua's seeds? Maybe there is something even more powerful about the music."

5
JUPITER

WILL

The *Dunamys* continued its journey, crossing the asteroid belt in route to Jupiter. That day Will was hanging out with his buddies, the ones he knew back in the days of the Air Force Academy back on Earth. Iram, a tall, skinny guy with black hair, was introverted by nature, and Joseph, a short, muscular guy had a strong temper and outspoken personality. Now they were running missions together.

Iram was a little concerned about crossing the asteroid belt, but Will assured him the trip will be smooth because of the huge spaces between each asteroid. And in case they couldn't elude objects, the shield gave them extra protection. Will suggested taking a look in the areas under construction while they were on the way to Jupiter. Joseph explained that he had early training exercises in the morning, so he left while Will and Iram continued on together.

The engineers were finishing the upgrades for the new common spaces inside the *Dunamys*. It looked almost like a mall, and passengers were encouraged to open stores and restaurants there. While walking around, Will and Iram ran into Michael, the former owner of The Vintage Proverb coffee shop, where they'd all hung out with Joshua.

Will hadn't seen the man since Joshua's funeral. "Glad you are opening another coffee shop."

"Yeah, I figured why not? Besides, I have a new partner."

David's dad joined them.

"Mr. Peterson!"

"Hi, Will, I guess you heard the news. We are opening the Vintage Proverb here on the *Dunamys*. I hope my son and his girlfriend will sing for us like they used to back in our town.

Girlfriend? I thought they weren't official. Will tried not to frown. "I'm sure they will. Now all the eighty-six hundred passengers will have the opportunity to hear them." Will tried to keep up his friendly smile, but it was hard.

All of a sudden, a strange transmission came out of the speakers, similar to the one when they'd reached Mars.

"Here we go again!" Will inwardly sighed with relief. Now they could stop talking about David and Elizabeth. And he could excuse himself from the conversation altogether.

"I'm going to check with Major Rogers to see what is going on. See you later, folks."

Will arrived at Major Roger's office near the bridge. He punched the doorbell. Immediately, the door slid open.

Will stepped inside. "Just reporting in case I'm needed, sir."

"You want some action, don't you?"

"Well, yes sir. Honestly, we haven't had anything going on for several days and..."

"Bored?"

"Yes, sir. And I just heard the transmission."

"We are tracking it now. It seems it is coming from one of Jupiter's moons. The language is strange and distorted, but it seems to be some kind of dialogue. It's hard to make sense out of it because of electromagnetic interference. Come with me."

They went to the bridge, where the controls of the *Dunamys* indicated that they were crossing the magnetic field of Jupiter. But the planet was still far away. It was strange, but Dr. Mendel confirmed that it was possible since this electromagnetic field was the biggest in the solar system. But they still couldn't explain the transmission since they believed the Ommites were far away.

Will wondered if the aliens had followed them somehow.

"Desperado has been very cooperative with us, giving us intel on the Ommites' tactics and culture, so we know it is not them."

"Is he still a prisoner or is he now a guest?"

"We consider him an asset. And we are treating him as a guest. We even assigned him living quarters, of course with a bodyguard as a roommate."

"So, he is a prisoner."

"It's complicated. We don't know what we are dealing with here, and he understands that. So, he has been very cooperative with us."

"More reason to give him more freedom to mingle with the other passengers. I think that is what Joshua would do."

"Perhaps, but for now..."

Commander Partridge ordered four probes and a full squadron to go ahead of the *Dunamys*. He wanted them to test the new upgrades for the jets. But this time Will's name wasn't called.

"I'm taking a break, Major Rogers," the commander announced. "You are in charge of the bridge." Commander Partridge left.

The reports continued to come in. As the advance group arrived in the Jovian system, they found more than sixty objects orbiting the planet. They instructed the probes to circulate and inspect the main four moons—Io, Europa, Ganymede, and Callisto.

"We have visuals." Star placed one of the transmissions on the main screen. It showed the moon Io with a majestic sight of Jupiter on the horizon. The probe flew at great speed close to the surface.

"Are we recording?" Major Rogers asked Star.

"Yes, sir, from all of the probes."

"Is that classical music I hear?"

"Yes, sir. It is," Star said, lowering the volume.

"Leave it playing." Major Rogers smiled at Star. "I think it is appropriate for this moment."

"I'll never get tired of these amazing vistas." Star increased the volume a little bit as she spoke.

"'The Bringer of Jollity.'"

"What do you mean, Major Rogers?" Will asked.

"That is the title of this melody, composed by Gustav Holst."

"Cool!"

They continued watching the transmissions from the probes and reading the reports from the squadron while listening to the music.

"Sergeant Morant, I suggest you take some rest, just as your sister has done. And get engaged in more social life on board before you get called again. For now, we are just collecting information."

Will agreed to do as his superior said, but it wasn't easy. Adapting to the new social life inside the *Dunamys* had been hard for Will. He had made an effort to get to know some of the people on board by hanging out in the common areas, sometimes by himself and other times with his buddies from the squadron. But as he left the bridge this time, he went to a different deck that had even newer installations.

This deck had developed even faster than the other one. The new living spaces were opening, and Will felt as if he were walking around in a giant cruise ship with a whole mall inside. As he wandered, he saw Mayor Jacobs, who had overseen the whole project.

"Sergeant Morant, is everything okay?"

"Yes, sir. But I'm still adjusting to this new lifestyle."

"I understand. It's strange being in a big ship traveling through space. Making this place a home will take time. That is why I'm trying to help everyone to feel comfortable here. If you have time, I can show you some ways we're making sure this happen."

"Sounds good. I'm free, at least for now."

Jacobs conducted him to the elevator and down to the deck below, exactly in the center of the ship. They arrived at a boardwalk surrounded by several spaces that looked brand new. Pulling out his information tablet, the mayor showed Will the schematics.

"We've divided the populated areas into twelve neighborhoods:

1. **Happy Place.** A recreation area for kids and youth, with a kindergarten, a daycare, an elementary school and a farm.

2. **Southern Place.** A kindergarten, a daycare, a junior high, a high school and a gym.

3. **Legacy Place.** The auditorium, a plaza with a fountain, another gym and a botanical garden.

4. **Fruitful Place.** Another botanical garden, another farm, and a park, with a restaurant and a coffee shop.

5. **Fortune Place.** Storage facilities, supplies and a small restaurant.

6. **Rewards Place.** Vintage Proverb coffee shop, another restaurant, and a boardwalk.

7. **Expression Place.** A separate deck with an open space in the middle for events, with a view of the outside around it. Also, a boardwalk and small park.

8. **Fight Place.** A military area with a gym, a couple of debriefing rooms, a training area and one medical bay.

9. **Remembrance Place.** A large civilian medical bay, with a therapy room and a spa.

10. **Hearing Place.** A space for scientific research and crew debriefing. It contains a research garden, mostly consisting of trees from the alien seeds. A tech lab and a bio lab also occupy this space.

11. **Dwelling Place.** All living quarters located on the same side of the ship distributed over several decks.

12. **Ancient Place.** A preserved section of the original ship. It is not open to the public until we figure out what exactly is there. It is full of light and has some facilities

that we don't yet understand their use. For now, it is considered for authorized personnel only.

"As you have seen, many areas are almost complete, although the parks and the boardwalks were already in place when the spaceship arrived on Earth."

"I like the simple yet straightforward names! The more I think about it, these spaces seem to have been designed especially for us, either by Joshua or the one who sent him to us."

"I agree. We are planning an official opening ceremony soon, and I want David and Elizabeth to provide the music, along with the other musicians on board."

Will remained quiet.

"Elizabeth got very excited when I talked to them about it."

Will look at his communicator, which had beeped.

Mission training at 1800 hours, the message read.

What is it?" the mayor asked.

"I have to go. It looks like we have a mission on one of the moons of Jupiter. Thank you for the tour, Mr. Mayor."

"Anytime."

JEN

Several days had passed since they arrived in the Jovian system. When Jen arrived for duty on the bridge, she spent her time collecting information and watching the recordings of the transmissions, trying to make sense of it all.

The probes were still exploring the four moons, but they didn't detect any sign of aliens or other spaceships. The only interesting thing was the sound of strong winds.

While the *Dunamys* was getting closer to Jupiter's orbit at a great velocity, Commander Partridge asked them to keep watch for any signs of danger. Dr. Mendel found only one—a strong source of radiation coming from the planet.

But Dr. Mendel indicated that the next priority was to locate a source of water and energy for the ship. Jen did a quick bit of investigation from the probe's findings and found that the moon Europa was covered with large amounts of ice. She also reported energy sources on Io.

"Good job, Miss Morant!" Commander Partridge exclaimed.

"Thank you, sir. And one more thing. The source of the signal we all heard came from Ganymede, but I couldn't pinpoint the exact location on the moon."

"Major Rogers," the commander barked. "Send another probe to Ganymede!"

Everyone kept at their work. Jen spent hours analyzing data from the probes and decoding signals.

She sighed and threw up her hands. *Oh, come on, I can't decode this!*

"Are you ok, Jen?" Star turned her chair to look at Jen.

"I'm fine."

Star frowned.

"Don't give me that look." Jen faced Star. "I'm just frustrated. I can't seem to get relevant information from the probe–"

"Come on friend, I know you. What is going on?"

"I don't like complaining. You know I love my job."

"And you are so good at it. The people on the bridge really appreciate all your hard work. Deciphering signals, finding hints of danger, sorting natural signals from manufactured ones, and communicating messages to people and crew is a high-pressure job."

"That is my point, Star. I'm getting tired of being in front of a monitor. I wish I could talk to people more directly as well as leading the contact with new civilizations, like I did with the Ommites."

"Like an ambassador?"

"Exactly."

"But I thought you were scared."

"I was a little shaken at first, but I know I can do this."

"I understand, and I'm sure your skills will help you to get there, but we don't have much to do in that field right now. I think what you need is a longer break, say a few days. We have people trained to cover your position, and there is not much going on."

"Great idea, Star."

Jen thought about what Star said, she finally requested a break, which was granted by Commander Partridge.

Then she called Elizabeth, who asked Jen to meet her and their friend Doris in the new park in the center of the spaceship to hang out.

After a quick hug of greeting, Jen and Elizabeth began to walk and talk.

"I heard you and David were asked to perform in the common area grand opening tonight," Jen said.

Elizabeth nodded. "They want to open with our songs. Honestly, I'm kind of hesitant about it."

"Because of your experience back on Mars?"

"Yes, it was a little intense for me. But I would still love to do it, all I need is time. I have so many things going on in my head, and I feel I need a break."

"I know what you mean, friend. We have not even left our Solar System and we are already struggling—but on the other hand, this situation has made us grow. We are getting better at what we do. And you don't know how many lives your music is touching, like Desperado's."

"You are right. Doris was so inspired the other day that she asked us to join David and I. She plays the cello. . But we gave her a try, and frankly, her skills on the cello are impressive. I was surprised, really. She's such a private person. David accepted her right away. This encouraged me a little bit, but still..."

"I know you're feeling a little down but think about the many people who will be cheered by today!"

"Yes, you're right, Jen. The focus should be them, not me."

"Besides, I think you enjoy singing to God as much as he enjoys listening to you."

Doris joined the girls as they walked.

"Sorry I'm running late."

Jen nodded to Doris as she continued to talk to Elizabeth.

"What you do matters, but it is also something you enjoy. Just have fun and forget how many people are present. Do it for God. After all, he is the one who sent us this ship. Just make it an audience of one."

"I agree," Doris said. "We need to play and sing for Him first."

Elizabeth hugged each of them. "Thank you, girls!"

Hours later, the grand opening ceremony started in the brand-new auditorium. The venue made Jen feel like she was in a royal theater, with its plush seats and artistic decorations on the walls. Everyone had dressed up, and almost all the crew was present, except for the ones needed on the bridge. Senator Jacobs, now the Mayor of the *Dunamys* came to the stage.

"I know the strange alien messages we received disturbed us all. But even though we were led to a trap, we were protected and saved from our enemies. All of us who decided to go into this journey have taken a leap of faith in order to find another world beyond the stars. We came to trust in the one who sent us this beautiful spaceship, the *Dunamys* which, I believe, was made especially for us. This is the reason we are preparing better accommodations for the long journey ahead of us. I want to thank all of you who have created this special community for everyone on board, both passengers and crew."

Then he asked David and his dad to come to the platform. He held them up as an example of living a normal life aboard the spaceship.

David approached the microphone. "We are refugees in this vast ocean of stars, seeking the new home where we will not live as strangers but as citizens with a normal life. We'll create businesses, cultivate the botanic garden, and get together as a big family. We are all together on this great journey. With people we love and care for."

Then he called Elizabeth to the platform. She stood close to him and he reached for her hand.

Doris drew her bow over the strings of her cello as other violinists joined in playing "I vow to thee my country." The music swelled as if played by a grandiose orchestra even though they were only a few musicians. Then Elizabeth sang:

"I vow to thee, my country,
all Earthly things above,
Entire and whole and perfect,

the service of my love;
The love that asks no questions,
the love that stands the test,
That lays upon the altar the dearest and the best;
The love that never falters,
the love that pays the price,
The love that makes undaunted the final
sacrifice."*

"Join us to sing as one," David said with a smile.

As everyone stood up to sing, Jen felt the hymn's theme as one for their journey ahead.

After everyone took their seats, David and Elizabeth performed a couple of their well-known songs.

Then Mayor Jacobs returned to the stage, smiling. "Thank you, David and Elizabeth—and all the musicians! You always sing beautiful songs about God and the beauty of his creation. Thank you for encouraging us with your voices.

"Now it is time to inaugurate this great city. This place was built for the journey across the galaxy. It might be a long trip, but we are ready for it! Feel free to open restaurants, stores, places for rest and nourishment, and even fun. Now we'd like everyone to join us in the plaza!"

The plaza had a fountain in the center and boardwalks around it. At one end of the space was a

---

* I vow to thee my country. Public Domain Hymn. Music composed by Gustav Holst and Lyrics by Sir Cecil Spring Rice.

huge botanical garden, where all the fruits, vegetables, and cattle were raised. It included an area where trees from the small seeds grew. There was even extra space to expand later.

The mayor shouted, "Welcome to the *Dunamys'* Neighborhoods!" He cut the ribbon and opened the way to the upgraded living space for the passengers that had still been in development when they departed from Earth.

The people applauded, and everyone looked happy. Except for Elizabeth. Her typical smile was gone. She looked more serious than ever.

Suddenly a huge jolt shook the spaceship. Jen saw David quickly grab Elizabeth to prevent her from falling.

"Thank you, David." Elizabeth put her arms on David's shoulders, then let go as soon as the ship stabilized. "I'm okay."

"Don't worry, everyone," came the voice over the speaker. "We are simply crossing the magnetic field of Jupiter. There is nothing to be alarmed about."

Jen's communicator immediately alerted her, and she went to the bridge.

As she arrived at her post, she noticed a huge gravitational pull and an increase in their speed towards Jupiter. Immediately Jen advised the passengers to go back to their quarters until further notice. On her monitors, she saw people running, panicking, and then locking themselves in their rooms.

Commander Partridge's voice rang out on the bridge. "Bring the shields to maximum and initiate the reverse thrusters."

Jen held her breath. It seemed to her that a crash to the surface of the planet was inevitable.

They hovered very close to Jupiter's great red spot, the huge storm in the planet's atmosphere three times bigger than the Earth. Several clouds of yellow, brown, and red began to surround the ship, but the shield was strong enough to protect them.

"Increase the engines' speed and power," the commander said.

Star looked at Jen. Her eyes seemed filled with fear and doubt, Jen felt that way, too. It was getting harder to think clearly enough to make the necessary adjustments. Then a thought crossed her mind.

"Joshua said we shouldn't be afraid," Jen said aloud.

"How can that help us avoid being sucked into the red spot?" Star protested. "That's the biggest storm in the solar system!"

Suddenly, an intense lighting storm surrounded them while the ship moved deeper into the atmosphere of Jupiter. The *Dunamys* shook with every strike.

"Why are we getting deeper, Dr. Mendel?" Commander Partridge demanded.

"My readings shows, there has been increase in the mass of the Dunamys, since our departure from Earth, but it has doubled since we arrived at Jupiter, which of course means–"

"I get the picture. But how is that possible? Why didn't we take that into the calculations?"

"Sir, this increase is not easy to follow. Every calculation we make is not accurate enough, and this incremental in the mass made the gravitational attraction of Jupiter stronger than we expected."

As they moved closer to the center of the red storm, the winds increased in speed and strength alongside the lightning.

Then a sparkle of intense white light shot out from behind the *Dunamys*. In a fraction of a second, it moved towards the front of the ship. An incredible power increased the speed of the vessel.

Everyone seemed to relax as the mysterious light towed them through the clouds, far away from the storm. When it surrounded them for a few seconds, they realized they were on the other side of the planet.

Commander Partridge spoke first. "Someone or something is helping us."

"Sir, we picked up a transmission," Jen announced. "Just audio."

"Put it on, Jen."

"Why did you doubt it?" a voice asked. "Don't let fear dictate what you do."

"Who are you?" Commander Partridge asked.

"I came to help you. As I always have."

Quickly the stars appeared clearly again in place of the brown, orange, and yellow clouds of the planet. They were stable in the planet's orbit.

"Who are you?" the commander asked again.

"You still do not recognize my voice?"

"Joshua?" Commander Partridge breathed deeply.

"Thank you for saving us..."

"Anytime! Many others who started the journey you are taking have been lost here in this red spot, and many of those refugees have died here on Jupiter. This is the place where all the toxins and waste of the solar system get deposited and create storms of gas and debris burning inside. Despair, doubt, and fear make travelers unable to do anything to escape. But I know you, each and every one of you, and there is still faith and hope among you. This journey is not easy, but keep moving forward. Believe, and you will get to Zion."

"Transmission has ended, Commander," Jen said as the mysterious light dissipated.

After they escaped the gravitational force, they moved away as fast as they could. Major Rogers dispatched another probe while Commander Partridge approached Jen's board to see her data.

"It looks stable enough, right?"

"I think so," Jen replied.

"Star, come here for a second."

"Yes, sir"

"Take a look."

Star studied the screen for a moment, then nodded. "That would definitely work."

Commander Partridge immediately ordered them to land in a safe spot on Callisto and launch missions from there to collect resources for energy and water supplies.

Right after landing Jen noticed Commander Partridge's tone of voice had turned more peaceful and relaxed than before.

"Dr. Mendel, Jen, Star, follow me to the briefing

room," the commander said. "Major Rogers, you're in charge."

The group entered the briefing room, each taking one of the seats close to the rectangular table in the room. Jen felt much more at ease as the danger had passed.

"What's on your mind, Miss Morant?" Commander Partridge asked.

"I have peace, but I think we need to consult Joshua more often."

Dr. Mendel nodded. "I agree with Jen. We need someone to shed some light into everything unknown in this journey."

"I realize that," Commander Partridge said. "We could definitely use some direction. I'm open to his suggestions."

"So, should we stay here in Callisto? Or what should we do?" Star looked around at each person in the room.

"Good question Star. We need a plan because I want the next missions to be well coordinated and smooth here in the Jovian system. That is why I choose Callisto. We can launch missions to the other moons from here. But let's ask Joshua first."

"Glad you are considering my advice in this situation Commander Partridge." Joshua appeared out of nowhere. "Landing on Callisto was the right move. From here you can replenish the *Dunamys* and continue with the repairs."

"Just as I thought," Commander Partridge added.

"But beware the enemies. Some will try to persuade you to go back, and others will try to deceive you. Prepare yourself to stay firm to continue the path." Joshua finished talking and then disappeared. Immediately, they activated the shields just in case.

WILL

Will sat with the other pilots in the briefing room.

"Ok gentlemen, this is the reason you have been training for the last few days. Io is a moon full of volcanoes, lava, and geysers, so use the precise precautions you learned in the training exercises. Right now the *Dunamys* is scanning the exact location of energy sources that will be transmitted to you shortly. The objective is to acquire the gas coming from the geysers and bring it safely to the Dunamys. You have a 'go' at 1300 hours."

Will was dispatched to escort the exploration shuttle going closest to the biggest geyser. As they neared, he noticed the gas coming out was blueish, unlike geysers on Earth. The report sent by Dr. Mendel indicated that this specific geyser was different from any others. Will circulated around it while the exploration shuttle funneled the gas into the tanks onboard. A few hours later, they prepared to return to the *Dunamys*, which was still on Callisto.

The itinerary was to rest for a couple of hours before sending another mission to the next destination, Europa, to look for another essential element: water.

Once again, the shuttle was dispatched, followed by Will's escort. They arrived to find a terrain covered with ice and full of cracks. They needed a stable place to land. Finally, the crew found a flat, solid place. Once the shuttle landed, the expedition began to drill ice to collect it for water.

JEN

Everyone on the bridge was watching the mission very closely. And as always, Jen was concerned for her brother. But then she reminded herself he was well trained to do this job just as she was doing hers, even if gathering information inside the ship did have fewer risks than her brother's.

Dr. Mendel sat in the empty seat next to her. "Everything all right, Jen?"

"Yes. Just thinking. Do you need anything?"

He was quiet for a moment, his eyes on her screen. "I've wanted to ask you about Joshua since you have been closer to him than almost anyone."

"Have I? Anyone who believes in him can be close to him. Do you believe he is alive?"

"I'm not entirely sure. I do believe it is possible. But what I'm concerned about at the moment is the increase in the mass of the spaceship. As we add resources to fix and maintain the spaceship, our weight will increase even more. Are you sure Joshua—or his hologram or whatever he is—knows what he is doing?"

"I do. And so far, he hasn't failed us, Dr. Mendel."

"Yes, I guess you are right."

"By the way, the report from the exploration team just came in. Their analysis shows that the water is rich in minerals and drinkable."

"Very good, but I still want to pass it through the purification process."

Jen activated her communicator and spoke to the shuttle. "Tell the exploration team to store as much as they can."

An alarm interrupted the conversation. Jen swiveled her chair. "What is it, Star?"

"Commander, we've detected a violent quake on Europa." Star and Jen locked eyes for a moment, then each turned back to their computers.

"Jen?"

"I'm on it, sir."

"*Dunamys* to Shuttle exploration team. Please respond."

No answer.

Jen tried again. And again. But everything remained silent.

WILL

From his orbiting ship, Will noticed the shaking. It

affected everything, including the shuttle. He glanced at the surface of the moon and saw a huge crack in the ice racing towards the exploration vehicle. The driver accelerated. Then another crack split off from the first one and began a direct course towards the shuttle. They were running out of time.

The exploring vehicle slid, then started to spin, tossing the pilot and copilot onto the ice. Their voices cracked through the communicator.

"We need to get to the shuttle! Run!"

Will held his breath and listened, powerless to do anything from his position above them.

The crack finally reached the vehicle.

"Just a few steps! Come on!"

Will watched them run until they finally reached the exploration vehicle. Other reached out and pulled them inside, but Will could still hear their conversation.

"I'm so sorry, sir. We lost the last cargo of ice."

"It's okay, Joseph. You collected enough already."

"Are you guys, okay?" Will inquired through his communicator.

"Yes, sir."

"That's the most important thing. Please depart quickly. The crack will reach the shuttle soon."

Within moments, the shuttle rose. The ice cracked beneath where it had been sitting. Will and his squadron escorted them back to the *Dunamys*, still stationary on Callisto.

Everyone seemed a little shaky as they

disembarked. Will found Joseph and Iram on the flight deck.

"Will you both please join me in my quarters?"

Once Joseph and Iram arrived in Will's room, he closed the door behind them.

"You both know that the next stop is Ganymede," Will began. "The transmission we picked up was coming from there. We need to use extreme caution after the last encounter on Mars. We don't want that same kind of situation. The commander asked me to put my entire squadron on yellow alert until we find out what's down there."

"What do you have in mind, sir?" Iram asked.

"Once we arrive at Ganymede, I'm pretty sure Commander Partridge will send more squadrons, including ours, to gather more information. I want you both to send out more probes. I know that's already been done, but I want a close surveillance of our own, just as a backup. Meanwhile, keep this a secret. We don't want to alarm the passengers or anyone else."

"Understood, sir."

6
GANYMEDE

JEN

Commander Partridge ordered the navigator to move the *Dunamys* into Ganymede's orbit and advised many of the crew to take a break before arriving. Jen took advantage of this time to join David and Elizabeth in the new coffee shop. While there, they listened to their favorite band, The Shawn Duet, on the speakers.

"Wait, I remember that song," Elizabeth said.

"Of course you do. It played on our first date." David answered, picking up his guitar.

> *"Forget not my love, forget not my darling*
> *And here with you crossing this bridge*
> *With the only one for me*
> *With you my darling, holding your hand."*

David began to sing, staring into Elizabeth's eyes. She joined in, smiling.

"Yes, you are the only one for me."

"I just remember. That was the day we were ice skating," Elizabeth said when they finished singing.

"And you fell on the ice." David grinned.

"Ice! Oh yes, that was embarrassing!"

David turned to Jen. "We were skating and singing that song we both knew."

"And I fell!" Elizabeth blushed.

"But I picked you up right away!"

"Yes, you did, David. It was so sweet of you!" Elizabeth smiled

"How romantic," said Jen, wishing she could fall ice skating and be picked up by that special one.

"What's that noise?" asked David.

"What noise?" Elizabeth tilted her head to listen.

A sound like thousands of voices singing in a high pitch reached Jen's ears, but it was very low. Almost imperceptible. As they listened, it got louder and louder.

Jen called Star at the bridge. "Star, are you listening to this?"

"Yes, it is all over the ship. The closer we get to Ganymede, the louder the voices become."

"Or maybe more voices are being added to the initial voices."

"Good point, Jen. It does sound like more voices are being added to the frequency."

"It's similar to a Gregorian chant, slowly changing to higher notes," Elizabeth interjected.

"I don't like this; it is so creepy," Star whispered. "I'm shaking."

Passengers all over the ship fell silent, leaving the chanting as the only sound.

Jen shivered with fear. Then she stood. "Enough of this ominous sounds! I'm going to the bridge right now!"

"Jen, don't leave!" Elizabeth grabbed her arm.

"It's ok, Elizabeth, I'm going to find out what is going on, and I'll let you know."

Jen arrived at the bridge to find everyone paralyzed, sitting still and listening to the voices. Even Commander Partridge was affected.

Then the singing stopped.

"We have to leave this place at once," the commander cried. "Take us away from here!"

As he spoke, the ship picked up transmissions from a different direction. Once the transmissions ended, they began again, like they were part of a cycle. All in the same alien language they had encountered on Mars.

"Dr. Mendel, what are they saying?"

"Surrender or you will be destroyed," Dr. Mendel translated. "I repeat, we are the Sarkos fleet. Surrender or you will be destroyed."

"This transmission is not from Ganymede but from space, in the opposite direction." Commander Partridge looked deep in thought.

Suddenly, powerful rays attacked the ship.

"Attention all passengers," Jen said over the intercom. "Go to your security rooms right away."

"How are we doing?" the commander asked.

"Not good. We're moving too slowly in comparison to the attackers."

Commander Partridge took a deep breath. "Then we don't have any other choice. We have to counterattack."

"Commander?" Star's voice broke into the awkward silence. "Don't you want to call Joshua?"

He looked startled, then thoughtful. He nodded decisively. "Yes, I won't do anything before consulting him. I learned that lesson."

Joshua appeared before them. "Go ahead and attack. Do not surrender to the aliens." Then he vanished again.

Commander Partridge sighed. "I was hoping he would help us, like the last time. But we will do what he said. Give the order, Star. We will attack."

"Right, sir." She turned to her communication device. "Attention all squadrons. Prepare for battle. This is not a drill. I repeat, this is not a drill."

As the squadrons went into battle mode, the commander called Major Rogers, Star and Jen to the briefing room.

"I've sent for Desperado. We need information from him. If he is on our side, we need to find out what he knows about the Sarkos."

"They want us to surrender. I am afraid they might do to us the same thing they did to the Ommites," Star interjected.

"The Ommites mentioned the Sarkos," Jen remembered.

"Exactly. Maybe Desperado can help us negotiate with them," Commander Partridge suggested.

"With all due respect, sir, I don't think it's possible." Major Rogers paced the office. "I don't know much about their culture, but–"

A member of the crew entered, bringing Desperado with him.

Commander Partridge turned to the alien. "Desperado, thank you for coming."

"Thank you for giving me a chance to prove myself, Commander."

"I need you to tell Jen as much as you can about the Sarkos. What are their weak points? How can we fight them? Can we negotiate peacefully with them?"

Desperado's face grew distressed. "The Sarkos have enslaved entire civilizations and you speak of standing against them? No one has enough power to do that! And they will not negotiate, they only conquer."

"Regardless, please tell us what you know. And Jen, please call Joshua again. Perhaps he will tell us how to defeat them." Commander Partridge returned to the bridge.

WILL

Will and his squadron shot out of the *Dunamys* first since they had been on alert and ready.

Iram called to Will through his communicator. "I wasn't expecting to engage in battle right that soon, sir!"

"I know, but I believe you are up to the challenge. You got this."

On the way out, they encountered several enemy spaceships flying in the shape of a triangle. The ships were almost heart-shaped with what looked like eyes on the front.

Behind Will's squadron, others were joining the fight. But the alien spaceships sent intense pink rays at them. The firepower was overwhelming.

Will followed what looked like the lead ship and targeted it, but he was too slow. A ray struck his left wing, making his jet spin out of control.

"Sir, are you okay?"

Jaw clenched; Will tried to balance his fighter. "No worries, Iram. I'll find a way to stabilize. Just keep fighting."

Will continued to spin, on every rotation he watched another fighter jet explode. Every now and then, an enemy ship went down.

All of a sudden, the battle stopped. Everything

went quiet. Before Will could communicate with anyone, he heard voices, like a huge choir, humming, Synchronized, like the buzz of bees. The same voices they heard before the attack of the Sarkos.

The voices grew louder as Will's ship continued to whirl.

Suddenly, a great explosion sent millions of colors into the air. The voice of the choir rose again. In desperation, Will turned off the engines just before the world around him went black.

*****

When Will opened his eyes, he was lying on a table looking up at a white, semi-transparent dome, something like clear quartz or glass. Above the dome, the area looked full of caverns. He turned his head. Several lights shone around him as well. He seemed to be in a different kind of alien spaceship, made of what looked like diffused light in an oval shape.

"Welcome to our mining outpost, human."

Will turned to see who had greeted him. The lady was very tall. She had short, blond hair, and thin eyebrows. Her eyes were large, her neck long and narrow, and her mouth small. Her skin looked paper white. She wore a bright white dress with gold decorations and a crown surrounded by a golden force field. On her chest, a plaque looked like a diamond. She walked gracefully into the room, almost like her feet didn't touch the floor.

Will raised himself on his elbow and surveyed the building in front of him. It was made of porcelain or ivory with diamonds and other precious jewels all around. It almost looked like a temple.

"My name is Ergon. We call ourselves *Religare*. We are a reverent civilization and enemies of the Sarkos. Welcome to Ganymede, our outpost in your solar system."

Commander Partridge stepped into the room, and Will felt relief at seeing at a familiar face.

"The Religare saved us from the Sarkos," the commander said. "They also know how to fix the problem with the extra weight on our spaceship. They are a very advanced civilization. I'll explain it all to you on the way to our new home."

"Our new home? But what happened? How did I get here? How long have I been unconscious?"

"25 hours. I'll tell you the whole story later."

Will stood, surprised that he didn't ache all over. He felt fine. Together they walked over a bridge and into another building.

"We are deep beneath the Ganymede surface, inside a giant dome made of some kind of glass. Don't ask me how, but here we are protected from space radiation and from the cold as well as receiving a perfect supply of oxygen."

"Wow! That is impressive!" Will admired their architecture and technology as they made their way into a big house made out of the same material he had seen on the other buildings.

Everything inside was luxurious, flashy, and modern. He noticed other aliens who looked like Ergon, tall, long neck, pale skin, big eyes and small mouths. But none of the others had crowns.

Is Ergon their queen?

"These people know Joshua," Commander Partridge said. "They said they can get us to Zion without the problems we've been facing if we travel with them. But they need us to work with them for a while. Actually, the tall lady you met is one of their leaders."

Will wanted to understand but felt confused. It sounded too good to be true.

"Where's Jen?" he asked.

"She's preparing for the meeting."

"What meeting?"

"She will start negotiations with The Religare. Your sister has become quite an admirer of them."

"Sir, I mean no disrespect, but this all looks very familiar. Do you recall what happened on Mars?"

"I remember, Will, but the Religare are different from the Ommites and the Sarkos."

"But there's something fishy here. Aren't we supposed to continue according to Joshua's itinerary and the information we received after eating the fruits?"

"Yes, Will, but as I said, they know Joshua, too. Think of this as a shortcut. And besides, they saved us from the Sarkos."

"May I join the meeting?"

"Of course. You are one of the closest of us to Joshua. But keep any unnecessary comments to yourself and let us negotiate."

JEN

Jen arrived at the big tower and took the elevator to the top. When she stepped out, she could see through to a big room with a rectangular table in the middle. Everything gleamed white, all made of the same materials. By the time she arrived, Commander Partridge, Mayor Jacobs, Dr. Mendel and Will, were already there, each seated on a cube outside the room.

Before they could enter the meeting room, the aliens checked them for security reasons. They were then led to another room, where a plaque of a silver-like metal was embedded on the wall. The aliens asked them to place their hands on it, one by one. As they did, the plaque turned black.

"All of you have a high level of contamination," one of the aliens said. "Every creature that has been in contact with the Sarkos, or with someone who has been in contact with them, is impure."

"Please sit down," said another tall alien said to the men. Then he escorted Jen into another room.

"Sorry for the inconvenience, but we need to purify you." The Religare voice came from outside the room.

Suddenly a powerful light clicked on, and Jen recognized the sound again, like a huge choir like bees buzzing. The same sound they had picked up before their encounter with the Sarkos. But this time the voices were more harmonic, and louder. Then several showers of gas and liquids fell over her.

When the process finished, her clothes started to glow. They looked brand new, but with a diffused light in them. Then the door that led to the hallway opened. Will came in as she was escorted out. Finally, they were all clean and sitting   silently in the big room.

WILL

Will wanted to talk to Jen, but the silence and the whole protocol made it feel awkward. Besides, he'd been ordered by Commander Partridge not to say anything unnecessary.

The aliens instructed them to sit in specific seats. Then Queen Ergon arrived. This time she didn't have a forcefield on her.

Queen Ergon led the conversation, she and the other Religare asking several questions of the *Dunamys* crew. The crew themselves asked a few questions.

"We have to take care of the others we rescued from the battle as well," the alien said. "And we need to purify the rest of your crew and passengers."

"Of course. I–" Commander Partridge's words were cut off.

"Then we are in agreement. You will remain here, working for us, and in exchange, we will take you to Zion, protecting you all the way there."

Mayor Jacobs leaned forward. "But we still need to talk with the rest of the passengers, and—"

"We are an advanced and powerful race, far more advanced than you. And we have been exploring space for many years. Trust us. We know what is good for you."

The aliens motioned for them to stand, then everyone from the *Dunamys* was led outside the room while the Religare continued conversing inside.

"So, the lady that visited me was the queen?" Will looked back in amazement.

"Now you see. Good people, these Religare," Commander Partridge whispered before making a sign to Will to remain quiet.

Will strained to hear what was going on behind them. The queen's voice rose above the others.

"They will if they know what is good for them. That is their only choice. Prepare their new homes immediately."

JEN

Jen was glad to head back to the *Dunamys*, which had landed outside the city. Escorted by one of the Religare, she boarded one of the small ships made of the same semi-transparent material in their buildings, the substance which looked like pearl. The ships were the shape of an elongated egg or a drop of water and with golden wings like a firefly. She was instructed to give an update to the rest of the people on board. Walking inside she went right to the elevator and then to the common area where the new coffee shop was. There, David and Elizabeth were talking with David's dad. Jen stood a little way off and could hear their conversation.

"I don't know about this," Elizabeth said. "There's something weird about these beings."

"They said they know Joshua and they want us to remain here in Ganymede," David said, "but we're supposed to continue our journey after leaving the solar system. At least, that's what Joshua said."

"You're right, David," his father said. "This doesn't make any sense."

"We should contact Joshua and check with him. He always knows what to do," Elizabeth insisted.

Jen walked up to the table. "You are right, Elizabeth, but I know he will be ok with this. They are offering us so much protection and technology, and they will take us safely to Zion."

"For free?"

"All they ask is for us to remain here for a little while and work with them."

"With them or for them?" Elizabeth asked.

Just then, Will's voice called out. "Guys, can you hear me?"

"Will?" David's eyebrows rose. "Where are you? How are you contacting us?"

"This is a low radio frequency. The Religare can't pick it up, at least as far as I know. Too primitive for them. I can't get inside the *Dunamys*. There are Religare guards' ships all over ..."

The transmission was interrupted for a moment.

"Will?!"

"Jen? How did you get back in the ship?" Will's voice returned.

"They wanted me to deliver their message to everyone." Jen answered.

"Listen, Jen. I think they're lying. This purification stuff – I don't know what it is, but since we got it we all feel weak."

"Now that you mention it, yeah. I felt kind of tired and heavy after all that. But I don't think–"

David solemnly reached for Elizabeth's hand.

"Jen, remember what Joshua said? Many will try to deviate us from our journey. And besides, the *Dunamys* was given to us for a reason."

"Will is right, Jen." Elizabeth said.

"Okay, let's say you're right, that this Religare group wants to keep us away from our journey. In that case, what are we going to do? They have us surrounded, and they are way more advanced in technology! Ugh!" Jen rested her head on the table with a groan.

"Jen? Are you okay?" asked Elizabeth.

"I feel heavier all of the sudden," Jen whispered.

David turned to his dad. "Bring her a coffee, please."

Will's voice returned. "I think it finally began to affect her, David. It seems that when we resist their influence, a heaviness manifests itself."

"And they want to do this to all of us? No thanks!" Elizabeth added.

"Elizabeth is right," Dad's dad said as he set a cup of coffee in front of Jen. "This is not good. I don't like how they want us to earn the trip to Zion by working for them."

"Will, did Joshua mention these people before? Did he ask us to follow them?" David asked

"No bro, never," Will answered.

"Ok ... I guess you guys are right." Jen lifted her head and sipped her coffee.

"We're trying to find out what these guys are up to, but it's hard. It almost seems like they're reading our minds." Will, continued.

"We need to call Joshua," Elizabeth urged.

"Yes, let's call him right now," David said.

Elizabeth agreed.

Will's transmission distorted. After a few unintelligible sounds, his voice vanished, leaving only static.

"Will, respond! Please respond," cried Jen.

"We can't keep talking. Let's call Joshua now." Fear colored Elizabeth's voice. David took her hand and together they all went to the bridge, gathering more people along the way.

"Joshua, please," Elizabeth pleaded. "If you are here, please respond. We need your help, please."

People searched all over the common areas and the bridge, but no one saw Joshua. Still, they continued calling to him.

WILL

Back on the citadel of the Religare, Will and Major Rogers were escorted back to the big room at the top of the tower to meet with Queen Ergon.

"I know you want proof that you can trust us," she said. "I hear you want to see Joshua. Well, here he is, with us. Listen to him."

"Queen Ergon is right. You have to remain here," said a voice from an unknown origin.

"Joshua, is it you, my friend?"

"Yes, Will. This is me."

Will wanted to believe, but the voice sounded a little different than the one that had come from the light that rescued them from Jupiter's red storm.

"If it's you, why did you ask us to take this journey?" he asked.

"I wanted you to meet the Religare. Now all you have to do is to work with them. It's going to be hard work, but in time you will be granted access to Zion and become an official citizen there as I promised."

All of a sudden, Will felt a peaceful wind pass by him. It was refreshing. Then Will remembered his first encounter with Joshua and the spaceship and how the journey's destination was promised to them, that they were free to accept the journey or not. Joshua had said that once they arrived in Zion, they would be accepted just because they had made the trip to get there. And he remembered the peace he had felt about it.

"You are not the real Joshua," said Will firmly.

Suddenly everything went dark, no light except the diffused ones glowing from the gems on each Religare's chest. It lit their faces from below, making them look creepy. Everything seemed to be frozen. Suddenly Joshua was there holding a lantern with a light ten times brighter than the Religare.

"Follow me," he said.

Will immediately followed him, as did others from the crew. They passed through the gate of the city and continued walking until they found themselves on board the *Dunamys*.

"David? Elizabeth?" Will ran into the coffee shop.

David hugged Will. "Joshua is rescuing the rest of the crew now."

Will turned around to find all of the *Dunamys* crew, including Commander Partridge.

"Welcome back aboard, sir." Major Rogers greeted Commander Partridge with a handshake.

"Major, what's going on?"

"They were fake."

"Who?"

"The Religare. They were desperate for workers, I guessing in their mines here at Ganymede. They wanted to enslave us, too. They are almost like insects, like a hive of bees serving a queen."

"What about Desperado?" Jen asked.

As she spoke, Desperado walked into the coffee shop. He was covered with bumps and bruises.

"They said I didn't deserve to live," he gasped. "They tortured me."

"Now you're safe." Jen hugged him.

"Sir, I think it's about time we trust Desperado," said Will. "He suffered even more than we did. I think he's on our side."

"We'll talk about that later. Right now, we need to leave Ganymede."

"I will get to my jet, sir, and—"

Major Rogers rested a hand on Will's shoulder. "No, Will. We will all remain inside the *Dunamys*. I believe Joshua wants us here together. For now, come with me to the bridge."

"It seems the Religare just discovered their prisoners are escaping and have decided to attack," Jen said from her seat on the bridge. "Here they come, hundreds of ships."

"How do you know?" Major Rogers leaned over her shoulder to view her screen.

"Because their ships have an elongated shape, like an egg, with golden wings. And they are attacking the *Dunamys*."

"Shields to maximum!"

The attack began before *Dunamys* could lift from the surface, and continued while the ship escaped. The Religare remained in pursuit from Ganymede all the way to the moon of Callisto. There, the lead Religare ships surrounded the Dunamys attacking it from every angle.

"They are trying to block our escape sir. We need to make room for the *Dunamys* to move away." Will followed Major Rogers outside the bridge, while the ship shook with each attack.

"You wanted some action, Will? I think this is the time." Major Rogers sent Will to lead the defense.

As soon as Will's jet left the *Dunamys*, he was face to face the enemy. They looked like a swarm of killer hornets and were just as deadly. The *Religare* moved more quickly than the Sarkos had, and their ships, like glowing fireflies, behaved so erratically that the fighter jets couldn't accurately fire at them. Frustrated with the whole situation, Will decided to remain close to the *Dunamys* to protect it from attack. Others followed his lead, staying as close to the ship as possible.

For a little while, they held off the attack. But it was getting to be too much. Suddenly Will noticed the winged egg ships whizzing away.

"Sergeant Morant, I think they are leaving," Iram said over the intercom.

Will scanned the area and noticed the same thing. The Religare retreated without any apparent reason. The battle was over.

The *Dunamys* landed once again on Callisto. Commander Partridge called the crew to the bridge for debriefing.

"What just happened?" Mayor Jacobs asked.

"We were deceived once again," sighed Major Rogers.

"So, we don't know if we can trust any aliens? What if Joshua is the same thing? What if he is fake and he wants to enslave us, too?" Commander Partridge sounded angry and confused.

"But he has saved us several times," Jen protested. "And he never asks for anything in return. He hasn't done anything but protect us and take care of us. He healed you, Mayor Jacobs, and you too, Commander Partridge. He actually gave us the choice to leave or stay on Earth. We had complete freedom to choose."

The others remained silent.

"The computer indicates we need to remain on course towards Saturn," said Star.

After a few minutes, they all agreed to continue the journey, believing that what Joshua had said was the right thing to do. Star set their course to the next planet, Saturn.

JEN

Hours later, Jen returned to her quarters, exhausted, physically and emotionally. Earlier she had learned that several of the passengers willingly decided to remain in Ganymede and take the offer of the Religare. She was disappointed that many chose that after seeing how Joshua had saved them so many times, but at the same time she also felt guilty because she almost believed the deception as well. As she was falling to sleep, her communicator indicated a call. She rushed to pick it up.

"Jen, do you have a minute?"

"Sure David. What's up?"

"Have you seen Elizabeth lately?"

"No, she isn't here in our living quarters. Is everything okay?"

"I'm not sure. Elizabeth and I went for a walk earlier today. We were watching the view of Jupiter as we moved away from the planet. I told her how excited I was for the upcoming presentations at the new Vintage Proverb, then we took some pictures of us with the view of Jupiter in the background. Then I told her about some plans my dad had in mind for the coffee shop. Suddenly her responses turned short and serious. I tried to hold her hand, but she wouldn't let me. Then she said she couldn't do this anymore."

"What?" Jen was fully awake now. And worried.

"She said 'what if one of us dies during this journey? What if all this is in vain?'

"I tried to assure her that I would protect her, that she wouldn't be alone, that I would be by her side every step of the way. And I reminded her that Joshua would always come to save the day. We have plenty of proof of that. But she started crying."

"Did she say anything after that?"

"She said she wasn't feeling sure about anything anymore. I asked if she still missed her parents. She said yes. I didn't know what to do except to hug her, but she pushed me away. I told her my parents love her as their own daughter, but she didn't respond."

"That is not good."

"I know. Then she told me I was making this too hard for her. She said she needed a break. And just like that ran away, leaving me in total confusion."

"I'm so sorry, David. I'm sure this is hurting. I don't know what to say, but—if I was on her shoes, I would act all the opposite of her."

"What do you mean?"

"But I don't know what is going on her mind."

"I was hoping you had heard from her."

"I wish I could say I had David" Jen hang up, felling a deeper sadness than ever before.

7

CASSINI

JEN

The click of the door to her living quarters woke Jen. She opened one eye to see Elizabeth quietly closing the door. Jen quickly pretended to be asleep. Minutes later, she heard the bathroom door close and the quiet sobs coming from within. After a while, the door opened again.

Jen blinked her eyes open. Elizabeth put her earbuds on and laid down on her recliner safety chair. Last time Jen had seen Elizabeth doing this she was mourning over leaving her parents behind.

Jen went back to sleep to give Elizabeth some alone time.

Hummm humm hum daaa!

Jen heard her roommate humming a melody. She sat up in bed to find Elizabeth looking at her song's notebook and humming.

How many hours have I been asleep? Jen got out of her bed.

Elizabeth startled. "I'm so sorry, Jen. Did I wake you?"

"No. I needed to get up. Songwriting again?"

"Yes, I was inspired."

"That's good, but—is everything ok?"

"Yes. Why?"

Jen tilted her head and stared at her friend.

"Well, fine." She set down her pen. "I'm not okay, not at all, actually"

"What's wrong?"

"I'm thankful that we were still alive, but I don't like it that we have so many enemies trying to stop our journey to Zion. It scares me. And my relationship with David is not in a good shape, either. With everything that is happening around us, it is all just too much."

The intercom crackled, and Jen and Elizabeth both looked at it. "Ladies and Gentlemen," Star's voice announced. "We have arrived at the orbit of Saturn. Feel free to take a look out your windows." Then an alarm sounded, indicating it was time for Jen to wake up.

"I'm sorry Elizabeth, I need to get ready to go to my post. Can we go for a walk later today?"

"Sounds good. We can visit the new plaza and the second Central Park."

"Great. Let's do that. For now, you need to get some rest."

"I am going to keep writing for a little while, then I will sleep."

Jen jumped in the shower before preparing a mug with black tea. After giving her roommate a hug, she left for the bridge.

WILL

When Will arrived at his living quarters, David was sitting in his recliner looking at his communicator as if he were expecting a call or a message.

"We just arrived at the orbit of Saturn," Will said.

"So, I heard." David didn't sound happy.

"Everything okay, man?"

"It is fine, dude." Now he sounded upset.

Is there a problem in paradise? Maybe everything wasn't as perfect as I though between David and Elizabeth.

Before Will could ask, David spoke again.

"Why now?"

"What do you mean, David?"

"Why do you care now if something's wrong with me? You've been keeping your distance, almost avoiding me, except for emergency or duty situations. It seems odd that we haven't spoken since Joshua died, even though we have been living together the last months."

Will fidgeted with his communicator. He was indeed avoiding conversation with David. All this time he'd said nothing more than a casual good morning or have a good day, short empty conversations.

"I'm sorry man. It's complicated. As you know, I' was busy with the academy and the whole process of becoming a pilot. All the new duties and stress."

David grinned, but his eyes still didn't look happy. "I bet ladies love that. Look at you, bro. You're a hero."

"Trust me, it is not as fun as you think. It's not like I'm a pop star or something, like—"

David growled, as if Will's answer made him even more upset.

Will held up his hands. "Okay, okay. Calm down. I guess we've both been having a hard time, right?"

David nodded; his jaw tight.

Will sat down next to him. "Is it Elizabeth?"

"Yeah. She said she needs a break."

"She broke up with you?" Will tried hard not to smile.

"I don't know!" David told Will the whole story. Then he cradled his head in his hands. "This is so hard. I love her so much."

I know what you mean bro.

Will didn't know what to say. Then his communicator beeped.

"Be on the bridge at 1700 hours. We have a mission to prepare.

"Another new adventure?" David asked.

"I guess so!" Will said.

"Have fun getting out at the alien sites and all. Meanwhile, we just wait here, admire the view, and have a hard time with people on board."

Will didn't say a word as he gathered his things.

"I'm sorry, Will. I didn't mean to say it that way, man. It's been a difficult week."

"I understand." Will put his hand on David's shoulder. "And I know the feeling! Ok, maybe when I get back, I could talk to her for you." Will decided it might be good to know what happened from her side of things.

"Sure, thanks, bro. But I don't think she wants to talk."

"Well, leave that to me. After all, we used to be close friends back in the day."

"Thanks, Will."

"Of course. I'll find her right before this next mission."

Will left quickly after that, He had so many mixed feelings about the conversation. He didn't know how to process the whole thing. But maybe he'd now have a chance to talk to her about her feelings.

JEN

Dr. Mendel set coordinates to station the *Dunamys* on the Cassini Division, the largest gap on Saturn's rings. As the spaceship slowly approached the ring, the gravitational forces of the planet tugged at the ship. But this time, the crew was prepared to avoid a gravitational collision. While the *Dunamys* maneuvered carefully to counteract the gravitational attraction of the planet, Dr. Mendel started his analysis of the rings.

Jen used the cameras to observe the passengers approaching their windows to take a closer look. Who wouldn't do that? The view was amazing, with the sun over the equinox illuminating the surface of the rings.

As the ship got closer, the particles from the rings began hitting the vessel. It sounded like hail. The noise got louder, then softer, then louder again as they slowly and carefully approached the Cassini division.

Then a bigger ball of icy rock came on the screen at the bridge.

"What is that?" Star pointed at the window.

"It is called Enceladus," Dr. Mendel answered.

"Sergeant Morant reporting for duty," Will said as he stepped into the bridge.

Dr. Mendel glanced at him. "Thank you for coming. We are preparing to collect several samples of a specific kind of rock from Saturn's rings."

"But aren't the rocks just made from frozen water, Dr. Mendel? Like ice?" Star asked.

"Most of them are, Star, but not all of them. Many think these rings were formed after a collision of moons. And we are detecting some metallic compounds present. Sergeant Morant, this is where you and your team come in. We need as many non-water rocks as we can get."

Commander Partridge stepped forward. "The objects orbit at 33,331 miles per hour or 53,640 km per hour. I don't want any accidents this time."

"No, sir." Will saluted him. "I'm on it. Calculating and compensating for the speed."

"This mission is extremely important," Dr. Mendel said. "We need these rocks to repair several vital parts of the ship. I've provided you with a detector and calibrated it to identify the specific kind of rocks we need. The same calibration has been provided to the jets and the exploration shuttle."

Jen jumped away from her board post to hug Will. "Please be safe."

Will nodded and kissed her forehead before he left for his ship.

"Wow," Star said, still gazing out the large window. "I'm just in awe! This place is huge, so many times bigger than the Earth. How small we all are!"

The *Dunamys* slowed down as it reached the middle of the Cassini Division, which had rings on both sides.

"And just think," Star continued. "Someone superior and intelligent created all this."

"And he was the one who provided us with this spaceship," Jen said as she returned to her post.

Jen checked the various cameras at her station to make sure all was in order on the *Dunamys'* decks. In one view, she noticed David walking around the first common area deck playing his guitar. From another, she saw Elizabeth lingering in the new Central Park, a deck below. While they both seemed to be admiring the view of the rings, Elizabeth seemed less astonished. After admiring the rings for a few seconds, she then frowned and looked down.

David, on the other hand, would often stop playing and place his guitar on the floor near the window, fixing his eyes on the rings as if looking for something.

Jen empathized with her friends. She felt bad for them. Could Joshua help them, even with this? Even if this could hurt her?

WILL

Will boarded the shuttle with Iram. He sent Joseph ahead in a jet as they approached the ring zone with the biggest objects floating around the planet. The pieces of ice and rock were as bright as mirrors, producing sparkles through the reflection of the sunlight. Will tracked the specific rock requested and moved the shuttle to an area where they could find more abundance of that material.

Carefully, the shuttle approached the area above the ring of rocks and debris to avoid any collision. Then, using the mechanical arms from the shuttle, Will grabbed small pieces of the rock and placed them inside the shuttle. Iram transferred them into a container prepared to simulate the temperature and environment of the rings.

Will looked out the window again. Some shiny objects winked at him from a little farther.

"Iram, can we get closer to that area?" He pointed at the sparkles beyond them.

"Are those diamonds?"

"I don't think so, but let's take some samples."

Suddenly Iram pointed to the *Dunamys*. "Hey, Will, look!"

"What?" He moved closer to the window.

"Looks like somebody is waving at us. Maybe you have an admirer."

Will rushed to the monitors showing the transmission of one of the cameras pointed to the *Dunamys*. It was Elizabeth, watching from the window of the common area. And she was waving at them. For Will, time seemed to stop for a moment.

"This is mission control, everything okay?" came a voice through their communicators.

"Roger. We're almost done. Everything is okay!" reported Will from the shuttle.

"Yes, sir. We are wrapping everything up as fast as we can." Iram went back to work.

Iram and Will classified each sample they'd collected, but Will took special interest in two specific rocks, one metallic and one crystallized. The crystallized rock looked like a diamond, and the metallic rock like gold or silver, or something in between.

Will hoped Dr. Mendel would be pleased with the variety they'd collected.

JEN

Back on the bridge, the crew monitored the progress of the exploration team. Suddenly, the computer sounded an alarm. Star studied the instruments and detected an object approaching the Saturnian system. A few minutes later, she called the team.

"Will?"

"Yes, Star?"

"You need to return to the spaceship immediately."

"What's going on?"

"You are in danger. Come back to the *Dunamys* right away."

"No problem. We just finished loading the last batch of samples into the shuttle."

They immediately departed, heading back to the ship, when all of the sudden a big chunk of debris hit the small craft.

"Will, are you okay?" Jen shouted at the communicator.

Silence.

Everyone on the bridge watched the shuttle float above the rings.

"Sergeant Morant, please respond." Star turned to Jen.

"Call Joseph immediately," Jen said.

"Joseph, can you see what is going on?"

"I can see it spinning, but the lights are on."

"Will? Iram? please respond," Star said again, the concern in her voice growing with each word.

"They are moving again. Slowly, but they are moving," Joseph added.

"Follow them," Star ordered.

"Yes, ma'am. They are moving towards the *Dunamys*."

"Good, keep us posted."

Jen looked for the camera closest to the shuttle bay and watched as the small craft made its way into the ship. "They're all on board." She sat back and blew out a long breath.

"Good, let's leave the ring zone." Commander Partridge sat back in his chair, as if he, too, had been concerned.

Jen asked permission to be relieved and went to look for her brother near the shuttle bay.

As she arrived, technicians were examining the shuttle carefully.

"Will, I was so worried." She hugged him.

"We lost the antenna, and part of our engines. It was all my fault. I was distracted."

"At least you and Iram are fine." Jen returned to her post thinking about the dangers Will encountered on every mission but also thankful for her brother's safety.

WILL

Will delivered his report to Major Rogers, then asked if he could keep some of the rocks he collected. The major agreed. The major then asked him to stay put during the next mission—to Enceladus, an icy moon of Saturn. Will wanted to protest, until he realized he had another priority. This would be a great opportunity to find out what was going on with Elizabeth.

As Will walked out of the briefing room, he studied the rocks from the mission. He'd kept the ones that were metallic and the ones that were crystallized. On his way to his living quarters, he called Elizabeth on his communicator. She answered right away.

"Hello, stranger!" She sounded happy to hear from him. "It's been a long time since you came to visit or wanted to talk!"

"I know, I know. I want to catch up with you, but first I think I owe you an explanation for why I haven't talked with you or David for a while. Can we meet to talk in person?"

"Sure."

"I heard the newest neighborhood has an awesome farm. We can talk as we walk on the boardwalk."

"What's it called?"

"*Fruitful Place.*"

"Sounds good, I'll meet you in about an hour."

"See you there." Will took a fifteen-minute power nap then jumped in the shower and prepared to meet

Elizabeth. Before he left, he put the rocks he picked up from his mission in a box to give her, an apology for avoiding her for so long.

As Will reached *Fruitful Place*, it occurred to him that the ship now felt like a small city, but not like any city on Earth. The cruise ship-like living quarters were connected by corridors which converged into big open spaces with a few big rooms around them. People often transported themselves through the corridors and decks with available scooters and a few small golf cars, though some preferred to walk or jog.

Will looked out the window and noticed a canopy of fire floating above the *Dunamys*. He realized it was the shield protecting the ship from freezing as they approached Enceladus.

Elizabeth walked toward him. She was wearing her gym clothes and looked like she'd been jogging for a while.

"Hi Will. It's good to see you." She gave him an awkward side hug.

"Good to see you, too." Will pointed out the window. "I never cease to be amazed. Joshua certainly thought of everything!" He continued contemplating the fire shield outside the window, the light with shades of orange and yellow colors reflecting above their heads.

"Yes, he's been with us all the way on this journey. I just hope that includes our relationships… Anyway, do you remember this?" She stepped closer to the window just as Saturn came into view.

"The first time, I showed you the stars on my telescope?"

"Yes, we were looking at this from afar and now we are close to the very planet we were looking at through the telescope."

How can I forget, Will thought, when I told you I would love to get a precious stone from it and make a ring to propose to the girl I loved. You said, "whenever you find the right girl." I never said it, but you are the right girl.

Elizabeth sighed. "I will never forget that evening—the ride on your bike, the picnic, that starry night. It was such a fun and sweet time. Before we were kicked out, that is." She grinned at him. "Anyway, what did you want to talk about, Will?"

"I−I−" Will snapped out of his memories. "I want to be sure you're okay after all we've experienced. And I want to apologize for being so distant lately. Especially since Joshua died back on Earth. I've been having a hard time since then, and I just..."

Come on Will, this is not the right time, just wait.

"What, is it Will?"

"Remember what I said that night as we looked at Saturn with the telescope?"

Elizabeth paused for a moment rolling her hair around her fingers. "You said... you said, your wish was to make a ring out of the finest rocks of Saturn's rings and give it to a special lady."

"Guess what lady I was thinking of?"

Elizabeth blushed.

"You."

"Thank you Will!" She held his hands.

"I know we've been friends for a long time, and when I heard you and David... well... It was hard for me, because I..."

Man, come on!

"Because I've had a crush on you ever since I met you, but I never found the right moment to tell you. I know this is not the right time but... I can't help it I–"

She didn't seem surprised, but she still blushed. "I'm honored, Will. Thank you for sharing your feelings. But why didn't you tell me back then?"

"I've never been good at this kind of thing. It is easier for me to pilot a fighter jet or drive a dangerous road. This is uncharted territory for me."

Then he told her everything he went through from the time he saw her the first time with David all the way to the present.

JEN

Jen returned to her post on the bridge after a short break, ready to monitor the progress of the second mission into Saturn's system. The *Dunamys* was stationary in orbit of Enceladus and another shuttle was dispatched to the frigid moon. Major Rogers was once again in charge of the bridge. He was not as intense as Commander Partridge, which made Jen feel more comfortable.

Jen noticed the south pole of the moon ejecting some kind of material. "What is that?"

"That is the reason we are here, Jen," Star explained as she followed the shuttle on her screen. "Those are huge plumes of water ejecting from the cracks at the surface, the sign of clean liquid accumulated underneath. The shuttle is going to gather some of it."

"No wonder we need to make stops on every planet. They all have something we need."

The mission progressed without any accident or problem. The shuttle collected great quantities of clean water after drilling the surface near one of the plumes. Then the shuttle returned to the *Dunamys*.

With nothing putting them in immediate danger, Jen decided to scan the cameras distributed among the twelve neighborhoods. She stopped on the image of Will and Elizabeth as they walked on the boardwalk by one of the farms. They were looking at each other with such intensity. She couldn't believe her eyes.

"No way!"

"What is it, Miss Morant?" Major Rogers asked

"Nothing, sir. I just... never mind."

Star moved closer to Jen's board. "Isn't that Elizabeth?"

"Yes, I can't believe it."

"I'm sure they are just talking as friends."

"I didn't think otherwise." Jen followed them as they entered the farm. It wasn't like an actual farm, like on Earth, but more like a living space similar to a botanical garden surrounded by the walls of the spaceship. The farm contained some fruit trees, a few cows, chickens, turkeys, and a tank of water for fish. Even though it wasn't large, it was enough to meet the basic needs of the people on board.

Suddenly Major Rogers was at her shoulder. "Why don't you take another break and join your friends, Miss Morant? Just be back in three hours to get ready for our next mission—to Titan."

Jen got up with a big smile on her face. "Thank you, sir."

WILL

Will finished talking to Elizabeth, relating his perspective from the time he met her all the way to the present without mentioning what he'd recently found out from David.

Elizabeth frowned, biting her lips, it was obvious she was getting nervous. As they exited the farm area, they came to a bench. She sat, arms crossed, head down.

Will was ready to reach into his pocket to get the present he had prepared for her, the rocks he got from Saturn's rings, when he heard Jen's voice.

"Hi, guys. Am I interrupting?"

Yes, you are, sis.

"Of course not, Jen." Elizabeth stood up and hugged her.

"Hey, sis!" Will said reluctantly.

Elizabeth turned to Will. "I'm so sorry. I really want to continue this conversation, so please let's talk more later. Right now, I have a lot to process, I just need some time alone."

"I understand. Take your time."

Elizabeth hugged him.

He talked with Jen for a few minutes, then Jen went to the other side of the deck to talk to some of her other friends. After she left, Will sat on the bench deep in thought. He watched families walking towards the farm, some couples holding hands, others hugging as they watched their kids chasing the chickens or petting the few cows. But their happiness was too painful.

He stood up and called Major Rogers. "Sir, this is Sergeant Morant. May I come to the bridge to check the data about our next mission?"

"Of course, Sergeant Morant. Come on over. We are just approaching the orbit of Titan."

As soon as Will arrived, he read the details of the mission prepared by Dr. Mendel. Their instructions indicated that they needed to get into the surface of Titan to obtain large quantities of the liquid found in its oceans. The analysis indicated methane mixed with small amounts of ethane.

Hours earlier, a drone had been sent across Titan. By the time Will was on the bridge, the footage and analysis had started to come in. The tactical instruments scanned for any possible sign of other vessels, while the science board scanned for chemicals in the atmosphere, environmental pressure, and any other compounds on the soil. Dr. Mendel confirmed the preliminary analysis of the liquid compounds from Titan. He determined that it was possible to harness them as a power source for their trip using a special converter. The atmosphere was rich in nitrogen and a little bit of methane.

"Ladies and gentlemen," Star announced over the com system, "we are approaching the surface of Titan, one of the moons of Saturn. It looks stable and calm, but the temperatures are very low. The protective shield will keep us warm, so we suggest you activate the heating in your living quarters only if it is absolutely necessary."

8
TITAN

WILL

When the *Dunamys* entered the atmosphere of Titan, they found a world similar to Earth, in appearance at least. They navigated across the moon, passing over a vast desert before crossing several low hills. The instruments analyzed every detail of the composition of the atmosphere, which was mostly nitrogen. They also found a huge lake, bigger than Lake Superior in North America, followed by a river. The area had several hills covered with solid ice surrounded by more rivers.

"Wow, it looks so much like the Earth on a late autumn afternoon," Star said.

Will approached Star's board to look closer. "So true, especially with the vivid oranges and yellows in the sky. The rivers and lakes are amazing, but I don't think there is water flowing through them."

"You are correct, Will," Dr. Mendel said. "Those are, in fact, rivers and lakes of methane and other hydrocarbon compounds."

Commander Partridge asked the crew to prepare for landing. The passengers were asked to take their seats and adjust their safety harnesses. They selected an area in a valley surrounded by the lakes. According to the logs, the place was called Xanadu. Finally, the *Dunamys* touched ground.

The area was surrounded by rocks with the appearance of black ice. The temperature outside read -142.6 F or -97 C, but this seemed to be the warmest area of Titan, since the average temperature was -291.01 F or –179.5 C for the moon as a whole.

Dr. Mendel immediately called a meeting with Will's squadron, along with Major Rogers, to assess how to proceed with the mission. They began by evaluating the footage and data from the probe.

"Rocks everywhere! What a desert!" commented Joseph.

"But rocks made out of ice, methane and other compounds, like ethane," Iram pointed out.

"This place reminds me of Earth, but at the same time the view is so lonely," Will commented while examining the footage.

"Do you think we'll be able to survive the rest of the voyage? So far, it's been full of traps and danger. Why didn't Joshua tell us about it all?" Joseph asked.

"I guess he didn't want to scare us? But so far, he's protected us, even while he's light years ahead of us,"

Dr. Mendel answered.

"How does he do that?" Joseph asked.

"I don't know. But I do know that for now there is no sign of any enemy here, and we have the chance to enjoy the view of this awesome place," Dr. Mendel said.

"Sir," Will interjected. "If you will notice, the temperature in here is very nice, not just because of the systems of the *Dunamys* but also because of the shield."

"You're talking about the cloud, correct?"

"Yes, but now it has turned into a fire again and is covering the ship. Same as I noted in my report from the Enceladus' mission."

Dr. Mendel immediately looked at the screen displaying the outside cameras. "You are right. How is that possible?"

"What is going on?" Major Rogers asked.

"This is impossible!" Dr. Mendel said.

"What?" Major Rogers sounded impatient.

"We are surrounded by combustible and flammable compounds. Any kind of flame should make everything explode within seconds. And besides, how can there be fire outside at all? Fire needs oxygen, and the presence of oxygen outside is very low. How is the fire burning?" Dr. Mendel shook his head.

Will smiled. "It's Joshua. I don't know how he is doing it, but he is keeping us warm in these cold temperatures."

"You talk as if he's still alive," Commander Partridge remarked as he entered the meeting.

"Sir." The others rose from their seats.

"At ease," he said. They sat down again.

"He is!" Will said firmly.

Dr. Mendel frowned.

"We will talk about this later, Sergeant Morant. For now, let's focus on the mission," Commander Partridge replied.

"Yes, sir." Will opened his tablet, ready to take notes.

Dr. Mendel continued his instructions. "As we mentioned before, this world is extremely cold. What you see outside are great quantities of liquid methane. On Earth, this takes the form of gas. Most of the mountains here are made of rock and very solid ice. That will tell you the magnitude of the low temperatures out there. The spacesuits will protect you from the extremely cold temperatures – they come with a thermal layer - and will provide you with oxygen. Nevertheless, I advise caution."

"How is it that the Dunamys is not freezing in this frigid place?" Commander Partridge asked.

"It seems that the protective shield surrounding the *Dunamys* has been calibrated to protect us from the extreme cold temperatures," Dr. Mendel explained.

"Impressive! Joshua thought of everything. It is like he knew all we would go through." Commander Partridge turned to Will, Iram, and Joseph. He pointed at the screen showing several tanks made of metal. "Your mission is to fill these tanks with the methane from the lake. We've prepared a special room the same temperature as Titan where you will place the tanks, then the room will normalize the temperature to the interior of the spaceship at a very slow pace. You must proceed with extreme caution; methane is highly volatile. The rest is standard procedure."

JEN

Later, as Jen hurried to report to her shift, she continued to think about Elizabeth, Will and David. It was complicated, for sure, and as much as she wanted to be away from the conflict, she was the one holding all the pieces together. As she opened the door of the bridge, she noticed everyone was busy. The crew was running more scans, not just of the surface but also the surrounding orbit, in case of enemy ships. But no threat appeared. Everything looked peaceful on Titan and also in orbit, no signs of any other aliens.

Major Rogers called her to the briefing room where he, Commander Partridge and Dr. Mendel were watching the video from the interrogation of Desperado about the Sarkos.

"It seems the Desperado's entire society is based on the mining of the rocks that produce the pink light, all for the benefit of their masters, the Sarkos. They are basically their slaves." Major Rogers explained.

Will shuddered as Dr. Mendel described the Sarkos, beings with a human form but dark blue, almost black, skin who stood between six and seven feet tall on average. They enslaved humans with long exposure to the pink light, which was some kind of radiation that turned their skin orange or reddish. It also had highly addicting effects. They had taken entire planets, transforming their population into minions to do the Sarkos' bidding.

Major Rogers showed them a computer-generated image of the Sarkos next to a picture of a human. The Sarkos were just a little taller, with hairy hands and glossy black skin.

"But this isn't like those who almost enslaved us, right? Weren't they bright white? I know they were really tall but there was no mention of the hairy hands," one of the tactical officers said.

"No, you are confusing the Sarkos with the Religare, the very tall aliens with long necks, big eyes, and bright white clothes that we encountered in Ganymede. We will analyze that enemy in another meeting. For now, let's focus on the Sarkos since they are actively looking for us." Major Rogers paced in front of the group.

"I want each of you to keep this information classified," Commander Partridge said. "We're doing research on these aliens because, according to Desperado, they are a very powerful enemy. And they are already aware of our presence."

"Sir, I'm keeping all squadrons on standby," Major Rogers said.

"Yes, please do. We need to prepare a strategy to face this enemy when we meet them again."

Everyone exited the briefing room and returned to their posts on bridge. Minutes later, Jen received the final report of the scans. The report concluded that Titan was safer than the other worlds they had previously explored. Jen immediately called Major Rogers and Commander Partridge to update them.

"Sir, I recommend a more intensive exploration," Major Rogers told Commander Partridge.

"Do you still think you can begin the mining operations right away?" Commander Partridge asked.

"Yes, sir. I think it will be safe with the right space gear. We can begin as soon as I have all the equipment ready for the mission, but our men are prepared and standing by."

"Very well. Send the mission as soon as possible." Commander Partridge left the bridge.

"He is really desperate for more resources. I mean, beyond what the mission instructions indicated." Dr. Mendel rubbed his eyes.

Major Rogers stood and paced the bridge area. "He just wants to be sure we have more than enough to face a possible war with the enemy. We're going to need more people to help on this mission, people with knowledge of chemistry, engineering, and even weather. Maybe you can go as well, Dr. Mendel."

Dr. Mendel shook his head. "I can't, sir. It's important for me to finish my research on the samples we got from Saturn's rings as well as figure out some needed improvements for the passengers' living spaces. But I can send some of my people from the science team."

"Sir, why don't you send some civilians? I know some who have advanced knowledge. Couldn't they help?" Jen asked.

"Like who, Jen?"

"Like David."

"The musician?"

"He studied weather in college," Jen explained.

"Really? I didn't know that. All right, Jen. Give him all the data we got from Titan and ask him to join us for the briefing room in an hour."

"Yes, sir!" Jen called David immediately, but he didn't answer. After the third try, she was able to speak with him.

"We need you on the bridge, David."

"Me? Why?"

"We need you for a special mission outside, if you are willing to help us."

"I will be right there."

Jen wondered if the situation with Elizabeth would affect David's and Will's role in the upcoming mission. But even if it did, she knew they were both the right people for their jobs.

David and Will arrived on the bridge at the same time. The crew continued to analyze the information sent by the probe. They got images of several sand dunes, the lakes, and a hazy view of Saturn on the horizon.

"That looks just like a sunset in Antelope Island State Park," David said as he watched the video sent by the probe.

"Where?" Star asked.

"It is a state park in Utah."

Dr. Mendel pulled David and Will near Jen and explained how they needed his knowledge of weather.

"But I just studied it in college," he protested. "I don't have any experience."

"Still, I'm told you were top of your class, Mr. Peterson. Besides, you're the only one on board with that kind of knowledge. The mission is safe," Dr. Mendel told him, "and you will have an escort of jets surrounding your shuttle. Also, you will wear a special suit to provide you with heat and oxygen."

David swallowed hard, then nodded. "I'll go."

"Excellent! The mission will take about four hours. If you have any problems, Sergeant Morant will communicate with us and will proceed with retrieving the probe we launched hours ago. Any questions?"

Will hesitated. "No, sir."

Dr. Mendel nodded. "Go ahead, then. And take care of the civilian, Will."

The team left to get ready for the mission while Jen's communicator flashed with an incoming call.

"Elizabeth?"

"David just messaged me that he and will are going on a mission together. Have they left?"

"Yes. They seemed a little tense, though."

"Oh, God, please, take care of them," Elizabeth prayed.

"They will be fine. Don't worry. I will be monitoring the mission closely.

"May I join you?"

"I'll ask and let you know. Wait a minute."

Jen requested permission from Major Rogers to get Elizabeth on the bridge. The permission was granted right away.

WILL

The mission team arrived at the planned site, a few miles south of the Xanadu region, where the *Dunamys* had landed. Immediately they boarded two jeep-like 4x4 exploration vehicles with cargo space in the back. There they placed the empty tanks prepared for the liquid from one of the lakes in the area.

The whole mission team watched the sky. It had similar colors as Venus, yellow and orange, but this place was totally different. More peaceful. And they all felt lighter, in comparison. In the sky, they saw Saturn, diffused by the massive amounts of clouds. But they could still see the sunset. David took pictures and video as they drove past mountains and rivers.

They stopped to check the landscape while the science team took samples from the desert and the rocks.

Will took some pictures, too. Then he noticed David checking some samples of the air with an analyzer.

"Okay, that is enough. We need to keep going!" Will called out.

They continued on their way in the exploration vehicles until they arrived at the shore of the lake.

"Looks like this is it." Will signaled the rest of the team to extract the hydrocarbon compound with the plastic hoses attached to the tanks. As they looked at the surface of the lake, they noticed that some areas looked like marble while others were highly reflective.

"Shangri-La. That's the name of this lake," David said as he climbed out of one of the vehicles.

"I can tell you did your homework." Will gave him a thumb up as they met on the ground near the lake.

"I'm trying to do my best!" Suddenly David jumped, soaring high in the air. "Cool!"

Will laughed. "As you remember from the report, gravity is a little lower here, so proceed accordingly. And be careful. I don't want to rescue you from an unnecessary danger."

"No problem, bro."

They hurried to bring the tank from their vehicle and placed a hose to suck the methane from the lake. Dr. Mendel had instructed them to maintain a very low temperature in the containers to keep the volume of the methane intact, otherwise it would turn into gas and its volume would expand, increasing the pressure of the containers. So, they turned on the special cooling system in the tanks to keep Titan's temperature inside of them.

While they placed their hands in the liquid, they noticed that the methane moved just like water.

"I hope we don't have any issues like we had on Europa." Iram looked a little uneasy.

"I don't think we will," said Will with confidence. "This moon looks more stable."

As they gathered some samples of the rocks and stored them in containers, Will noticed smoke rising from a mountain, like a volcano. But the lava flowing out of it was a white-blueish instead of red or orange.

"It could be water, ice, hydrocarbons, or a mix of all those, based on the weather conditions," David told him.

"Interesting. What else can you talk about the weather here?" Will asked.

"I'm on it." David peered up as if to study the clouds.

Will moved closer to him. Only then did he realize David didn't look happy.

"Hey Will?" he said. "Did you get a chance to talk to her?"

"Yes, I did. But I couldn't say everything I needed to say because Jen arrived all of the sudden."

"I don't know what I did wrong." David shook his head. Then he looked at Will. "Or could she be interested in someone else?"

Will was glad his space stood shaded his eyes.

Oh, man, what I have done. What if Elizabeth is thinking of me after I came clean about my feelings? I'm so selfish. *They had something good going on, and he is my best friend, even if that was ages ago.*

"I'm thankful Elizabeth is more than just a girlfriend to me," David continued. "She is also my best friend. She's the person I want to spend the rest of my life with."

Will noticed David had pulled up a photo of him and Elizabeth with her parents on the communicator attached to his suit. Will kept silent.

"I know it's hard for her to be away from her family. I'm so blessed to have my family here. Maybe I should be more understanding and kind to her." David bowed his head and closed his eyes. "Oh, God. Tell me what to do! How can I comfort her? how can I be more empathetic?"

As David opened his eyes, he had the look of someone having a Eureka! moment.

"You know, Will, I think I'm ready to let her go if that is what she wants. As long as she is happy, that is all that matters. After all, she is one of the sweetest girls I have known, and she deserves the best!"

Will squirmed a bit, wondering if he would be willing to do the same for her. Then he remembered something Joshua had told him during one of the first conversations they'd had at the coffee shop back on Earth. *There is no greater love than giving your life for the ones you love.*

Joshua had given his own life to save everyone.

"Ok, let's focus on the mission." Will didn't want to think about all that right then. They had a job to do.

David returned to studying the sky. Then he advised the team of his concern about the dark orange clouds approaching from far away. Those kinds of clouds produced electric storms with powerful lightning. They needed to move quickly. He told them he could already see the lightning breaking rocks, sounding almost like a storm on Earth. Then they heard a sound like an explosion just as a lightning bolt flashed in the sky.

The bolt of lightning had hit a small hill, breaking it in half. David advised them all to move away from the direction of the storm.

JEN

Elizabeth was starting to get worried "Watch out guys!" she said to the screen.

"They can't hear you, Elizabeth."

"I know, Jen. And I'm glad. Please don't tell them I'm here with you."

"I promise, not a word. But look, it seems like the storm is moving away from them now." Jen switched to the probe data. "See? Now the sky is a little clearer. I can see the sunset over the horizon."

"Wow, the sun looks so small."

"Yeah, almost like the moon in distance from Earth. And based on the report I read when we got here, the Saturnian system is now in its closest distance to the Sun." Jen felt a little more relaxed after the storm faded away from the exploration team. She also noticed Elizabeth had calmed, too, and was enjoying the view from the probe passing through a big valley covered in what looked like sand.

They followed the video feed until it landed in the valley near where the exploration team parked the vehicles. Jen immediately switched the view to the exploration team. They discovered the sand was very similar to the dust they had encountered on Mars.

"Jen?" Major Rogers stood behind her chair.

"I see, Major Rogers. The probe is now closer to the exploration team."

"Perfect. Ask the team to retrieve it."

Jen spoke to the communicator. "Attention exploration team, the probe is on your way out. Get ready to retrieve it."

"Thanks, Jen," Will responded.

"How is everything?" she asked.

"Fine. We are still collecting resources."

"Hi, Jen. It's David. We were a little worried about the storm on the horizon, but it is gone now. It was behaving weird for a storm. Maybe because it was caused by methane clouds. As soon as I read the data from the probe, I told the team it was safe to continue."

"Thanks, David."

"And now we have the probe." Iram signed them off as the team headed back.

WILL

Will asked David to continue monitoring the sky as they returned to their ships, watching for a possible storm or variation in the weather.

"I'll do the best I can," David said. "But it's hard to tell what can happen out here. I'll have to use the little I know about chemistry and weather studies. This is not a simple task. Titan is totally different than Earth."

Will nodded. Far away, he saw more lighting. Then the sky above them turned a little cloudy.

"I think we should get back to the shuttle," David said. "There is another storm coming."

At that moment a bolt of lightning struck about a mile from them. It sounded ten times louder than thunder on Earth.

"Good call, David." Will placed his hand on David's shoulder. "But we still need more resources."

"How are you guys doing?" Major Rogers asked over the communicator.

"We need more time, sir," Will answered.

"You have 5 minutes. Then I want you guys to wrap everything up. I want to avoid any trouble."

The mission team returned to the vehicles, but they continued their exploration in the opposite direction of the storm, driving in the direction of the sunset that seemed slow compared to Earth's. They stopped at a lake that reflected the setting of a small sun. The water looked just like a mirror reflecting everything, including the sky, so clearly. David took several snapshots and videos while the rest of the scientific team proceeded to take more liquid from the lake.

JEN

Jen and Elizabeth stood together at the bridge window watching the misty view of Saturn on the horizon with its reflection in one of the lakes of Titan.

"So pretty!" cried Elizabeth.

"I wonder the actual reason we were sent here. I don't think it was just for the view."

"I don't know, but it was worth it." Elizabeth sounded happy.

"I told you everything would turn out all right. If the Creator has the power to make all this and send us to these places safely, He will take care of us. Even the small details, like relationship issues." Jen didn't look at her friend as she said the last part.

"You think so?"

"Yes, I do." Jen returned to her board with a smile. Both continued watching the progress of the mission, which was taking longer than expected.

Then Commander Partridge returned to the bridge. "Everything going well, Miss Morant?" He moved closer to her board.

"Yes, sir. They are doing good. They just have a detour to avoid difficult terrain and to escape a storm moving close to them. But they will be fine."

"Good! Major Rogers, please continue monitoring the progress of the mission."

"Yes, sir. Are you staying?"

"No, you remain in charge, but keep me posted. And the rest of you, keep up the good work!" Commander Partridge's visit was so brief it left Jen wondering if he was okay.

Elizabeth asked Jen to show her the live feed of the horizon. When it popped onto the screen, Elizabeth smiled and began to sing quietly.

> *"The Sun is rising up*
> *with healing in His wings;*
> *So, I will sing to God in the morning,*
> *I will sing of his love.*
> *Cause he is my strength,*
> *my refuge in the storm*
> *Oh my God, I will sing to you.*
> *Cause you are my fortress*
> *And forever I will sing for you.*
> *I will sing of your love..."*

"You have such a beautiful voice," Star said.

"Thank you. I just love singing. I did that one at the opening of the living spaces. It is one of my favorites."

Star turned to face her. "Elizabeth, may I ask you a question?"

"Of course."

"Why do you always sing to God?"

"Because I love him. Don't you think this big, wonderful cosmos is something more than just a random coincidence of chemistry and physics? There is a creator, a supreme intelligence out there who started it all, and we are on the way to meet him in person. That is very exciting to me!"

"Yeah, you're right. That's why I joined the *Dunamys*, although I was thinking more about escaping the destruction of the Earth than meeting the Creator. But it is an exciting thought, like you said." Star stared down at her computer.

"Everyone has different talents, Star," Major Rogers said. "And you are the best at what you do as a second officer."

"Thank you, Major Rogers."

9
SATURN

WILL

*A*fter the exploration team arrived safely back to the *Dunamys*, they very carefully filled several special containers–created by Dr. Mendel with the knowledge he had gleaned from the computers on the *Dunamys*–with the liquid methane. Then they began the debriefing from the mission.

"I just noticed it is like our knowledge and level of understanding have increased since we started to eat the fruit of the seeds Joshua gave us. Before, I wouldn't have figured out so quickly the method of gathering these resources," Dr. Mendel noted.

"I have to admit, eating the fruit has proven to be very useful to us."

"Yes, commander, but it is also further proof that Joshua has delivered us so far, as he promised." Major Rogers nodded at Will, who nodded back.

"Then we have everything we need right?" Commander Partridge asked.

"Yes, and more than expected," Dr. Mendel affirmed.

"Good job, everyone. You are dismissed." Commander Partridge ended the meeting.

Will exited the briefing room. Although he was tired, he wanted to go anywhere but his living quarters. There was enough tension with David already, and although the mission had been successful, it had been stressful, too. He thought about going to one of the neighborhoods, but he wasn't sure which one. Then he remembered The Ancient, a mysterious area on board. He went to the elevator and stopped at deck 3. He exited into a long narrow corridor surrounded by white walls. As he ventured deeper into the corridor, the light seemed to increase in intensity. It reminded him of the first time he entered the spaceship, when he met Joshua for the first time. He sat down on the floor and rested back against the wall.

"You know, sometimes I wish you were here, like in the times back in the day on Earth when we hung out at the Vintage Proverb," he said out loud. After a moment of silence, he felt a fresh breeze blowing, but he didn't know what direction it came from. He thought it was from the vents, but he didn't pay too much attention to it. Instead, he listened to the quiet music, like a keyboard and some strings, playing around him.

That is strange, he thought.

"I have always been here for you. For everyone." Joshua's familiar voice filled the space around him.

"I know, but it is not the same."

"It is different. But don't worry. You took the right course of action. You were brave. And there are more victories to come!"

The peace Will longed for settled over him like a blanket.

JEN

The day after the mission on Titan, the crew prepared to journey to the next planet. However, Commander Partridge seemed uneasy after looking at some reports from Major Rogers. Jen pushed the button on her microphone, ready to announce their departure from Saturn's system. Before she could speak, Commander Partridge stopped her.

She turned off her microphone. "Yes, sir?"

"Call Mr. Peterson. Ask him to join us in about two hours. Also, call Desperado in for a short meeting as soon as possible."

When Jen brought Desperado into a conference room, Commander Partridge again questioned him about the tactics of the Sarkos.

"I've recently acquired some data which has me concerned," the commander told Desperado.

"May I see?" Desperado asked. Commander Partridge showed him his tablet, he scrolled down then quickly laid it on his chair.

"Is that bad?" Commander Partridge asked.

"Worse than you think. They are looking for you. Well, for all of us, actually. This is very clear. They are on the move, and they will be here soon, no doubt about it."

"That is what I thought."

Commander Partridge continued questioning Desperado, mostly to find out the tactics and attack patterns of the Sarkos and compare them with their current situation.

After an hour, Jen and Commander Partridge returned to the bridge. The commander gave the order to take the *Dunamys* to the surface of Saturn.

"Dr. Mendel, do you have the calculations?"

"Almost, Commander."

David entered as they were speaking.

"Mr. Peterson, I'm glad you could join us!"

"My apologies for the delay. I had to meet with someone. It was very important."

"No worries, you are just on time. What do you think of this?"

David looked at the monitors, trying to assess Commander Partridge's plan to go into Saturn's atmosphere, close to its North Pole.

"This is the result of different wind speeds colliding. It would be very risky such a wind's strength and a velocity, about 199 miles per hour or 320 kilometers per hour," David pointed out, concerned.

"Why do we want to go there?"

"I understand the danger, but it's important. And we don't have much time—or any other choice, really. We need to hide the *Dunamys* for a little while."

"But the speed and strength will tear the ship apart. We need to go somewhere calm."

"Is anywhere safe near the storm?" Dr. Mendel asked.

David walked to Dr. Mendel's board. "Well, the storm is about..." He checked some information, "about 186 miles high or 300 kilometers high. Maybe we could..." David looked zoomed into the center of the storm and pointed into a very small area.

"This could work. Let me check." Dr. Mendel recalculated the trajectories and looked up with a calmer expression. "We have the calculations, sir," he announced.

"Ok, so where are we going?" Commander Partridge asked.

"In this small area we can be above the surface and surrounded by the storm but away from it in a considerable distance because the center of the storm creates a swirling movement that goes deeper into the planet.

"Also," he added, "the magnetic field will mask our signature, but it might also interfere with our communications and systems while we are there. I suggest we activate the shields as long as we remain there."

"Very good. Take us to the destination."

195

"Yes, sir. We will be there in approximately 30 minutes." The navigator responded.

"Excellent."

Jen readied the microphone once more. "Attention, passengers of the *Dunamys*. We have detected the presence of the enemy and are proceeding with evasive precautions. Please go to your quarters immediately and fasten your seat belts."

"Mr. Peterson, please remain on the bridge." Commander Partridge asked. He pointed to a chair close to Jen. David sat and buckled in.

Jen wondered if going directly toward that huge storm was the right choice, but it was no longer time for thinking. They needed to act fast. The commander had made his decision—to move to the eye of the storm over the north pole.

"Increase speed," the commander ordered. Then he turned to Dr. Mendel. "Any suggestions?"

"This storm can block any detection for sure," Dr. Mendel replied, "but it could be dangerous, as David assessed."

"But the enemy is almost here, so we have no choice. We have to think about the well-being of all passengers."

"Sir, this storm is larger than any ever seen on Earth," David added.

Just then they felt a pull on the spaceship—and it wasn't only because of the large storm. It now appeared there were also two smaller storms underneath it. The entire ship shook, the vibrations even worse than they'd experienced before under the influence of the powerful storms. And in those cases, the storms had been far away. Already thunder boomed, and clouds circulated inside other clouds with great might.

"Okay, that's enough," Commander Partridge barked. "We have to get far away from this planet." He ordered that the ship be moved as far from the storm as possible.

The *Dunamys* pulled away from the planet's surface just in time.

*****

They stayed in Saturn's orbit for one more week to avoid detection by any enemy ship.

Before they prepared for departure to their next destination, Jen was scheduled for a break. She left the bridge and met Elizabeth at their living quarters.

"What a ride right?" Jen said.

"For sure," Elizabeth answered. "But we are safe. Hey—could I hang out with you and Star sometime today?"

"Actually, that is why I'm here. I just finished my shift."

"What about Star?"

"Let me check." Jen signaled Star on her communicator and asked her to join them.

They all rode the elevator to the deck where the

new Vintage Proverb was located. Jen and Star got coffee while Elizabeth ordered her usual cup of tea.

The minute they were all seated, Elizabeth spoke. "I had another conversation with Will, and it was very intense."

"What did he say?" Jen inquired.

"He wanted to know what I thought about his feelings for me and—"

"Hey guys!" David stood near their table.

"Oh, David." Elizabeth looked even more serious now.

"Elizabeth, I don't want to bother you since you are with your friends right now, but could we talk sometime soon?"

"I'm so sorry David. I know, I owe you an explanation..." she looked at Star and Jen.

"No worries, Elizabeth. We can talk sometime later. Come on, Jen."

"Elizabeth?" Jen eyed her.

Elizabeth looked hesitant.

"It's okay, Elizabeth." David touched her shoulder. "As I said, we can talk another time."

"You don't mind, girls?" Elizabeth looked at her friends.

"Not at all. We will have a chance to catch up later." Star hugged her. Jen did the same. Then Elizabeth walked away with David.

Jen was curious about the conversation, but it was hard to hear from where they now stood.

"So what is going on with them?" Star asked.

"I'm not sure. I think Elizabeth wants to take a

break from the relationship, and my brother recently shared his feelings for her."

"What?" Star's smile disappeared.

"Bad timing, I know. I tried to prevent that from happening, but by the time I got to them he had already told her. And then they talked again because I think they both wanted to finish the conversation I interrupted."

"So, Will has a crush on Elizabeth? Wow!"

"He has since we were younger, but he never told her until now."

For the next twenty-five minutes, Jen wondered if Elizabeth would come back. She and Star were both hungry now, so they ordered a small sandwich each.

"You are still here!" Elizabeth slid back into her seat and picked up her cold tea.

"Yeah, Star and I decided to go ahead and have dinner. Is everything okay, Elizabeth?"

"Well, I was telling you about my second conversation with Will before I left with David, right?"

"Yeah." Star looked at Jen. "And Jen told me he shared his feelings for you."

"He wanted to talk a second time, so we met at the Legacy Den and sat by the fountain. I didn't know what to say. I didn't know where to start. But he was mostly concerned about how I was doing. I told him I just needed some time alone, but then I broke down and told him the truth: that I'm afraid."

"Afraid of what?" Jen asked.

Elizabeth shook her head blushed.

"I thanked Will for being honest with me and said I was sorry if I hurt him because I didn't know about his feelings before. And now things are so complicated. I told him that I didn't know what I wanted and that I needed time to process a lot of things."

Jen's heart ached for her brother, for she felt she knew what was coming next.

"But you love David, don't you?" Star whispered.

"I thought I did, but I don't know."

"How did Will react?" Star asked.

Elizabeth smiled, but her eyes were sad. "He was great, actually. He said he didn't want to come between us. That he knows David loves me too. That he wants me to be happy. Will is a good friend. To both of us."

"Oh, wow! What a hard conversation."

"You have no idea, Star. He looked so sad when he left for his mission briefing—I think I'd made him late. I stood by the fountain feeling a little sad as well. I don't want to lose a friend like Will, and I have to admit, I have some feelings for him too. Then I looked through the window at the opposite side. The view of black space was slowly replaced by the view of different tones of beige, brown, white, and gray colors. Saturn's rings. Then I saw the planet so close to us."

"I remember that moment," Jen said. "It was an amazing sight."

"Yes. And it reminded me why I am afraid. I don't want to lose any more people I care about. I'm not sure the dangers and sacrifices of the journey to a planet of hope and happiness are worth it."

"Oh, Elizabeth!" Star reached for her friend's hand. "I wish you would have shared your fear with us."

"Yes, that would have helped. But at that moment I realized I needed to talk to David, so I did. He deserved to know. I told him I needed some time, but I still have feelings for him."

"How did he react?" Jen asked.

"He was very understanding. Right away he told me he would do whatever was necessary to make the relationship work, or he'd even let me go once and for all, if it was for the best."

"I hope a man loves me that much one day," Jen said. "What happened next?"

"He told me he still loved me, and reminded me of the first time we sang together, how clearly, we felt we were meant to be. He also reminded me that God has kept protecting us and guiding us all the way. That God promised I would never be alone."

"That was yesterday?" Jen asked. "And he came today because . . .?"

"He just wanted to talk a little more."

"Did you talk just now or are you meeting again later?" Star asked.

"Tomorrow, for dinner."

"Will you be, okay?" Jen asked.

"I will. Thank you, friends, for bearing with me in all this drama."

"That's what friends are for!" Star smiled.

*****

The next evening Elizabeth was in her quarters listening to music—a little bit of indie pop—when the music gave her some ideas for a new song. She paused the music and grabbed her journal and a pen to start writing. Then she resumed the song for a few seconds before stopping to write again.

"You are inspired today!" Jen said as she walked in the door.

"I am. I feel much better than many other days."

After all this time as roommates, Jen was used to seeing Elizabeth caught up in these moments of inspiration. For a few minutes Elizabeth wrote easily, but then she got stuck. She pulled her chair close to the window and admired the view of Titan in the distance as they passed by in orbit of Saturn.

"I don't know how to end the song," she told Jen. Then their doorbell rang.

She put her journal away before opening the door. "Hey, David."

"Hey, Elizabeth. Ready to go?"

"Sorry, David. I got so inspired to write a new song that I lost track of the time."

"No problem. I'll wait for you outside."

Elizabeth quickly put on a casual dress and some perfume and light makeup. She seemed nervous.

"You will be fine, friend. Just be honest and transparent with him."

"I want to make a good impression after all my attitude the other day."

"That is over. Just be yourself and have fun!"

"Thank you, Jen." Elizabeth hugged her and joined David in the hall.

WILL

Will spent the evening working out at *Fight Place*, the spaceship's gym, trying to forget the feelings rushing around his heart and the memories of his recent advice to David after they arrived from Titan, repeating in a loop over and over in his head.

Listen, man, I don't know the details of everything going on between you two, but I know that you both will be alright. Just tell her how much you love her and what you are willing to do for her. And listen to her. I'm sure she will understand.

Will could not believe those words came out of his mouth. The same advice he would have given to himself, the same thing he wished he had said to Elizabeth.

He added more pounds in every weight set, pushing his muscles to their limits.

As he took a break, he scrolled down his tablet looking at the pictures he'd taken on Titan, then the only picture he took with David by the lake. This triggered the last conversation he had with him. The conversation that had been so painful.

Thank you for talking to Elizabeth. I don't know what you said to her, but it worked. Thanks for being a good friend.

Then he gave him a small bag Will had kept for a long time.

Take it, she will love it.

It was the moment he knew he'd let Elizabeth go forever.

A tear dropped out of his eye as he put away his information tablet. He grabbed more weights and began to workout even harder. Suddenly, he threw the weights against the floor and screamed.

He sat there for a moment and collected himself. Then he went for a run on the treadmill.

JEN

Elizabeth came back to her quarters three hours later. Jen couldn't help but notice her roommate was shaking.

"What happened?"

They both sat in their recliners. Elizabeth closed her eyes and started talking.

"We went to the restaurant at *Fruitful Place*. It was weird because they were serving Asian food—you know they serve a different international cuisine depending on the day—and they were playing Japanese music. Then some bells jingled and the music changed to something a little more pop jazz. It was very interesting music."

"This is what you wanted to tell me?" Jen was so confused. She thought something had happened with David.

Elizabeth laughed nervously. "No. It was what came next. David called me close to the window to show me the way Saturn's rings shine against the sun that time of day."

"I know that view. It is lovely!"

"For a while we just stared at the rings that glowed brighter and brighter as the distant sun illuminated the small particles of rocks and ice. But then something even brighter caught my eye. It looked like a crystal reflecting a multitude of colors, like one of those particles from Saturn's rings had entered the restaurant in front of me. Then I saw it in his hand. I didn't understand for a moment, but then I realized he was holding a crystal he'd brought back from the mission to Titan. He promised again to take care of me no matter what the danger or uncertainty. He said he loved me—all my talents and all my flaws. He said I was sweet and beautiful and his best friend. Then knelt in front of me."

"Elizabeth!" Jen jumped up from her chair. "He asked you to marry him, didn't he?"

"He did," Elizabeth responded mildly.

"And you said . . ."

"Well, he caught me by surprise. I was excited, but I wasn't ready either. I smiled, I hugged him, and I told him I needed some time. I... I also told him that this is not what I meant when I said I needed something steady to hold on to. Then he put the ring on my hand

and insisted I keep it until I was ready to wear it. Then he kissed me on the cheek. He said we could take one step at a time." She held up the ring up for Jen to see.

The rock was like an opaque white diamond, extremely reflective, and attached to a silver-like band.

"Totally understandable!"

"We talked for a while after that. He reminded me that even though we are far from Earth, we have everything we need and we have been protected. This is a reminder of that. By the way, have you seen the pictures they took of Titan?" She shared the pictures from her communicator.

Jen nodded.

"Do you remember when Joshua said the Creator will open rivers in the desert and dry places? That's like Titan. He showed me that in that desolate world there is still beauty. He encouraged me to believe there is beauty and provision ahead of us, that Joshua will protect us, and that we are not going to be alone, ever. And one day, we will return for my family and the rest of the people we left behind, as he promised!"

"That's great. You guys are like me, I never get tired of admiring the view. And when I do, I always remember the things Joshua taught us."

"I'm so thankful. Now every time I look outside, the view is a reminder that the Creator will take care of us."

"You will figure it out, friend, one step at the time."

"Yes!" Elizabeth smiled.

Peace settled into the room, which continued when the *Dunamys* started to shake. Then a voice on the intercom instructed all passengers to fasten their seat belts. Jen's communicator buzzed. *We have been detected by the enemy alien ships. Report for duty.*

10
URANUS

JEN

The tension on the bridge was felt so intense as soon as Jen entered the bridge, more than the usual.

"Miss Morant just in time." Commander Partridge motioned her, Mayor Jacobs, Major Rogers, and some other crew members into the briefing room with Desperado to review footage from a vessel coming towards them. Desperado analyzed the data while the rest of the crew continued preparing for evasive maneuvers.

"It's no use," Desperado said. "The Sarkos attack from a main spaceship using hundreds of smaller, hunting spacecraft—ah, the *Dunamys* doesn't have a chance."

Commander Partridge turned to Star. "Show me the Sarkos lead ship at the highest magnification possible."

"Yes, sir." She zoomed in on the huge triangular spacecraft. It appeared as dark gray green with a crimson glow and red lights. Then what Desperado had told them was confirmed. Coming out of the large ship were hundreds of smaller vessels with similar colors and shapes.

Commander Partridge returned to the bridge, the others right behind him. Jen reached her station just as Commander Partridge ordered maximum speed to their next destination. But the enemy followed them closely and easily. Desperado tried his best to help with the tactics while the rest of the crew discussed the situation. Then Commander Partridge silenced everyone with a raised hand.

"Activate FTL light speed mode," he ordered.

"Commander," Dr. Mendel stood. "The system hasn't been fully repaired. I'm not sure—"

"Activate it. We have no choice."

Dr. Mendel nodded to his assistant. The *Dunamys* leapt forward at an extremely fast velocity. The systems indicated that they were outrunning their enemies. Within a few minutes, they approached the next planetary system.

As everyone on the bridge scrambled to check their consoles, the *Dunamys* started to spin on its axis. Half the systems went down.

Jen gripped the arms of her chair, eyes fixed out the window. As she watched, the Uranus system rotate from the top down, over and over in slow motion, like a pendulum ride in a fair. Jen finally looked away to avoid getting dizzy. At the same time, she tried to activate the alarm system, she struggled to reach the switch to activate it, and finally after stretching herself up, she got it. She noticed Star trying to keep herself stable on her seat as the *Dunamys* continued spinning.

"This is beyond our capabilities!" Commander Partridge held onto his chair.

Finally, the navigator stabilized the *Dunamys*.

"Sir?" Jen tried to get Commander Partridge's attention. When he turned to her, he appeared extremely upset. Jen startled. "Sir, I just wanted to ask what I should say to the passengers."

He thought for a moment, then said, "Notify everyone that we have arrived in Uranus' orbit but don't mention the enemy ships."

"Yes, sir." Jen passed along the information as instructed.

Suddenly, the general lights flickered off. Now the only systems working were the life support, the intercom, and a few emergency lights. Commander Partridge wiped sweat from his forehead.

Then Jen noticed something else wasn't right. She felt way lighter than usual. She noticed the ends of her hair floating upwards. Some of the information tables and communicators lifted off the table. She unbuckled her security belt and navigated around the room like she was swimming in water.

"Wow! This is awesome!" Jen laughed softly, excited after doing some flips.

"Artificial gravity offline," Sounded repeatedly an alert on the system's intercoms.

211

Desperado seemed confused. Perhaps because it wasn't anything unusual for him, but Jen was enjoying the moment.

"What is going on? Why are the gravity systems down?" Commander Partridge inquired.

"Aren't you worried?" Desperado asked Jen. "The systems have gone offline, and the Sarkos are still after us."

"I guess you're right. I should be worried. It's just that I've never felt this before. But I also know and trust Joshua. He will get us out of this."

"You seem very confident he will save you. What if he doesn't?"

"I know he will. He always does!" She floated back to her seat with a smile on her face. She fastened her seat belt again and put her hand on Desperado's shoulder "He will save the day like he always does. You don't know him as I do."

"I don't doubt what you believe, but you don't know the Sarkos as I do." He frowned. "They are brutal and merciless."

"Miss Morant, Desperado has a point. Please focus."

"Yes, Commander. I'm sorry."

"And will someone please fix the artificial gravity?" Commander Partridge demanded.

Immediately a group of spaceships appeared in front of them—the Sarkos, ready to attack.

Finally, Major Rogers voiced the decision he had wanted to avoid at all costs, a direct confrontation.

"Star," Commander Partridge said. "Call all the squadrons to launch."

"Please wait, sir!" Major Rogers stood. "We need to ask Joshua we don't want to make more mistakes."

Joshua didn't appear, but his voice spoke. "Extend your sword to the north and fire."

"Dr. Mendel, did you hear that?" the commander asked.

"Barely, sir. 'The north?' There is no north in space."

"What do you think he meant?"

"I don't know. Maybe this ship has some sort of defense weapons."

"Find them before it's too late."

Dr. Mendel floated his way to his research lab to consult his notes and previous research papers on the *Dunamys*.

WILL

Will, continuing to try to burn off his emotions through exhaustion, was seated at the multi exercise station when he felt the weight he put in the machine wasn't enough. He kept adding to it, but it still felt like lifting nothing. He wondered if he was getting stronger or if something was wrong with the machine.

As he let himself out of the chair to add more weights, he realized he was floating. Immediately, he called the bridge, but he didn't get any answer.

Maybe they are working on the gravity issue. It will probably be fixed in a few hours. I might go to sleep as well while I'm waiting. He advanced through the corridor by moving his arms and legs with difficulty, but he remembered his training to move quickly in zero gravity, so he advanced floating pushing himself through the corridors. When he reached the elevator, an announcement came over the intercom system.

"Attention all pilots," the voice said, along with alarm sounds. "Report to battle stations immediately. This is not a drill. I repeat, this is not a drill. Prepare to face the Sarkos."

Because the gym was located in a section mostly used by military personnel, Will didn't have far to go. He joined his squadron and prepared for battle against an enemy they had never faced before. Although he was tired, he rushed into the tunnel leading to the jets bay, where the pilots usually emerged like a football team coming into the field. But this time, everyone was floating their way out as fast as possible due to the absence of gravity. Will climbed the ladder leading to the cockpit, turned on the engine, then disconnected the fuel and energy systems from the *Dunamys*.

"This is Sergeant Morant, ready to depart."

"Roger. Lead your squadron to 12 o'clock sector alpha."

Will launched his jet, emerging from one of the tunnels. Other jets launched from other tunnels. As soon as the Sarkos saw them, they launched an intense laser attack against the *Dunamys*, trying to destroy its engines. But the jet fighters led by Will thwarted the attack. Meanwhile, other squadrons defended other angles of the *Dunamys*. Adrenaline rushed through Will's body.

Then he grew frustrated. Every enemy they encountered was more superior than them. They were faster, more organized, and used different tactics. The Sarkos fought differently than the Religare, which acted like a swarm of bees attacking from different directions. Instead, the Sarkos moved like darts in straight lines aiming to destroy specific targets.

When Will realized this, he decided to figure out their targets and defend from there. To go on the offensive. But as the battle progressed, they were barely held their defensive positions.

All the fighter jets reciprocated bravely, but they were overwhelmed by the maneuvers of the enemy.

Will did his best to keep up with every enemy ship, but as soon as he shot one, it only spun out of control without creating much damage. Regardless, he kept firing, trying to get to the main spacecraft. And as soon he got close to it, he noticed a second wave of alien ships advancing without hesitation. Then he remembered the information from the tactical meetings—that the Sarkos attacked from one big enemy ship.

"Iram, Joseph, let's go." Will's friends peeled off and followed him to the main ship. They fired as much as they could, but it didn't result in much damage to their enemy. It was impossible. They couldn't win.

Will called his squadron to retreat, to return to the *Dunamys* to protect it.

"Sergeant Morant, you have four enemy ships on your tail!" one of the pilots yelled over the communication system.

Will tried to race away, but it was useless. So, he turned around to confront them head on, flying up and then down, firing constantly. Then he was hit. His jet boosters exploded. He couldn't move, couldn't defend himself.

Then he saw another wave of enemy ships coming toward him.

"Alert! Enemy within firing rage," came a voice from his speakers.

Will held on and cried, "God, help me, please!"

Suddenly, the closest enemy ship exploded, right before it fired to finish him.

"Sorry for coming late to the party, Sergeant Morant." Iram's voice sounded in Will's ship as he watched Iram, accompanied by the rest of his squadron, arrive to protect his jet.

But Will was still adrift. He wasn't unable to respond. Exhaustion overcame him and everything turned dark.

JEN

Dr. Mendel called the bridge from the room where Dr. Hackett had grown a few *logos* trees. He was breathing with a lot of effort. "Joshua?"

Major Rogers moved closer to Jen's board. "Dr. Mendel, is Joshua there with you?"

"No, but I heard a soft voice say, 'The key is in the *logos* trees!' that is why I came here."

"Did he say anything else?" Major Rogers asked.

"Not really."

"Good, proceed with your report."

"My previous analysis indicated that the trees were producing some kind of energy source and I just finished tracking it. So, I detected the same energy signature over the spaceship, but it was particularly stronger in one specific area. I'll show you."

A 3D hologram of Dr. Mendel appeared on the bridge.

"Interesting. So now can you tell us what we need?" Major Rogers swiveled his chair to face Dr. Mendel's form.

"Yes, I think I found the defense mechanism." He activated holographic controls on several boards.

"How do we control it?" asked Commander Partridge.

"Joshua mentioned a sword. What could that mean?"

Star studied the controls on the bridge until she found a small holographic projection hovering over a panel in one of the back corners of the room. She extended her hand to the new holographic screen. As soon as she did, a sword-looking pointer appeared. "I think I know what he meant, Commander."

Commander Partridge walked to the 3D screen with the sword-looking object on it. He touched it, suddenly able to control the sword as though he had virtually grabbed it. Immediately, he aimed it at the main Sarkos vessel.

A target appeared, inscribed with a sign in an alien language. Dr. Mendel translated it. "You will know the truth and the truth will set you free."

Commander Partridge pushed his arm forward, and the screen zoomed in on the area of the enemy vessel he was looking at.

"How do I fire this thing?" he asked.

As he said the word "fire," the spaceship launched a concentrated beam of light onto the large alien ship. It blew into a million pieces.

A shout of victory went up on the bridge–until Commander Partridge pointed out several pink lights emerging from the explosion.

"All surviving fighter jets, return to the *Dunamys* immediately," he ordered.

The fighter jets arrived, towing some of the damaged ones with them. Forty percent of the pilot fighters were wounded. Fifteen percent of them had died.

From a distance, Jen saw a few pilots celebrating the victory as they hugged each other, but others were very sad. She searched them all for Will's face, but she couldn't find him.

Desperado came to stand next to her. "I'm sure your brother is fine; he is a great pilot."

No one else said a word.

*****

A few hours later, Dr. Mendel finished half of the repairs, restoring gravity and the rest of the lights. It had been a very tough battle, but the people of the *Dunamys* attempted to go back to their new normal life. Jen remained on the bridge, working hard, but also trying to figure out what had happened with her brother.

Iram told her his jet had been shot, and she knew that the few doctors and nurses on board were working around the clock to attend to the wounded. Hoping he was in the medical bay, she finally asked to be dismissed. She immediately ran to the elevator and rode right all the way down to *Fight Place*. From there, she walked through the gym, the training area, the briefing rooms and, finally, into the medical bay.

The facility had been fully finished since they left the orbit of Mars, and fortunately, some of the *Dunamys* passengers were physicians and nurses. The bay was small but could sustain up to twenty patients at one time. It was enough for their current circumstances.

Medical personnel rushed to and fro in the area, the door sliding open and closed every few minutes. Military personnel guarded the entrance, not allowing anyone to enter except the medical team.

"Please," she pleaded. "I'm part of the crew, and I think my brother is in there." She showed her badge.

The door slid open. Dr. Hackett greeted her. "Let her in, please."

Jen hurried in before anyone could change their mind.

"I'll take you to him." Dr. Hackett explained that Will was unconscious, in one piece but with injuries. "He needs to remain in bed for several days or a week to recover, but he will be fine."

Jen sat by the side of Will's bed as Dr. Hackett left to check on other patients. "Oh, Will." She pushed his hair from his pale face. "You have to get better. I know life hasn't been easy for you, letting Elizabeth go, then getting injured in battle. I wish I could do something to help. It feels like just yesterday that we found this spaceship. And now look at you—a hero. You've saved so many lives, Will. I think it's only fair for you to get well now."

She called Elizabeth to update her on Will's condition, but Elizabeth didn't answer so she left a brief message, dropped her communicator, and started to cry.

Her grief was interrupted by a knock on the door. She stood up, wiped her tears, and opened it to find Desperado. She hugged him and thanked him.

"I don't understand you guys," he said with admiration. "You fight the Sarkos with bravery and keep hope and faith in the impossible. These beings have enslaved hundreds of civilizations without resistance, and yet you chose to oppose them. Whoever your God is, He is certainly awesome! And I'm sure your brother will be okay. I'm sure of it."

As he walked away, Elizabeth came in.

"Hey, wow, you came fast!"

"I was close, so I came as soon as we got your message."

"So sorry for what happened, Jen. In a way, I feel responsible." Elizabeth bit her lip.

"What? No, it is not your fault, Elizabeth. You had to be honest with him, for his own sake. I'm sure it didn't affect the way he did his job."

They hugged each other.

"Please, oh God," Jen pleaded. "If you're hearing us, please heal my brother." Then Jen noticed a nurse waiting, not wanting to disturb.

"Just need to check on my patient," she said.

Jen thanked her, then she and Elizabeth went to the waiting area. They sat down. Everyone was silent. Then David walked in. He hugged Jen right away.

"Jen, I'm so sorry this happened to your brother." That hug didn't last long enough for Jen.

This is just what I needed. "Thank you, David!"

Elizabeth and David hugged casually.

"Attention, please," came the announcement over the speakers. "We are free from enemy ships, and we are in orbit of planet Uranus. You are welcome to check out the views and relax as we orbit."

"Is that Star?" Elizabeth asked.

"Yep. She is taking my place for a little while."

"I want to be honest with you guys," Elizabeth said. "I still feel this tension in my heart about everything. I know we had been protected all this time, but this constant visiting of new planets and resting for a while until the next conflict or enemy or whatever happens is a little unsettling. Will has been injured. Many passengers were left behind to become slaves. Others have died. And we haven't even left the Solar System yet."

"I know," Jen said. "This is hard for me, too. But Joshua said this wouldn't be easy, that we needed to fight the way out."

"That still doesn't make the situation any more comfortable for any of us!" David sounded upset, too.

"Trust me, if anyone can understand that right now, it is me. My brother lying in bed is a reminder of the perils of this journey!"

"You are right, Jen. So sorry." David answered.

David and Elizabeth each hugged her, then left to let her rest. Jen went back to the side of Will's bed and sat down. She studied all of Will's monitors and tubes. Then she cried again until she fell asleep.

*****

"How is everything going?" Dr. Hackett greeted someone outside Will's bedroom. Jen went to the door to see who was there.

Dr. Mendel waved at her as he continued speaking with Dr. Hackett. "So far, we have about seventy percent of the damage repaired. We need to gather more resources to finish the repairs and restock our supplies. How are things going here?"

"Taking care of patients, and doing more research on the *logos* trees. So far, there seems to be a connection between the spaceship and the seeds, but we don't know any more than that. Except . . ."

"What is it?" Doctor Mendel asked with curiosity while Jen listened attentively.

"While I was doing research, I heard a voice saying, 'His name is *Logos*.' Of course, we know the trees are called logos but I think he was referring to something else, maybe."

"Perhaps we should check with Joshua. Still, you are the best qualified person to figure it out." Doctor Mendel turned to Jen. "Miss Morant, how is your brother doing?"

"Still unconscious, but other than that he seems well, I hope."

Dr. Hackett put a hand on her shoulder. "Will is tough, and we are taking good care of him." Then he turned to Dr. Mendel. "I will do more research on the seeds and trees, but for now I have my hands full with all the patients from the last battle. We will meet later to discuss it."

"Thank you, Dr. Hackett."

The men shook hands. Dr. Mendel said goodbye to Jen.

"Wait, please," Jen called. "Is anything I need to know about happening on the bridge?"

"Not really. We are about a thousand miles from planet Uranus. The gravitational forces seem to be weaker than the ones on Saturn, so we are in stationary orbit. According to the mission logs, there's something we need to pick up from the planet."

"Right!"

"I know you are anxious to go back to your post, but I also know Will needs you, and you need the rest."

WILL

Will opened his eyes and saw a big bright light over his head. Slowly that light turned into four squares of LED lights on the ceiling. Then he looked around and recognized the medical bay on the *Dunamys*. He tried to move, but his arm was connected to a Medline pole hanging on the right side of his bed. Some sort of serum flowed into his veins.

"Jen?" he called.

"Will?" He heard her voice outside of the small room. She slid the door open and walked in. "You're awake! Are you feeling, okay?"

"What happened?" he asked.

"Your jet was hit. You've been in the medical bay for quite some time. I don't know any more than that."

Then he noticed someone had left a card beside his bed. Jen had seen it there, but had it been left by Elizabeth or David, Desperado or the commander?

"I saw that, earlier, Will. Maybe a possible admirer?"

Will tried to laugh. "I was just fulfilling my duty, doing my part, like all of us on this journey."

"Well, you know, brother, we girls like brave, bold, and sharp guys, especially if they are heroes."

"Please." He picked up the card and opened it.

Thank you for keeping all of us safe. You are an awesome guy!

Get well soon!

A *friend.*

"Who is it from?" Jen asked.

"No idea. Hey--what about the enemy ships?"

"They're gone. We're safe."

"Good to know." He relaxed back on his pillow. "I can't wait to get back to duty."

"Are you serious? Don't even think about it."

The nurse from earlier showed up again and tended to some of his wounds. "Glad you are back with us, Sergeant Morant."

"Augh!" He hissed as the nurse removed bandages from his right arm. "I'm fine, you know."

"Sure, you are. I suggest you stay put for a while, Sergeant."

Jen patted his arm. "We are safe, thanks to you, Will. Mission accomplished. Get some rest." She kissed his forehead. "I'll come to visit you later, bro."

After Jen left, Will wondered about the anonymous card. And he wondered if David had proposed to Elizabeth after Will gave him the rocks from Saturn's rings. It was hard to let her go, but he knew it was the only way to show her how much he loved her. He knew she would be happy with David, so he tried to erase her from his heart. Finally, he fell asleep.

JEN

Jen joined David and Elizabeth in the coffee shop. They had just ordered their favorite drinks. She told them that Will was conscious. The news encouraged them, gave them hope that God would keep them safe for the rest of their journey. Inspired by the deliverance from their enemy, they decided to continue composing the song that Elizabeth began to write earlier, in her diary. They showed it to Jen. It was a song of gratitude and admiration of the Creator and His salvation, but also a song of encouragement to the people on board the *Dunamys*.

"Do you think we should perform it tonight?" Elizabeth asked David.

"Well, it's not finished yet."

"I know, but I think it will cheer people up. And the music you added to the lyrics is fantastic!"

"Thanks. I agree that this one will really encourage people, but let's take our time on it and finish it right so people can enjoy it better!"

"You're right." Elizabeth smiled, something Jen hadn't seen in a while. "Thank you for being willing to help me finish my song!" She hugged him.

"Of course, anytime." David stood up. "I got to get going. I promised to help my dad for a little bit. Have a great day."

"You too, David."

"So how are things going with him?" Jen asked with curiosity as soon as David left the coffee shop.

"We are sort of dating, I guess. It is more... casual now. No sense to rush things, right? I mean, worst case scenario, if we break up, we could still be friends, I hope. But I don't want to think about that, right now I'm content with the way things are. Now what about you, friend? Any guys around?"

"Mmmm, not at the moment. Maybe it is not my time, but I hope for it one day." Jen suggested Elizabeth go for a walk around Central Park.

*****

Jen decided to report to the bridge a few hours later despite her leave of absence. When she arrived, there wasn't much going on. The *Dunamys* was slowly circling Uranus without much noise detected from the instruments.

"Jen! What are you doing here?" Star hugged her.

"Just checking on everything."

"How is Will?"

"He is recovering better than the doctor anticipated. He is tough, you know."

"I'm sure he is." Star winked at her.

"So, what's going on?"

"We have a new mission. We are going to take rock samples from Uranus's rings and from one of its moons, Ariel."

"Cool! I might check with the science team whenever they get them. I've always wanted to see the stars and planets up close, but I never dreamed of actually holding pieces of them in my own hands."

The commander entered the bridge. Everyone stood and saluted. Then he ordered them to approach the ring made up of the finest particles that surrounded the planet. Star read aloud the information coming to the screen.

"Uranus's axis is tilted at an angle of 98 degrees. Nobody knows why. Also, the main magnetic field is tilted 59 degrees."

They moved closer to a section of the rings that held smaller fragments of rocks and ice. As *Dunamys* passed by the fine grains of the rings, the ship slowed down to remain in orbit.

Jen, as the rest of the crew were able to see the pieces of ice and debris moving from the northern to the southern hemisphere. It was strange. Then she got closer to the front window to get a closer look at Uranus. The surface was plain, some kind of gray, blue or turquoise color.

The exploration shuttle was dispatched with Iram and Joseph escorting them, and the crew followed their progress closely from the video feeds from inside and outside the shuttle. Once they got stationary it was easy to get samples from the rings, like catching fine mist. They collected the samples for a while, then, suddenly, the mission was disrupted by the planet's magnetic attraction.

"It seems your math fails, Dr. Mendel," Commander Partridge noted.

"I beg your pardon, sir, but my calculations were correct. There must be some kind of variation in the—"

The shuttle moved to the other side of the planet. Iram activated the emergency rockets, but it was too late. The gravitational forces were very strong, more than anyone had been expecting. Little by little, clouds of gas – blue, white, gray, and pale green–appeared from the cameras on the shuttle. Then small fragments of fluffy snow started to cover its windows.

"Sir. We've lost contact with the shuttle," Star announced.

Commander Partridge immediately ordered a full scan of the area.

"I can't find them, Commander. But..."

"What is it, Star?"

"I detect an even stronger gravitational force from that specific area."

"What? That's weird."

"For some reason, the magnetic shield and the gravitational forces of the planet are stronger there than anywhere else."

"That doesn't make any sense." Dr. Mendel came to look at Star's screen.

"I know it wasn't in the briefing from the science team," Star said, "but this planet has different attributes than the others we've encountered."

Commander Partridge sighed. "We need a rescue team."

II
MIRANDA

WILL

Hours later, Will woke up again. He felt much better after his long nap. He turned around after he saw another card laying on the side table.

"Another card?" Jen smiled as she entered his room in the medical bay. "Who is this secret admirer, I wonder?"

"Oh, you know, sis. I have so many." He laughed.

"Well, I'm glad you're keeping your humor—and your humble attitude." She laughed back.

"You can read it if you want," he offered, handing her the card.

"Oh, this one is from Doris! I haven't heard from her in a while." She read the card. "She's planning to open a restaurant on the *Dunamys*! Very cool."

"Yes! I was glad to hear she's doing well."

"Is she another fan of yours?" Jen smirked.

He laughed.

"Well, on a more serious note, your friends, the ones who actually rescued you—"

"Iram and Joseph? What happened to them?"

Jen bit her lip before speaking. "They've been lost in a mission close to the orbit of Uranus. Commander Partridge is sending a squadron for search and rescue."

A few minutes later, David and Elizabeth arrived in the medical bay. They both hugged and greeted Jen, who was sitting nearby while Will was being cared for by a nurse.

When the nurse was finished, they greeted Will. For a few minutes they just chatted, remembering the adventures they'd had back on Earth trying to smuggle Joshua away, how the events had unfolded so quickly, and how they'd survived every mission on each planet of the Solar System.

"Do you remember when I picked up my music box and showed it to Desperado?" Elizabeth reminisced.

"Yeah," said Jen, "I remember. "

"I sang that song to Desperado and even though it was an old hymn it seemed to have a great impact on him. I know when we sing about the Creator something powerful happens inside us." Elizabeth pointed at her heart.

"And as we've been observing Uranus and thinking about all the times, we've escaped danger, Elizabeth was inspired to write a song we are now finishing." David smiled.

"We're planning to perform it at David's Dad's

coffee shop as soon as it's ready," Elizabeth finished. "I think it's a fun and inspiring song!"

"Wow, can you guys give us a preview?" Jen asked. "We'd like to hear it."

"Why not?" Elizabeth agreed, handing David his guitar.

"I thought you'd never ask," David chuckled.

As they performed the song, Jen smiled and joined them in the singing.

"Wow! It's really, really good!" Jen said, eyes wet when they had finished.

"Yeah, it's powerful," agreed Will.

"And there is one more thing we want to share with you. Will," David began, but Elizabeth interrupted him.

"We can talk another time, David. Will still needs some rest and we really need to get going. But I'm so happy and relieved you are alive and well!" Elizabeth give Will a gentle hug.

"See you, buddy!" David waved goodbye.

"Thank you for coming! I really appreciate it!"

"Anytime! Get well!" As they made their way out of the room David asked Elizabeth why the hurry.

Will held his breath, trying to hear their words.

"David... I have to be honest ..." They were gone. No more chance to hear what she was going to say.

He turned to his sister. "What is going on Jen?"

"Well, there is something about them that I didn't tell you." Jen bit her lip again.

"I know that face, Jen. It means bad news. You

know what is going on, don't you?"

"I do, but I don't know if I should tell you."

Will felt his heart beating faster than usual. "I prefer to know now rather than later. Please tell me."

JEN

Jen left the medical bay and went directly to *Rewards Place*. There, close to the Vintage Proverb Coffee Shop, was Doris' new restaurant, The Golden Rose. The place had a cozy, family environment. The wooden furniture and decorations on the walls gave it a country style look. Jen wondered where she got all that wood for the place. Jen waited at the entrance until she heard Elizabeth arguing with David at a distance. It was the first time she heard a heated argument between them. Discreetly, she approached a bench surrounded by trees, using the trees to hide her. She got close enough to hear the discussion.

"He did what?" David raised his voice.

"Please keep quiet! I didn't know you would react this way."

"What way?" David had lowered his tone of voice a little. You think it is fair that you and Will hid those two conversations from me?"

"I'm sorry, David but you already knew I wasn't sure about my relationship with you, and I have known Will a little longer than you."

"But we are still dating, are we not?"

"Yeeees, but not officially. I mean, kind of. You see why I wanted to take things slowly? I don't want to make things awkward for anyone. That is why I didn't tell you. I know he is your friend."

"Or I thought he was."

"He is. In fact, he told me he hid his feelings for a long time. He told me he was willing to let me go and lose me forever to make me happy."

"So did I, if I recall correctly."

"I know, you both are amazing! David, please don't be angry with him. This is all on me."

"No, it is not. No wonder why he got those stones for me. He didn't do it for me. He did that for you!"

"What are you talking about?"

"Oh ah–" David paused, placing his hand on the back of his head. "I have to do the right thing, I guess. The ring I gave you. Will got the rocks to make it."

"Wait, so the ring you gave me after you proposed was actually from Will?" Elizabeth paused for a moment. "That explains a lot–"

"Well, technically he willingly gave me the rocks to make it, you know."

"I can't believe you didn't tell me."

"I thought it was irrelevant. After all, it was my idea, after I talk to Will and–never mind."

"Are you sure, David?"

"I–I guess we both held back information from each other." David's tone was sad. He stood up.

"I guess we both didn't think it was important for the other." Elizabeth lowered her head.

"So where does this leave us?" David squatted to look up into Elizabeth's eyes.

"I don't know, David. That is exactly why I wanted to slow down."

"I'm sorry. We can still date and try to figure it out."

"Let's talk about this when we are a little calmer."

They hugged half-heartedly, and David departed. Jen immediately returned to Doris' restaurant. She found a table and sat down to wait for Elizabeth. A few minutes later, she arrived, her eyes red and puffy.

"Elizabeth, are you ok?"

"No, not really, but I don't want to talk about it right now."

"Okay, friend, let's go inside."

They went to the counter to greet Doris.

"Hello girls, I'll be with you in a moment," Doris said as she finished attending to another customer. Then she asked one of the servers to lead the ladies to the table prepared for them.

They sat down and picked up their menus. The plastic laminated card had a golden letter R golden surrounded by a couple of roses. The offerings included chicken salad croissant, turkey and Swiss panini, sausage and cheese panini, cranberry salad with pecans and walnuts, and some soups. Everything looked so good that Jen couldn't decide.

"So... How is he doing? Really," Elizabeth asked.

"The nurse told me he might be back on duty soon."

"I didn't mean that. You know what I mean. I was wondering... how he's *feeling*."

Jen sighed. "I told him David proposed, and I told him you decided to wait. I hope you don't mind, but he insisted. It's like he already knew. But I kept it short, and I didn't share anything else. I promise."

"It's okay, Jen. Thank you for trying to be discreet."

"Are you ladies ready to order?" Doris gave them both a quick hug.

"I don't know yet, everything looks so good! You are so talented!"

"Yeah, you play strings, you're good with flowers, and now look at you—a great chef. Congratulations!" Elizabeth smiled, but it didn't reach her eyes.

"Thank you!"

"How did you get the supplies you needed for all of this?" Jen asked with curiosity.

"Good question, Jen. We had a lot of food supplies when we came on board. Those were distributed to the restaurants and shops in the neighborhoods. So far, they have lasted a long time. But in the future, we want to use the farms and the botanic gardens to provide our ingredients. We have plenty of chickens, turkeys, fish, and sprouts. But we still need to manage our resources well. We don't want to run out of supplies."

"That is understandable. We all are making sacrifices. But thank God we have enough food for everyone," Elizabeth said.

"I know, it's like it has been multiplied," Jen added.

"By the way, how is the newest engaged couple in town?" Doris asked enthusiastically.

Jen waved at Doris to signal her to not go there.

"Oh, we are not . . . Doris, how do you−?"

"A lot of people saw the proposal back when we were in Saturn's orbit. People talk. I'm sorry if you were trying to keep it a secret."

"No worries." Elizabeth frowned.

"Gossip inside the spaceship. Seriously?" Jen complained.

"David proposed, but I didn't say yes," Elizabeth explained. "I told him I needed some time to process everything that has happened. We had some misunderstanding about that. I mean, David gave me the strength to come on this journey in outer space. He has helped me through the whole thing, even when it was painful. I guess I am thankful to him," she said, but there was little joy in her voice.

I guess she is ready to talk now, Jen thought.

"So, you think you owe him something?" Jen asked.

"No. I mean, I never saw it that way." Elizabeth frowned.

"But he loves you!" Doris said.

"Yes, but right now it is complicated."

"At least you have someone." Doris leaned forward. "He proposed in the most romantic way. How many girls have an engagement ring made out of Saturn's rings?"

"Yes, but the whole situation is not as glamorous as you think," Elizabeth responded.

"Can I see it?" Doris requested.

Elizabeth reluctantly held out her ring for Doris to admire.

"The truth is, David confessed that Will is the one who gave him the rock and the metal from the rings of Saturn for my engagement ring. I was upset. Also, I told him about my conversations with Will."

Doris scrunched her nose. "I'm not following you."

Jen decided to spare her friend the discomfort. "You see, my brother has been in love with her for a very long time. So back on Earth, he told Elizabeth he would love to get a ring out of Saturn's rings and give it to the girl he loves. But he never told her how he felt about her until recently."

"That's what I told David." Elizabeth moaned.

"Wow! How did he take it?" Doris asked.

"We argued. I guess we need to talk when things cool down. I mean I love David, but that doesn't mean I don't have mixed feelings. This is so complicated." Elizabeth rested her head over her hands on the table.

WILL

Major Rogers visited Will in the Medical Bay. Will thanked him then requested an update on the current mission, since he was concerned about his buddies. Major Rogers agreed, but with a little bit of reluctance. After he updated Will on his squadron, he also filled him in on the status of the *Dunamys*. Major Rogers left him with the video logs of the exploration team. Will immediately opened logs to learn what was going on. The videos included the conversations streamed to the *Dunamys*.

He read how as the shuttle approached the other side of Uranus, the gravitational forces increased significantly. The spaceship activated the engines to counteract the gravitational forces. Then they lost contact with the shuttle.

Will opened the next log. Commander Partridge dispatched a search and rescue squadron to explore the last area of transmission.

Intrigued, Will went back and searched earlier logs from the shuttle mission. He found one dated about three hours before the last transmission. Iram and Joseph and the shuttle were facing a bizarre climate of ice particles in the upper atmosphere of Uranus. Joseph and Iram activated their protection shield and advised the shuttle to do the same. Iram also advised the science team to slowly increase the shuttle's heat. The ice around them started to melt little by little. But the gravitational forces were still strong. They were losing oxygen, so they turned off the heat, allowing ice to drift onto the shuttle again.

For several minutes, they remained inside the clouds—inert, unable to move. Then they heard a sound like rain falling onto the craft. The sound became stronger and stronger. At first, they wondered if it was hail, but when they looked, they saw the particles were bright, reflective, and large, like diamonds of different sizes and shapes. A particularly large one struck the ship so hard that Iram and Joseph fell forward. The transmission continued but no voices were heard. The video feed showed them unconscious.

Will opened another log previous to the last transmission that included the video feed. Iram woke up and looked out the window again. Something in the middle of the clouds caught his attention—something moving, something bright and fast. It seemed to be a light, and the light shone brighter and moved faster as he watched.

"Joseph... Joseph, wake up!" Will heard Iram say.

"What? What is it?"

"Look! There's something outside!"

Joseph immediately jumped up, his face clouded with worry.

"Tell me it's not another enemy. No, please, no."

"I don't know what it is."

Suddenly a scream like the scream of an eagle sounded. Then Will saw a creature similar to an eagle but giant, made completely out of light. The creature realized Joseph and Iram were awake and immediately swooped closer, its screaming beak open wide.

"You have a visitor, Sergeant." The nurse voiced over the intercom outside the door.

Will paused the video log from the mission and took off his headphones.

"Let him in please."

Elizabeth entered the room. She looked more serious than she had earlier.

"Hi!" called Will as she entered. "Thanks for coming again."

"How are you?" Elizabeth asked.

"Much better. And you?"

"I'm...fine. So, when are you getting out of the hospital?"

"I'm stuck here for a while. Doctor's orders. But I can't wait to go back in action. They're keeping me out of all the fun." Will tried to get more comfortable in the bed.

"There is something we need to talk about."

"Sure, what is it?" Will asked, ready to listen attentively.

JEN

Jen returned to her post while the rescue mission was still in progress. The squadron followed the trail of the engines to an upper layer of Uranus. There, the system detected a high concentration of rocky objects flying around the shuttle at great speed. It immediately became clear that the team was in a great danger.

"Sir, we found them, but they are trapped in a weird kind of storm. A diamond storm," reported the rescue team pilot.

"What? Please repeat, Captain Frisbie."

"It is raining diamonds down there. I'll send you the information."

"Jen, did you receive it?"

"Yes, sir. The shuttle and pilots are trapped in crystalized rocks flying around at a great speed. The data says carbon rocks, so, yeah. Diamonds."

"*Dunamys*, this is the shuttle..." The communication cut off.

"Exploration shuttle, please respond." Jen tried to boost the signal. "Exploration shuttle, please respond."

"Anything?" the commander asked.

Jen shook her head. Her only hope was to request the rescue team to help boost the signal, since they were closer, and forward it to the *Dunamys*.

Then a spaceship appeared out of the light. The shuttle. Everyone cheered. But as the light came closer, they realized it was in the shape of an eagle. Just as they saw it, it flew away at a great speed.

"Exploration Shuttle, can you hear me? This is Captain Frisbie. Please respond."

"This is Iram. They are fine. We are escorting them back to the *Dunamys*. Over."

The shuttle and the squadron of jets finally arrived safely on board the *Dunamys*, bringing samples of the rings and part of the atmosphere. And a few samples of the diamonds. But they couldn't explain the encounter they'd had with the creature of light. The report just read, "We were pulled out by a mysterious alien creature in the shape of an eagle made out of light."

The *Dunamys* departed the orbit of the planet, leaving behind a beautiful sight as the rings of the planet reflected the sunlight.

WILL

Elizabeth looked at Will like she was trying to find the right words to say. After a pause, she said, "I know you got the rocks from Saturn's ring. David told me."

"Oh, really?"

"That was very sweet of you. I just want to thank you."

"I'm happy for you. I really am," Will said, trying to smile. He put his hand on her arm.

"I don't want to hurt you." Elizabeth reached out to Will's hand.

This is it, man. Be strong. This is going to hurt!

Will exhaled. "I know."

"But David and I are not engaged, as many people think."

Really? So, this means...

Elizabeth kept talking. "I just realized I'm not ready for a formal commitment, and I don't want to lose you both. This is getting too complicated for me."

"Thank you, for your honesty, Elizabeth. I just want you to be happy. I really do. If I need to let you go, I'm prepared to do it."

"Thank you, Will." She nodded. "But this will take a while for me to sort out. What I mean is, I need space, sometime apart. There are so many things I have to process."

"I totally understand," Will agreed.

"But I wanted you know I know what you did to get this ring. It means a lot to me. Thank you so much for understanding. I hope you get better soon." Elizabeth left in a rush.

Wow, this is tough. Then he reached his communicator and called David. A few minutes later, David arrived in Will's room.

"Listen, man." David approached Will's bed while making a fist with his hand. "Elizabeth told me about the past conversations between her and—"

Will help up a hand. "I'm so sorry, David, I wanted to tell you, but I didn't know how."

"Tell me that you secretly loved her all this time?"

"That's why I was avoiding you guys. It was hard for me."

"And you still talked to her after I shared with you all about my relationship with her?" David paused for a moment, his jaw clenching. "I thought you were my friend."

"I'm still your friend. I shouldn't have said anything to her. I'm really, really sorry, David. That's why I decided to give you what I got from Saturn. I knew I was wrong in sharing my feelings for her. I knew I had to let her go. Please forgive me?"

"I forgive you, Will. But to be honest, I'm not happy with what you did, even though I realize you met her before I did."

"Did she break up with you?" Will asked.

"You would love that, wouldn't you?"

"No. I mean, I just want her to be happy. Look, she was just here. That's why I called you. I told her I was willing to let her go."

"It doesn't matter anymore. I don't want to see your face again, dude!"

"I understand." Will pressed his lips together, trying not to say too much. "But what are we going to do? We are roommates."

"I will request a transfer."

Will hesitated, then spoke. "I do hope we can mend this friendship."

"Maybe with time. Maybe. But this one is tough." And with that David left.

The nurse came into the room and asked Will to lay back on the bed. She proceeded to check his vitals.

Will couldn't hold back a few tears. Then he grabbed the anonymous card he had received earlier. He read it, then he threw it on the table beside his bed.

"Do you want to take another nap?" The nurse said after administering his medication.

"Yes, I need it," Will murmured.

"I'll make sure nobody disturbs you."

Before she had left the room, he fell asleep.

JEN

The next scheduled mission was to the moon of Miranda. Jen adjusted the feed from the probes sent to inspect it while the *Dunamys* got into its orbit. She zoomed into the surface and passed the feed to the large monitors on the bridge. Huge hills covered the moon, some topped with snow and others without it. The ground looked like it was made of different pieces of rock and other materials roughly put together. As the *Dunamys* passed over the hills, Major Rogers deployed the explorer team commanded by Captain Frisbie.

The team was divided in two, one to take samples from the rocky areas and the other from the frozen areas.

As they separated, the *Dunamys* monitored the activity from above.

"Everything is huge on Miranda," Captain Frisbie reported. The bridge watched as the team jumped high and fell slowly due to the low gravity.

Dr. Mendel registered some minor tremors in the surface but nothing worrisome until the teams reached their spacecraft with the samples. Then the tremors increased exponentially in intensity.

"*Dunamys*, we have a problem." The explorer sounded concerned.

"We see it. Return here immediately. That's an order."

"Aye, aye, sir!"

Immediately Jen piloted the probe closer to the team's position. The ground of the moon began to split open. As the men tried to enter the shuttle, one of them fell into a crack.

"No!" he screamed.

Two more followed him.

"Sir, we have a big problem!" Jen shouted to the bridge.

"What is it?" Major Rogers came to her station.

"Three of our people just fell into the cracks!"

"I see. I'll be right there." Captain Frisbie's voice came over the communicator, and Jen realized he'd heard the conversation. They watched from the live feed as he arrived on the scene.

"Maybe the low gravity will slow their fall," Major Rogers mumbled.

Captain Frisbie exited his jet. Holding onto a rope attached to his craft, he jumped in after the men. Jen lowered the probe to peer into the crack. As hoped, the low gravity slowed the captain's descent and the fall of the men. But despite the slow falls, the three other men had reached the bottom and were hurt. One of them had injured his neck, another his stomach, and the third his head.

The captain tied the rope around the first man. The other team members pulled him up. Then Captain Frisbie moved to his right to reach the second man. He followed the same procedure. Finally, he reached the last one. He checked for the man's vitals, but there was no pulse. The fall had broken his neck.

The bridge was silent as they watched Captain Frisbie close the man's eyes and yank on the rope to be pulled up again.

As Captain Frisbie and the exploration shuttle prepared to take off, another violent earthquake rumbled the moon. But this time the shuttle left the ground before it was too late.

Jen continued to listen to the conversations. She heard they had taken the wounded men to the military medical bay where Will was. She put her earpods down and breathed deeply. "I need a break. Permission to be relieved."

"Of course, Miss. Morant," Major Rogers set his hand on her shoulder. "Take your time."

WILL

Will overheard the doctors talking about how the new men had been wounded. The danger of their whole mission struck him once again. The solar system was a very well-known place, and yet it wasn't. They continued to confront situations out of their control. How much more dangerous would it be visiting unknown star systems?

Will overheard some people talking outside his room. Other patients? Medical staff?

"This is pointless. We are risking our lives for something we have no evidence exists. It's just a few holograms and the word of an alien pilot that now is dead."

"I heard many of the passengers think the same way."

"Yeah, I think several people are finally waking up to the reality that this journey isn't worth the high risk."

The voices grew quieter. Will strained to hear.

"There is a movement spreading across the ship to protest and go back to Earth, back to our old lives. If the planet is going to be destroyed, we can wait for it in peace instead of going through all the danger and difficulty we had been facing."

Then the voices faded away. Silence followed, then the sound of footsteps rushing.

"Doctor, he's bleeding."

"This one too, sir."

"We need to operate. Hurry, take them to surgery. Quickly!"

An hour later, Will heard more whispering. He listened hard, then wished he hadn't. One of the men had died in surgery. The other one, the one with the wound on his head, was still alive but in a coma.

JEN

Jen went straight to *Fight Place* after a short nap. She was coming to understand Elizabeth's feelings of a few days before. Not everything on the trip was as glamorous as she'd thought it would be. They were on a treacherous journey full of perils.

Major Rogers pulled up next to her in one of the small golf carts used to travel across the ship. "Miss Morant, are you going to visit your brother today? I was just with him briefly. I'm told he might be released soon."

Jen took a deep breath, immediately feeling less heavy. "I'm so glad. Where are you going now?"

"I'm going to see one of my contacts. It might be a serious issue, but I'm not sure. If you can spare a few minutes, it would help if you would come with me. You are one of a few people from the crew who I trust."

Jen wondered what he meant, so she decided to go with him and visit her brother later. She got into the golf cart, and they took off.

They stopped at one of the living quarters. Major Rogers rang the doorbell.

A man slid the door open. He eyed Jen suspiciously.

"You can trust her," Major Rogers said. "She has been a pillar of the project since the beginning."

He let them both in and slid the door shut right away. "I found something beautiful and valuable. But we can't tell anyone yet."

"What is it, Arthur?" Rogers asked, raising his eyebrows. "I don't have time for games. I'm hearing rumors of an enemy infiltration, and I need information."

"I have the information inside this little box."

"Show me."

Arthur's hands shook as he opened the box. The object inside shone like a pink sapphire, its reflected pink light filling the room. Jen's sight changed, as though captivated by a strong obsession.

12
NEPTUNE

WILL

"Are you sure you want to do this?" the doctor asked after his examination.

"I'm totally fine, I can handle it," Will insisted.

"Your injuries are not completely healed, but your overall health is better, considering what happened. I don't recommend you go back in action just yet. You need to lay low for a while."

"Thank you, doctor. I am just going to make myself available. I'll go to the bridge and see what is going on."

"Okay, but I urge you to rest."

"I will. Thank you for everything." Will left the medical bay and walked to the bridge. He stopped at the door and waited for a moment. Surprisingly, it was so quiet, not many people coming in or going out. As he walked past the briefing room located close to the bridge, he heard Commander Partridge yelling at someone.

"Are you sure about this, Dr. Mendel?"

"I am, Commander. As you know, our spaceship has gained mass exponentially since our departure."

"And yet we're still collecting resources from the planets. This journey is too risky. It's one complication after another."

"But, sir, those resources represent only about 0.05 % of the actual mass increase since we left Earth."

"So, what is the issue?"

"We don't know. Nevertheless, if this continues, by the time we leave our solar system, our total mass will be double what it was at our departure."

Will heard a slam, like someone punching a desk. Then the room went quiet for a moment.

"I need you to concentrate on the origin of this problem with the excessive mass of the spaceship. Give it a hundred percent of your time."

Will shuddered. The danger seemed to be inside the ship this time. He pushed the reception button to announce his visit to the bridge. "This is Sergeant Morant reporting. May I come in?"

The door slid open. Will entered to find the crew making preparations to arrive at Neptune.

"Hey, Will," Star grinned at him.

He walked over to her. "How is everything going?"

"Good. Much more relaxed than the previous days. Shouldn't you still be in bed?"

"Nah, the doctor gave me an earlier release, just with certain conditions."

"I see you still have bandages."

"I'll be fine. When are we expected to arrive at Neptune?"

"Four weeks, even at the minimal speed, thanks to *Dunamys'* technology. Otherwise, the trip would take four years. Oh, watch out." Her voice lowered. "Here he comes."

Commander Partridge entered the bridge without saying a word to anyone.

"He doesn't look happy," Will whispered as the commander sat in his chair resting his head on his right hand.

"He has been quite upset about all the troubles and problems we've found along the way," Star whispered back.

"I don't blame him. It's been one thing after another lately."

"But I think he is also tired of always waiting to hear instructions from Joshua. You know, to him Joshua is just a hologram that tells him what to do or not to do. He blames Joshua for all the risk and lives lost lately."

"Well, Joshua did warn us of dangers, and he also said it would not be easy. But still, we voluntarily took this journey."

"That is not all, Will. I've been hearing rumors of passengers and others wondering whether the whole journey is worth all the danger we've encountered so far."

"That doesn't sound good."

"Star," Commander Partridge yelled from his chair. "Announce that we are on the route to Neptune and locate Miss. Morant."

"Wait, is my sister missing?"

"Yes. Her shift time is almost over now, and she hasn't responded to my messages." Commander Partridge frowned.

"Let me try." Will called Jen's communicator, but he didn't get any response. Which was odd. She usually picked up his calls right away. He was worried. He left quickly to go look for her.

JEN

Jen wandered through several different neighborhoods. She was disoriented and having a hard time trying to recollect the last few hours. Her memory was a blur.

She remembered that Major Rogers had been with her when the little box revealed the gem with the pinkish shining light. Jen had noticed the major's eyes go wide and sparkly, as if seeing the most beautiful thing in the universe. Even Jen herself felt captivated by the jewel.

She also remembered Commander Partridge entering the room right after, joining them with a few exchanges of dialog. Jen had felt she wanted to run away, but she was unable to do so, allured by the shining lights and reflections. Slowly, hypnotic voices had pierced into her ears, and then her heart, touching her emotions. The voices were different from the Ganymede voices produced by the Religare's artefacts.

These were more subtle, like voices of the sirens in the old folklore told by sailors, soft singing like the whisper of wind blowing over the sea.

"We need to go back to Earth," she remembered hearing Commander Partridge's say as her vision distorted.

She'd remained quiet, closed her eyes, then rushed out of the room. A few minutes later, she found herself at the *Hearing Place*. She was shaking, barely able to walk.

"Go to the *logos* tree and eat its fruit, *rhema*." The whisper was so clear in her ears.

Finally, she found herself in the botanical garden where the trees of the alien seeds grew tall. She grabbed fruit from one of the trees and tried to eat it, but everything seemed to be in slow motion. She felt as if she was about to pass out. But she managed to take one bite.

"Help!" she cried.

Moments later, a familiar voice calmed her. "Breathe! Just take a deep breath."

Then she fainted.

And now she was walking again.

Suddenly, she recognized the new Vintage Proverb. She was supposed to meet Elizabeth here, wasn't she? She glanced at her watch. Things were beginning to seem clearer. Yes, they had planned to meet--an hour and a half ago!

Jen ran to the shop and found Elizabeth sitting at a table outside. Jen sat down and ordered a coffee.

"What's wrong, Jen?"

"It is a long story." Jen tried to focus, but she felt disoriented again.

"I was about to leave, but I'm glad I stayed a little longer. I wanted to show you something." Elizabeth pulled a big velvet bag out of her purse.

"Oh! The music box that had attracted the attention of the Ommites."

She nodded. "I still wonder how they were able to hear it out of all the other sounds inside the spaceship. Why was my little music box such a big deal for them? Could its music—or any music—attract other aliens?"

"I don't know." Jen opened the box and the sound rushed out. "Nothing seems to be happening now, so I guess we're safe."

"Perhaps you are right, but I still wonder. I keep examining it, but there is nothing special about it. It's only a good memory with sentimental value. But what I was really hoping was that music would allow us to encounter other enslaved civilizations and bring them freedom, to let them join us in our journey to Zion. That is what I would love to do." Elizabeth contemplated her music box.

"I've been talking with Desperado," Jen said. "The enemy appears to be a very sensitive society."

"But that's also a weakness, isn't it, Jen? Remember their issue with the pink light?"

"Yeah, but I now understand that."

Elizabeth looked up, startled. "What do you mean? That thing, whatever it is, enslaved a whole civilization. What you mean you understand that?"

"I can't exactly say, but I kind of get it. But your music had an impact on them. As it does on all of us."

"Thanks, Jen. I love making music. That's why we're thinking of recording the song that we just finished, regardless of the awkwardness between David and I, he really is a professional, separating our craft from the personal affairs. I hope we can fix that, but for now I am excited about our first recording."

"I'm sure your music will be a flag of freedom and peace for many."

Elizabeth smiled. "What about you? How is your job at the bridge? Any promotions expected? After all, you have been more than just a communications officer, and you've done a very good job. I am sure Commander Partridge could assign you to an ambassador position or something like that."

"Maybe, but right now it is complicated."

"Oh, by the way, I forgot to tell you Star called me asking for you earlier."

"Oh no! I missed reporting my shift!" Jen stood quickly, ready to head to the bridge. As soon as Jen stood up she saw Major Rogers walking by. He seemed confused, or at least a little disoriented.

"Jen?"

"Major Rogers? Where did you come from?" Jen asked.

"I don't know. I don't remember." He shook his head. "I was in a dazzling place where I saw Joshua. He gave me instructions for a mission. He seemed like a real person, not a hologram, so I wrote down everything that he told me. But when I read it back, it was gibberish. Then I came here."

"We need to go to the bridge and talk with Commander Partridge," Jen urged. "I think he was there too."

They left together in a rush directly to the bridge looking for Commander Partridge, but he was in the briefing room with some of the passengers. They waited patiently until the meeting was dismissed. Then they went in.

The people leaving the meeting looked tired and upset, but Jen didn't think too much about it. At that moment, she just wanted to know what happened to all of them after the exposure to the pink light. And she wanted to find out if Commander Partridge had been there as well or if that was her imagination.

"Glad you both decided to join us!" He spoke as if he was upset with them.

"I apologize, sir. That is exactly the reason we are meeting with you now." Major Rogers related everything he remembered, from meeting with Arthur to the rock or gem emitting the pink light and after that. Jen did the same, explaining she remembered seeing him in the room with them.

"That is the strangest story I have ever heard, even for our circumstances. I don't recall being there, but if the story is true, it means you both have been compromised. I suggest you remain in the isolation chambers until further notice. You may go pick up a few things from your living quarters first."

Before he dismissed them, he assigned a guard to each of them. They were escorted to their living quarters and then to the isolation chambers.

WILL

When Will found out what happened to his sister and Major Rogers, he decided to find answers. He thought maybe Dr. Mendel would know the details, so he went to visit his living quarters. He rang the doorbell and waited patiently.

"Yes?" Dr. Mendel only cracked the door. He seemed secretive. Or afraid?

"Could I talk to you for a moment?" Will asked.

"I don't have too much time. I have to report to the bridge."

The door slid open enough for Will to step inside.

"I understand, but I'm worried about my sister and Major Rogers. How can we help them?"

"We would like to do research but, we don't even have a sample of the rock."

"Do you know who exposed them it?"

"No idea, Will. But we are monitoring them, so no need to worry."

"How long are they going to be in isolation?"

"I don't know. We are consulting with Desperado since he has knowledge on the pink light. Just be patient, they will be fine. Meanwhile get acquainted with the next planet, I'm sure you will need all the information you can get."

Dr. Mendel left held the door open, for Will to stepped into the hallway and then he locked his door.

How strange! What is going on?

Will though as he strode toward the elevators.

*****

At the end of the four weeks, the *Dunamys* reached the Neptunian system and still Will hadn't been allowed to pilot his jet. Instead, he had been asked to temporarily take his sister's function. His first day came right on time for the approach to Neptune's orbit. As he entered the bridge he laid eyes on the blue planet. It was similar in appearance to Earth, a reminder of the oceans they hadn't seen in a long time.

"Attention, everyone," Dr. Mendel called out. He had temporarily assumed Major Rogers position on top of his other duties. "I have carefully calculated the strength of gravity here. With this information, we will be able to stay in orbit around the planet and even get deeper into it."

"Does he mean we are plunging into Neptune's atmosphere?" Will asked Star.

"Well, not exactly plunging, but softly going into the atmosphere." Star said.

"The data indicated fast winds, but according to Dr. Mendel, the spaceship's protective shield will compensate for it and protect us."

As they entered Neptune's atmosphere, it looked

as if they were in a tunnel. Rays of different tonalities of blue advanced toward them at high speed. As they moved, they emitted a supersonic sound with a little echo.

Now they needed to get samples of each layer of the atmosphere, so the *Dunamys* deployed a couple of hoses to collect them. Somewhere in the distance they could see darker clouds moving in a different direction from the rest of the clouds. Dr. Mendel sent a probe to look beneath the storm.

The results were very interesting. The atmosphere was full of gasses—hydrogen, helium, nitrogen, and some oxygen. Further below, the probe found boiling water. As the probe went deeper, temperatures got even higher, and the pressure was one hundred times stronger. Then the pressure destroyed the probe.

Commander Partridge mumbled in annoyance. He didn't like losing more resources.

The *Dunamys* proceeded through the atmosphere with caution, measuring to find the safest area for the *Dunamys* and for the exploration shuttle. The mission was sent with the same personnel as before, Joseph and Iram escorting them. The goal was to get close to the water and gather as much as possible.

"It feels like we're in a submarine out here," came one of the voices from the shuttle intercom. "Like navigating in an ocean of water and liquid nitrogen."

Will was happy to be able to help during the mission, taking some of his sister duties at the communication board even though he wasn't part of the action. Although Commander Partridge had accepted his temporary position with reluctance.

"There are some small, shiny objects attached to the spaceship," Will noted. Commander Partridge didn't respond. "Maybe it's nothing," he muttered to himself as he continued monitoring the progress of the mission.

A few hours later, Iram, Joseph and the science team arrived safely back on the *Dunamys*. Will was glad his buddies were safe, but he wondered about the tension on the bridge. He was in a position new to him, but it didn't feel anything as Jen had described it. She talked about the attitude of the Commander at the bridge and the energy of working as a team.

In fact, he also was worried about his sister, who was still in an isolation chamber. Will regularly took her food and left it at the door. He did the same for Major Rogers in his isolation chamber. At least they each had an intercom system. Will often talked with Jen and shared with the major about the objects on the shuttle before returning to the bridge.

The report from the science team finally arrived. They had harvested a few hundred gallons of the liquid and began processing it to get pure water since it had nitrogen mixed with it. Will passed the report to Commander Partridge, who still seemed quiet and upset. As soon as he read the report, he exploded in rage.

"We only get this much purified water? How is it going to last for the extra months? This is unacceptable!"

Dr. Mendel advised a mission to the moon Triton. The journey was in the itinerary already, and he believed they could find water there.

Commander Partridge yelled for them to get on with it, then sat down holding his head again, as if he had a headache.

The exploration shuttle was sent to Triton with another set of pilots as escorts. Dr. Mendel suggested that they might have to drill to get water from under the surface.

Upon their arrival, Will received the images sent by the shuttle and proceeded to share them on the main monitor of the bridge. They observed Neptune setting on the horizon across a hill.

"I'm so thankful we are still alive in spite of all the dangers we have encountered," one team member said.

"Not to mention, we've had the privilege of seeing the wonders of other planets," another answered.

As Will listened to their conversation, he found himself agreeing with them. As the exploration team set up the drilling machine on the surface of the moon, Commander Partridge crossed the bridge and stood behind Will.

"Turn that off! That's an order," he barked.

"I'm about to approach Triton to follow up with the mission—" the pilot's voice came over the communicator.

But the commander pushed the button to end the transmission. Then he turned to the crew.

"Attention everyone. Despite the mission in progress, I want all of you to focus on keeping the *Dunamys* here, in orbit, until further notice."

"But sir, the team." Will wanted to explode but managed to keep himself under control.

"They will be fine," Commander Partridge said. "This is an order, and it is final. Stay put. Everyone." Commander Partridge left for a meeting, reportedly with some passengers.

"What is going on, Star?"

"You mean with Commander Partridge?"

"I mean with everything. You can't deny there is a lot of tension in the air."

"More than usual, yes. And I'm worried about the mission. The idea was to get us closer to assist the team in case of an emergency, but now…" Star looked out the window.

Will laid a hand on her arm. "We will keep an eye on them while he's away. Besides, those missions take time."

Dr. Mendel came over to them and spoke softly. "Will, I spoke to Major Rogers, a guy named Arthur is the one responsible for smuggling the pink rock so, we need to find this Arthur fellow, and quickly—before he exposes other people. And it is urgent we get samples of that gem or rock or whatever it is to study its effects."

"Got it." Will pulled up the passenger manifest and browsed through it. There were three people named Arthur, so he suggested bringing each of them in for questioning. But with extreme caution. Dr. Mendel approved the plan.

At that moment, Commander Partridge entered the bridge again.

"What's going on, Commander?" Dr. Mendel asked.

"Turn back toward home. Right now."

"You mean back to Earth, sir?" the pilot asked, his eyes wide.

"Precisely!"

The navigator hesitated but obeyed, putting in the coordinates for the destination of Earth.

Will didn't like this. Not at all. But he didn't move or make any comments. He discreetly eyed Star, trying to capture her attention. She seemed extremely worried. He had never seen her so jittery before.

"Sir," Star approached Commander Partridge's chair. "May I ask why we did a course change towards Earth? According to the mission schedule—"

"I know what I'm doing, Star. We need to save as many people as we can, so please carry out my orders."

"Commander Partridge, I think Star has valid concerns." Dr. Mendel came to stand beside her. "I don't think this is a good idea, and the exploration team is still in Triton. Is there any specific reason why—"

"I'm simply not willing to risk more lives. Please continue with your research and leave the leadership chair to me."

"Very well, sir, I will return to the science research area."

"Yes, Dr. Mendel. You are dismissed." He yelled.

Will knew something was totally off. Then he remembered what Jen had told him—that Commander

Partridge was present when she and Major Rogers were exposed to the pink light.

"Permission to be dismissed, Commander Partridge." Will requested.

"I need you here, Sergeant Morant."

"I need to check on my sister, sir. As always, I will keep it short and take the necessary precautions."

"Make it quick."

Will walked out of the bridge a couple of minutes behind Dr. Mendel. "Dr. Mendel," he called as he jogged toward the man.

When Will reached him, he said, "Follow me."

They walked at a normal pace, rode the elevator, then arrived at *Hearing Place*, where the scientific research was conducted. Once inside the research facility, they called Joshua, but this time, he didn't respond.

"Okay, maybe there is something else we can do." Dr. Mendel gave Will a couple of earpods.

"Listen carefully," he said as he put another pair in his own ears.

Will heard the audio from the briefing room near the bridge. It was Commander Partridge's voice, and it seemed several people were with him.

"Nobody suspects anything, right?" the commander said.

"Well, sir, I think some of the passengers might suspect we've changed course."

"Where do Major Rogers and Dr. Mendel stand?"

"We don't know what side they are on, but I

assume their loyalties are with you, as are the majority of the crew." Who spoke for the crew, Will wasn't sure.

The commander spoke again. "There are still plenty of passengers and pilots who want to continue this journey. We need to figure out what to do with them. I mean, I know Joshua saved me, and many of you had experiences with him, too, but at this point you'd have to be nuts to continue on. We've already lost so much. If it wasn't for this flashing rock, I wouldn't have had the strength to make this decision."

The sound of a small object placed on the table was followed by the sound of many voices, then silence.

Dr. Mendel pulled out one earbud. "This is not good," he whispered to Will.

Will nodded. "Now we know for sure that Commander Partridge is compromised."

"And we need to do something about it."

Will nodded. They removed their earpods and entered the isolation chamber area.

JEN

Jen spent the four weeks in isolation reading and checking the notes she'd made since they departed Earth. And she got to visit with Will through the intercom. David, Star and Elizabeth also visited her a few times, but it wasn't enough. The isolation was breaking her. Overwhelmed with sadness she closed her eyes for a while.

"Jen, are you awake?" Will's voice called through the intercom.

She scrambled up from the recliner and sat close to the door. "I didn't think you'd be here until later."

"This is not an official meeting. I came to get you out."

Jen gasped. "You can't, I'm compromised. I don't even know the extent of the influence of the gem on me."

"You are fine, maybe a little disoriented but nothing else."

The door slid open revealing her brother wearing a cap on his head. He held a card key and another cap for her. Looking down she saw a guard lying unconscious on the floor.

"What is going on?"

"Put this on." He handed her the extra cap. "You have to come with me. Dr. Mendel is getting Major Rogers. We have to stop Commander Partridge."

"Let's go." Dr. Mendel and Major Rogers walked past them, signaling for them to follow.

"Do you remember the behavior of the Ommites on Mars?" Dr. Mendel asked Jen.

"Yes, they were deceived. It was like they were...obsessed."

"Do you remember the reason?"

"According to Desperado it was the pink light that enslaved most of their planet."

"Exactly!"

"Dr. Mendel! Do you mean that gem Major Rogers and I saw earlier is the pink light?"

270

"I'm afraid so, Jen. And somehow it has enslaved Commander Partridge."

"And it almost got me, too," Major Rogers said. "I didn't know what to do, so I did the only thing I could think of—I ate from the *rhema* and cried out for help. At that moment, Joshua appeared, and immediately I felt a strength like never before in my life. I snapped out of the confusion and weakness."

"And I did the same, I think. I barely remember," Jen said.

Will shook his head. "Wow! Just like Desperado and many others."

"Yeah. And unfortunately, Commander Partridge is not the only one affected. There are several people with him."

All four of them left the isolation chambers area. From there they boarded the elevators and went to the auditorium at *Legacy Place*. There, several of the passengers were gathered for David and Elizabeth's event to celebrate their first recordings, organized by David's dad.

How is she doing this, performing and recording an album after what happened between them? I guess she is stronger than I thought.

Major Rogers, Dr. Mendel, Will, and Jen sat in a far corner surrounded by empty chairs. Most of the others took seats closer to the stage. They talked quietly as the couple rehearsed for the performance.

"The problem," Dr. Mendel said to the group, "is that Commander Partridge has ordered the spaceship to turn back to Earth."

Jen gasped. "But that isn't right. We can't go back after all we've gone through. The *Dunamys* is almost repaired, and we've gathered supplies. And besides, we're so close to the end of our solar system."

"I agree, sis, but we can't contact Joshua. Trust me, I tried."

"I had heard many people actually want to go back to Earth," said Jen sadly.

"I guess they'll be relieved when they find out we've changed course then."

Jen noticed a flashing on Dr. Mendel's belt. It was his communicator, indicating a call on a private channel.

"Dr. Mendel, do you read me?"

He picked up his communicator. "Yes, Star. What's going on?"

"Can I talk to you in private? I think something is wrong."

All of them immediately knew Star's concern.

"Jen, Will, and Major Rogers are here with me. You can trust them."

Dr. Mendel gestured them to come closer to listen while Star related everything that happened on the bridge since they'd left—including a potential division among the crew and passengers.

"Thank you, Star. Keep me posted." Dr. Mendel turned to Major Rogers. "Major, I have a plan. We'll go to the engine room while Will keeps monitoring the main briefing room. Jen, tell David and Elizabeth what has happened. I have the feeling they will be a big help."

The two men left Jen and Will watching the rehearsal, although Will was also listening carefully to the audio coming from his earbuds.

Minutes after the rehearsal ended, Jen saw David talking with Mayor Jacobs at the stage while Elizabeth was holding a few dresses on hangers.

Jen left Will still seated in the back and got closer to the stage. Yet she maintained a bit of distance. She didn't want to bother them, but she also wanted be sure no one else was around.

"Jen, what are you doing here? I thought you were in isolation," Elizabeth said as soon as she saw her.

"I'm fine now. It's a long story."

"So does that mean you are clean?" Mayor Jacobs asked.

"I think so." Jen answered, getting closer.

"Good to hear." Mayor Jacobs gave her shoulder a pat. "After watching the rehearsal, I think this show is going to be the best!" Then he took David over to the corner to talk to him.

Jen was a little worried about Mayor Jacobs. She didn't know if he could be trusted.

"Sorry I have been so busy, Jen. There is so much going on," Elizabeth said.

"How are you doing with the situation with David?"

"We talked and decided to keep our relationship professional. I enjoy making music with him, but the rest is not the same. We talk but we keep our distance."

"How is Will feeling?" asked David returning from his talk with Mayor Jacobs.

"He has been covering for me at the bridge, but honestly, I'm concerned about him. He has not fully recovered after his injuries. He is doing better though, although everyone, including the doctor, keeps telling him to take it easy. He insists on being back in action. He's there in the back." Jen pointed to where Will sat.

Elizabeth turned and waved to him.

Will jogged up the aisle toward the stage while removing his earpods. "Jen, did you tell them?"

"Tell us what?" David asked.

Will looked at David. "I know things are a little tense between us, but there is something bigger at stake here. We need to talk to you both. We've got an emergency."

"Let's go backstage," David suggested. "We'll have some privacy there."

13
TRITON

WILL

“What is going on? Why the *Dunamys* stopped? Why are we not moving?” Will heard Commander Partridge screaming around, while he continued to listen on his earpods. He was surprised the listening devices planted by Dr. Mendel haven't been discovered yet.

Immediately Will went outside the auditorium and looked for the closest window. Neptune looked farther away, but they seemed to be getting closer and closer to Triton, one of Neptune's moons. As he looked outside through the window, he continued listening.

“Sir, the navigation system isn't working.”

“I order you to continue our course toward Earth immediately.”

“I would, sir, but I can't.”

“You are relieved. Star, take over the helm.”

The voices went quiet, but Will heard steps and the sound of digital devices in operation.

"Sorry, sir," Star said. "But he's right. The navigation system is locked and won't allow us to move."

"I said turn back immediately!"

"It's impossible, sir. Ouch!"

Will noted the sound of something hitting the console and then the floor. The audio was coming from the bridge, not from the briefing room.

"I'm afraid you are no longer in control of the *Dunamys*, Commander Partridge." Major Roger's voice sounded like it was coming from the speakers.

"Major Rogers? What are you doing?"

Will held his breath, torn between needing to listen and wanting to run to the bridge to help Major Rogers subdue Commander Partridge.

"First, I'm stopping your attempt to return us to Earth. Then I'm starting an investigation into what you're up to."

"You won't stop me!"

Will cringed at the sound of chairs sliding over the floor. Then something heavy hit the control boards.

"The spaceship descending to Triton using a safety protocol," Dr. Mendel said.

"No!" Commander Partridge cried. "This is mutiny, treason! Initiate Korah protocol!" he ordered something or someone.

"What is wrong with him?" Will mumbled. Then he re-entered the auditorium and joined the others again backstage.

"What is going on, Will?" David looked concerned and confused.

Will ignored him, placing his hand against his ear trying to hear better.

"It's time!" Commander Partridge said. Then Will heard the door sliding open.

"I have to go to the bridge. Now. Jen, can you update them?"

"Will, do you really trust me?"

"Sis, I have the feeling I can trust you more than Commander Partridge. That's enough for me."

Will raced away while continuing to listen to the audio feed.

He arrived at the bridge to find the door standing open. He hurried inside. Star lay on the floor, bleeding from her head. He knelt beside her.

"Are you all right, Star?"

"I'm fine, Will." She sat up and touched the cut. "It's just a scratch. And a headache, I think. But what just happened with Commander Partridge?"

"I don't know, but I'm going to find out. Maybe Major Rogers can take command. I'll try to locate him."

Suddenly the *Dunamys* trembled. On the bridge, everyone grabbed onto anything they could find at hand. Then the front window was covered by plumes of gas mixed with a dark gray liquid.

"It looks like some kind of eruption," a crew member said.

"Triton has several geysers," Star responded as she tried to hold herself steady on one of the consoles. The *Dunamys* began to shake once again.

"But why does it all look so black?"

Star was about to answer, but the shaking grew worse. She could barely stand.

"Star!" Dr. Mendel rushed to catch her. "We need to take you to the Medical Bay."

"If you take command for the time being, I'll go there." Star slung her arm over his shoulder.

"We have no other choice. Will, take her to the medical bay for me. I have to command the ship. Although from what I've been told, it doesn't look as though we are going anywhere for the time being."

JEN

Jen chose a secured area backstage before sharing with David and Elizabeth everything that happened with Major Rogers and her when they were exposed to the pink light.

"I'm glad you guys are free from that influence." Elizabeth smiled.

"That's not all, though," Jen went on. "It seems several people want to go back to Earth, including Commander Partridge."

David put a hand on Jen's shoulder. "I know this seems overwhelming, but I believe we will get out of this. We always have before."

"I hope you're right, David," Elizabeth responded, exhaling.

A commotion outside the auditorium interrupted them. Jen peeked out the door, careful not to be seen. People were gathering at the boardwalk. Commander Partridge and a small group of security guards surrounded the crowd.

"Go to your quarters," the commander barked. "That's an order! Until we get back home, no one should leave their living quarters. We're thinking only of your safety."

Jen eased the door shut and told David and Elizabeth what she'd seen and heard. Then she warned them to stay away from the multitude, to remain inside the small auditorium.

"This is not good!" David whispered.

"I'm calling Major Rogers. He will know what to do." Jen pulled her communicator.

"What if they hear you?" Elizabeth asked.

"Don't worry. We are on a private frequency."

WILL

Will was on his way back to the bridge, after dropping Star at the medical bay at *Remembrance Place* when he noticed someone following him, He ducked into the emergency stairs and went to *Legacy Place*. He continued walking normally, but as he passed the storefronts, he glanced at the reflection in the windows and noticed the same figure still behind him and getting closer.

When he reached the plaza near a fountain, he found people being forced to their quarters. But there hadn't been any official announcement by the military.

He picked up speed, trying to lose his tail. He arrived at the botanical garden and dove into the bushes to avoid walking out in the open. He gasped when someone reached out and pulled him through a hidden door.

"Major Rogers!"

"No time. I have to get you up to speed."

They remained hidden until others passed by.

"We need to go back to the bridge and take control," Rogers insisted.

"You're the one who sabotaged the *Dunamys?*"

"Not sabotaged, redirected. And it wasn't me. Well, not exactly. He told me what to do."

"Who?"

"A mutual friend."

"Joshua?"

"Yeah. You guys were right. He is not just a hologram. He is alive.".

Suddenly Joshua stood there with them.

"Woah!" Will stepped backward. "I didn't notice you here."

"Many have fallen in the trap of their fears, their passions, and their hopelessness. They now fully believe the lies," Joshua said.

"That's what happened to the Ommites," Major Rogers said.

"Yes, and Commander Partridge and many others have become addicted to the pink light," Will said.

"Jen and I almost fell for the pink light, too, it was something kind of—mystic. But something protected us. I am still trying to figure it out." Major Rogers added.

"The gem only enhances what is already in the heart. Giving them a false illusion and keeping them addicted to the light of the gem. That is what has enslaved them," Joshua explained.

"You mean Commander Partridge has been wanting to go back to Earth all along?" Will looked from Joshua to Major Rogers and back again.

"Not exactly. He had doubts and fear, yes. He hesitated, as did many others. But then he changed his mind, turning one eighty back to where he started. But as I told you from the very beginning, everyone is free to come on this journey or remain on Earth."

"But Commander Partridge has no right to make the decision for all of us." Major Rogers's frustration was evident.

"I will help you," Joshua said.

Before Will could ask how, Joshua was gone.

But suddenly Will knew what to do. "Where is Jen?" he said.

"She's still at the auditorium with David and Elizabeth. I just talked to her a few minutes ago. For now, let's go to the bridge!"

Upon their arrival, they found all the crew mobilizing to assist the exploration team.

"Dr. Mendel!" the ship's pilot cried. "I can't move the ship at all. We have been unable to regain control of the *Dunamys*."

"I know. We are going to be on Triton for a while. In the meantime, we need to sort out our situation on the inside of the *Dunamys*," Dr. Mendel responded.

Will took Jen's seat while Major Rogers took Star's. "We are here to help," Will said.

Dr. Mendel nodded, then addressed the bridge crew. "Commander Partridge has been compromised. He is now a threat to our mission. Therefore, he has been relieved of duty. For now, Major Rogers is assuming command of the *Dunamys*. Please follow his orders."

Major Rogers approached Dr. Mendel. "Are you sure about this? You know I might be compromised," he said quietly.

"The fact that you're helping us and opposed to going back to Earth is a good sign. You're the right man for the job."

"Thank you, Dr. Mendel." Major Rogers shook the doctor's hand.

"But I would ask that you stay close by. I'll need your advice."

Will immediately restored communication with the exploration team and turned on their cameras.

"We're approaching a geyser," one of the team members told them. "But we're having to be very careful due to the ice on the surface."

The feed went up on the screen. It was a strange sight. The geysers were black and gray, and the gas rising from them was turned at a forty-five-degree angle. They watched as the team gathered samples to keep in the tanks and then returned to the shuttle.

Everyone on the bridge breathed relief, until another team member spoke.

"Please help. We are being pulled towards the planet Neptune. We request immediate assistance."

"Any idea what's going on?"

Iram spoke next. "We analyzed the data, and it appears that the gravitational attraction of Neptune is not only responsible for the pattern on the geysers on Triton, but it is pulling our ship off course and towards Neptune.

"Understood, exploration shuttle. We are sending a rescue team."

"Wow!" Iram said again. "How beautiful!"

Then the transmission cut off.

"Shuttle, please respond!" Will tried to reestablish contact, waited for several minutes, then tried again. "Sir, they are still not responding."

"The rescue team has been dispatched?" asked Major Rogers urgently.

"Yes, sir. They're on the way."

At that moment, another transmission came through. "*Dunamys*, this is the exploration shuttle. We are safe on board."

"What? How is that possible?" Will asked in surprise.

"We don't know. It was that bright light, the one that looks like an eagle. It pulled the shuttle back into the cargo bay of the *Dunamys*."

"Are you okay?"

"Affirmative. And the cargo is intact."

JEN

"Oh, Will! I'm so glad you made it to the bridge!" Jen said over the communicator. "Commander Partridge's people are everywhere now."

"I know, sis. It took a while to find a way to the bridge without being discovered. Now we can enact our plan."

"Awesome, I will get to it as soon as possible."

"Dr. Mendel is working on the communication board. He wants to talk to you."

"Jen?" Dr. Mendel's voice sounded tired. "How are David and Elizabeth holding up?"

"They know what to do and are ready to do it. And it's perfect because it is part of their first album launch."

"Excellent. Will, please set up the communications board," he instructed.

"Hey you!" yelled a voice nearby. "No one is allowed in here. You must go to your quarters."

"Got to go, Will," Jen whispered. "I think we've been discovered."

"Be careful and let us know if you can make the plan happen."

She hung up. Steps inside the auditorium came closer to backstage.

"Joshua, can you please help us?" said Jen. "Otherwise, we'll be taken prisoner, and no one will stop Commander Partridge. We'll return to Earth, and this whole trip will be for nothing."

The intercom above her head squealed a moment, then Major Roger's voice came through. "Attention of all passengers and crew of the *Dunamys*. This is an important announcement. Commander Partridge and others on board have been compromised. Their intention is to abort our mission and return to Earth. I'm asking every officer and crew member to assist us in continuing our journey to Zion under my command."

"You were right, Jen," Elizabeth said. "Now what?"

Jen called them close so she could whisper in case the guards were still lingering in the auditorium. "You know what to do, right?"

"Yeah," David nodded. "We need to sing a reminder of the purpose and hope for this journey. If the Creator himself has sent this lifeboat to escape the demise of our own planet and go to a paradise place that he has prepared for us, it will be worth all the trouble. I know we will be protected as we've been in the past."

David inched open the door. All the guards were gone. Jen prepared the audio equipment and called Doctor Mendel to coordinate everything on the bridge.

"Ready to launch your album?" she asked David and Elizabeth.

"Yes!" They grinned at each other.

"Then lead us in singing for freedom and hope."

The couple climbed onto the stage to start their concert as Dr. Mendel set up the sound to be broadcast all over the *Dunamys*. As they prepared, Major Rogers sent a group of security personnel to keep the music from being interrupted again. Those who desired to enter the auditorium were ushered inside.

"David!" Elizabeth said as she looked out over the auditorium. "There's your dad."

David's dad stood at the edge of the stage looking up at them. "Let's do this, son. Just be yourselves. Do what you always do when you are on your own."

Jen smiled to see the support from David's dad. Then she went to the audio mixer and monitored the streaming to the bridge and, from there, to the rest of the ship.

David's dad came on stage and took the microphone. "Hello, everyone. Here is the moment you've been waiting for—your favorite duo, David and Elizabeth!"

The people stood up and applauded. Jen realized that her friends had become more popular than ever before. After all, their songs inspired hope, joy, and faith in all the passengers of the *Dunamys*.

Then Jen also remembered that Dr. Hackett told her that they had something special. That during the time they had been on the ship, the *logos* trees grew faster than they had on Earth, and he believed the music produced by the couple had something to do with that.

"Thank you very much, friends," David said. "We want to make an announcement. As you know, Elizabeth and I will be releasing our first recording soon. We called it *Horizons*, and tonight we will be broadcasting this concert throughout the entire ship so everyone can enjoy it."

People clapped again, then Elizabeth started to play her guitar. The people sat down.

"Please join us in singing to the Creator, who has protected all of us during this journey. Also, please join us in prayer for many of our friends who are in the medical bay, especially the pilots who have been a blessing in our journey," she said.

As the couple sang, Jen remembered the times they'd been protected during the journey, and she noticed Elizabeth smiling as she played with a joy that Jen never had seen before. For the last song, the couple beckoned Chloe, the cello player, and asked Doris to join them as a background vocalist. Both had just arrived at the auditorium as part of Jen's plan.

Wow Doris sings too! Not a trace of the old lady we knew back on Earth.

As she watched them take the stage with David and Elizabeth, an overwhelming peace inundated Jen, like the feeling of resting in a light boat in calm waters.

WILL

A group of Commander Partridge's guards surrounded the bridge doors and forced them open. They entered, with Commander Partridge leading the way.

"So, we have a mutiny on board?" He pulled a box out of his pocket and opened it so everyone could see the pink light within. "Now, you will comply with my orders. You will give back control of the *Dunamys* and go back to the route I set. That's an order!"

Will and other crew members closed their eyes, refusing to be exposed to the pink light. Commander Partridge's guards took them by force, one by one, to show them the contents of the box. Just as Will was about to be forced to look at the pink rock, the final song on the intercom system began.

I will search for you
I will search for you
With all I am
I need you more than water
more than the air
Oh my God, save me
Because only you can deliver me
Because only you can deliver me.

I will search for you
I will search for you
With all I am
I need you much more
more than yesterday
Oh my God, come visit me
Cause I won't leave till I see you face to face
Cause I won't leave till I see you face to face.

The music streamed into every dorm, every public space, and every meeting room all over the ship.

Will cried with his eyes closed, trying to avoid exposure to the pink light, wondering what do to next. Then he heard a subtle, small voice instructing him to grab the box and some tools from the emergency safe while everybody else was frozen. He slammed the box closed and ran towards the weapons room in the opposite side in the same deck of the bridge area.

There, he placed the box inside of a laser canon. Then he returned to the bridge to fire it outside the ship. As soon as he sat down, he noticed Commander Partridge and the people who were with him wandering off confused, as if they had just woken up from a dream.

"Will? What is going on?" asked one of the crew members.

"I'm not sure, but I think the threat is over."

"Where's the box, Will?" cried Commander Partridge. "What did you do with it?"

Without answering, Will fired the canon, then he reached the weapons controls and pointed to the small box and fired the small laser weapon. A pinkish flash of light appeared through the large window. Will knew then that the pink rock was finally destroyed.

"What's going on? Why are all these people on the bridge?" asked Commander Partridge after a long pause.

"It's a long story, sir," said Major Rogers, breathing deeply.

"Oh. Now I remember." Commander Partridge grabbed his head as if he had a headache.

As David and Elizabeth's song finished, the audience cheered and clapped and asked for one more song. Joy flooded Will's heart again with a hope stronger than ever before.

"What just happened?" the pilot asked.

"I think I know the answer," came a soft voice.

"Joshua!"

Joshua appeared in front of them. "Your eyes are the windows of your soul. If your eyes have goodness, everything you are will be filled with light. But if your eyes become dreadful, your whole being will be filled with darkness."

"What do you mean?" Will asked.

"The power of the pink light brought up the darkest side of each person. Some remained strong against it, and some were weaker, to the point of being enslaved by it. But for most, it just brings to light what was already in their hearts."

"But how did we break out of its influence?" Will asked.

"Real conviction—hope, love, life, and the true light."

"I don't understand, Joshua," the navigator said.

"You will. All of you will understand more clearly. But fear not, because the best is yet to come." Then Joshua disappeared.

"What are we going to do with all the people who wanted to take us back to Earth?" Will asked Major Rogers after a moment of silence.

"As Joshua said, for some reason the pink light brings out the dark side of each one of us. All I did was run away from it, but some embraced it. I think that is what happened with Commander Partridge, Arthur, and the others. It's too powerful to resist once you've opened the door. Maybe that's why it's the main power of the Sarkos to slave entire civilizations. I'm sure we can find a way to overcome its power. I'm sure Joshua will tell us how. But for now, I think we need to put them in isolation and see what they want to do now that the pink light has gone." Major Rogers rubbed his forehead. "And I want more officers to replace them. And, we need to be sure there are no more pink rocks on board."

"Yes, sir."

JEN

After the show, Jen turned everything off and went to the stage. David and Elizabeth were thanking their audience for their support.

Then Dr. Hackett arrived. "Hey, guys. Congratulations."

"Thank you, Dr. Hackett."

"I need to speak to you both."

"Sure, what is it?" David asked.

"Not here. Let's go to a private place."

*****

The following day Jen returned to the bridge to report to her usual post. On her way, she found Star, who also was reporting for duty.

"Glad you are okay, Star."

"Thanks, friend. I was dismissed from the medical bay after a short rest. It was just a minor concussion. It has been a very difficult day. There are so many changes on board. And I heard many people still want to go back to Earth."

"The same people who were with Commander Partridge?"

"Yeah, and others have joined them. Pilots, crew members, and many of the passengers. It's hard to watch."

"What are we going to do?"

"I heard that Major Rogers is with them in a meeting right now."

Even as they spoke, Major Rogers was walking toward them. He looked exhausted. He breathed deeply and adjusted the collar of his shirt.

"I'm so glad Dr. Mendel removed the mics from the briefing room and the bridge," he said to them. "It has been stressful."

"What did Commander Partridge say?" Jen asked, too curious to wait.

"He admitted that while he was under the influence of the pink light he acted impulsively, but his resolve has not changed. He and the others have decided to go back to Earth."

"But what about Joshua? He saved us again, and—"

Major Rogers shook his head. "I told them the same, but they asked 'What about the next time or the next?' For them, Joshua is just a hologram. I'm sorry, Jen. They concluded that t's too dangerous out here without knowing what we could find in other star systems."

Major Rogers was quiet for a moment. "I need you to do me a favor, Jen. It is the last request from Commander Partridge. He wants you to announce this to the whole ship."

Jen received a text on her information pad. She cried as she read it. "Permission to speak freely, sir? I really don't want to do this, but because Joshua said we all are free to choose, I guess we should."

Jen wiped her eyes and prepared to make the announcement.

"Attention everyone—every passenger, military member, doctor, businessman, man, and woman aboard the *Dunamys*. As you know, many among us have decided it is too dangerous to continue this journey across the stars. This journey hasn't been easy for sure, but the Creator of the universe is the one who sent us this vessel to escape the destruction of our planet. He has protected us and led us during this journey. But we recognize, as we were told from the beginning of this journey, that we are free to go or stay behind. Each and every person has to make their choice to stay or to continue. Therefore, Commander Partridge has requested me to announce that he is going back to Earth and—" Jen took a deep breath, trying to hold back more tears. "And if anyone wants to go with him, gather your things and meet him at the cargo bay tomorrow at this time to depart on the shuttles. Please let us know what you decide as well. That will be all."

As Jen returned to her leaving quarters, she overheard fiery discussions among passengers. Friends of the people who wanted to leave tried to convince them to stay, but it was pointless. Many had already made up their minds and wanted to leave as soon as they could.

The following day, Jen and others from the bridge joined departing passengers and crew in the cargo bay. Among them were Commander Partridge, a couple of the bridge crew, several pilots, and a big group of passengers—a total of two hundred and fifty people. They filled some exploration shuttles, and some jets.

Those remaining had nothing to say, but their sadness was evident as the pods shot into space. Then the rest of the crew returned to their duties.

Major Rogers, now Commander Rogers, prepared to depart to the next destination, Pluto. From there, they would go to the edge of the solar system. They turned on the engines, and Commander Rogers gave the order to set the course.

Suddenly Desperado entered the bridge. "Sorry for interrupting, sir, but I just received a communication from some of the other *Ommites*. There is a great army of Sarkos coming our way. We will be outnumbered."

Commander Rogers looked at the remaining crew and everyone fell silent.

14
PLUTO

JEN

The *Dunamys* continued its journey towards the outer solar system, following the mission plan given by Joshua. The passengers were quiet. They no longer walked in the main plaza or visited the coffee shop or the other new venues.

On the bridge, the tension felt even stronger. After the departure of Commander Partridge and the others, everyone was discouraged. It got even worse when they learned the Sarkos were approaching their coordinates to intercept them.

The silence was interrupted by a notification from the main console on Jen's board. Apparently, they had entered the orbit of Pluto, but instead of the dwarf planet, they saw a vast group of rocky objects.

Star read out the records from the computer. "We are near an area called the Kuiper Belt—like an asteroid belt, but the objects are bigger."

Finally, the instruments located Pluto, an icy world with a brown-reddish color, darker in some areas more than others. It had a thin atmosphere rich in methane.

For their next mission, they needed samples of the grain of Pluto, but there was an even more important aspect of the mission that remained unclear. As the spaceship approached the dwarf planet, Commander Rogers dispatched the exploration shuttle like always.

After giving that order, he met with their senior officer and some of the crew, including Jen, to assess everything that was happening. They needed to solve the problem in the increase of mass. Dr. Mendel did an exhaustive check of the engines. He communicated with the engineers while the rest of the team revised the other systems, including energy, shields, the launch deck, the botanic garden, the laboratory, the medical bay, the exploration compartment, and every neighborhood on board. They found nothing to justify the increase of mass of the spaceship since their departure. It was odd, as though the spaceship was carrying a burden that grew heavier and heavier during the journey.

And there were other issues, like the imminent arrival of the Sarkos trying to stop the *Dunamys* from leaving the Solar System.

All the meetings, the research, and the overall situation started to wear on Jen. Her physical energy, her desire and motivation to keep working at her post waned. She yawned constantly and almost fell asleep.

Jen jerked awake. "Commander Rogers, could I request a break? I need some time." She rubbed her eyes.

"Are you okay, Jen?"

"Just need some rest, maybe some coffee."

"Sure. Take at least an hour. Actually, Star? You should take a break as well. We have a long day ahead of us."

"Yes, sir." Star signaled Jen to follow her. They exited the bridge and went to the new break room, which used to be part of the briefing room close to the bridge.

"I have to be honest with you, Star. I'm starting to get worried," Jen confessed as Star prepared two cups of Yorkshire Gold Tea. "Hey--where did you get that, Star?"

"I purchased several boxes from the old Vintage Proverb before our departure from Earth. When Commander Rogers asked me to set up the new breakroom, I brought them up here."

"Thank you, Star! This brings back so many good memories." Jen sipped her tea. "I didn't want to get in the way of the crew with complaints or pessimism, but now I can see why Commander Partridge wanted to leave. Not that I agree with his decision, but now I understand where he was coming from. Honestly, this is tough."

"I know, Jen. Trust me, you are not the only one who feels that way. But I'm pretty sure we will survive what is coming next."

The door slid open. Elizabeth entered and greeted them.

"What a surprise! What are you doing here?" Star asked as she hugged Elizabeth.

"Remember the day Dr. Hackett explained how everyone had been delivered from the influence of the pink rock when they heard our songs? And how our music contributed to the growing of the alien seeds? He doesn't know what the connection is, but he told us our music is making this a better place. He said he might need us more than he previously thought, so he asked to meet us here. It is a long story. I decided to come early and say hello to you both."

"What about the other thing?" Jen asked her.

"David and I talked after the whole crisis passed. He finally understands why I was so hesitant about the relationship. As I said earlier, we are taking it easy. We agreed to be good friends for now. After all, we are a professional duo."

"What about the ring?" Jen asked.

"I will return it to him. It's the right thing to do."

"And how do you feel about the whole thing?" Star asked.

"I feel relieved."

"I'm happy for you Elizabeth. And look." Star pointed to the small window in the breakroom showing the moon Charon and the planet Pluto. "Look how far we are in the solar system. And we are still alive and well. There is hope."

Jen was amazed at how her friends could be so positive and hopeful after everything that happened. Especially David and Elizabeth.

"Awe! Is that a heart?" Elizabeth pointed at the dwarf planet.

"It really looks like it, especially with the maroon colors," Jen said.

"Those red spots are called tholins," Star added. "They are rich in organic compounds. We are going to mine them on the next mission." Star brought the box of tea bags to the table. "Want some?"

"I do," Elizabeth said, taking a bag. "Thanks, Star."

After she made her tea, Elizabeth pulled out her communicator. "Listen to this." She hit play on the music player and they all listened.

"What do you think?" Elizabeth asked.

"I like it," Star said. "So inspirational and uplifting!"

"Wait a minute, I know this one. Isn't this the song you showed me a while ago?" Jen asked, recognizing the tune.

"Yes, although this version is much better than the first one I shared with you."

"It sounds incredible."

"It is almost done. We still have to add a few details, but I believe this is close to the final version. I think we will add this song to our album."

"Congratulations!" Star smiled.

"Thank you. This song will be a nice surprise for people since we didn't perform it at the concert."

Star and Jen's communicators went off while as the song finished.

"Seems our break has been cut short." Star sighed. "Let's go, Jen."

They returned to the bridge leaving Elizabeth to wait for David and Doctor Hackett.

WILL

Will was eager to participate in the next mission to Pluto, but again, Commander Rogers refused. Instead, he asked Will to assist Iram and Joseph as they prepared to escort the exploration team. The team would be wearing special suits for the cold since the thermometer indicated around 55 degrees Kelvin, which was -360.67 degrees F., or −229 degrees C. The mission was basically a mining operation.

Once the team was off, Will hung around with Jen at the communications board monitoring the mission, following them with the live camera and mics on the team suits, hearing their conversations. This time, Iram and Joseph, lead an exploration team descending on the planet. As they got closer to the big glacier area, they could see the highest peak in Pluto, called Tenzing Montes, but it was too dark to see it well. They took many samples of the maroon ground then continued onward. Will watched Iram stop to take a picture of the distant hills.

Iram and his team followed the exploration team until they arrived at a vast, craterless, frozen plain.

"*Dunamys*, this is Iram."

"Go ahead, Iram," Will responded.

"We are close to the Tombaugh Regio, the huge icy surface. It appears to be divided into irregularly shaped segments ridged by narrow troughs."

"Good. Please take as many samples as you can," Dr. Mendel requested.

"Yes, sir. We're on it."

All of a sudden, an alarm went off on the bridge. Then Iram spoke. "Sir, the temperature just dropped to..." He checked his instruments. "Minus 360 degrees."

"That's what you said earlier."

"Yeah, but that's Celsius, sir. It's now minus 616 Fahrenheit."

Suddenly, a dark shadow blocked the view of the far-away sun.

Will reached around Jen and spoke to the exploration team. "Please zoom in on the sun."

The camera moved as indicated, revealing what looked like a dark cloud with several shiny, reflective dots.

"Dr. Mendel, do we have telescopic cameras?" Will asked.

"Yes, but we have never used them. Why?"

"Take a look." Will pointed to the sun's position and provided the exact coordinates.

Dr. Mendel's face turned pale. He immediately checked his information pad. From there, he activated several systems on the communications board. Then asked Will to sit down to move more of the settings on the console. He looked back and forth from the information tablet to the communication console. Then he stood up.

The chair spun as he walked away. He held his head and paced the bridge area, his face sweating. Dr. Mendel checked his tablet again. His fingers shook as he typed.

"Oh no!" Jen screamed. She pointed to the screen on the communication board.

The apparent cloud was a group of spaceships—perhaps thousands of them—swarming like wasps ready to hunt.

"You've got to go, now!" Will yelled to the exploration team.

"All right people, you heard the boss. Let's move it!"

Iram and Joseph hurried the exploration team to the shuttle, then they boarded their jets.

"*Dunamys*, this the exploration team on Pluto, over. Our instruments are frozen. We will try..." Static overcame the words.

"Exploration team, please respond." Will tried to boost the signal but all he got was more static. "This is *Dunamys*, over. Please respond."

Jen approached the communication board to help, but the interference seemed to have originated on Pluto. Several minutes passed in silence, until a short circuit kind of sound interrupted it.

"*Dunamys*, this is Iram and the exploration team on Pluto, over."

"Go ahead, exploration team. We hear you."

"Please help me!" called a voice from the shuttle entrance.

"Iram? Who is it? What's happening?"

After a few tense minutes, Iram returned to the communicator. "Sorry. Joseph found Tom lying on the ground unconscious. His suit had a huge rip, like he slid and caught it on something. We've laid him on the floor."

Another few silent moments passed. Then Iram said, "The medic says Tom's still breathing, but barely. I'm starting the shuttle engines now."

From the outside feed, the bridge crew watched the shuttle lift slowly from the surface, every part of the craft covered in extreme frost.

"Mission accomplished, but we have a huge problem. There is a very large group of—" A faint voice came from the communicator.

"We know. Please return as soon as possible."

"Roger that. We are returning to the *Dunamys*. Please send a team of medics to meet us."

"Will do." Will signaled Jen to request medical team assistance in the shuttle bay.

"Thank you for assisting me on the communication board, bro."

"Any time, sis." Will stood up. He felt a pain poke his side, but he didn't pay much attention to it. Instead, he went to meet Iram and Joseph to find out exactly what had happened.

He exited the bridge, went down the elevator, then took one of the golf carts to go to the shuttle bay.

Upon his arrival, he saw Tom, one of the members of the science team who went to explore Pluto, lying on a bed ready to be carried out by the medics.

"What happened?" Will asked Iram.

"When the exploration team arrived at the shuttle, I noticed Tom was missing. I called him with my communicator. He didn't respond. Joseph offered to look for him while I was trying to communicate with the *Dunamys*. Anyway, while I was checking for the interference, I recorded this."

Iram held up a screen. It showed footage of a triangular ship hovering and spinning over Pluto. As soon as it was spotted, it flew away at a great speed.

"Wait, go back. Now zoom in." Will gritted his teeth. "I knew it."

"What is it?"

"It is... ough!"

"Are you okay, Will?"

"Yeah. Muscular pain, nothing major. What worries me is this." He pointed to the footage.

"Are you guys, okay?" Commander Rogers asked when he arrived in person to check on his team.

"Yes, sir. We have issues with the temperature drop but other than Tom, we are okay. However, I think we have a bigger problem."

"Yes, we know. We saw them coming. We are working on it. Please, all of you, check into the medical bay right after the debriefing."

Will asked Iram to show the footage to Commander Rogers. Together, they returned to the bridge. They analyzed the gathered data and arrived at the same conclusion—the Sarkos moved in after the exploration team left the dwarf planet.

Will suggested passing Pluto and going as fast as possible in the opposite direction of the enemy ships while still continuing in the same direction as the itinerary they were following.

Dr. Mendel indicated that their route would cross the Kuiper Belt, the groups of asteroids and planetoids they saw earlier. "Although there are great distances between objects, we must navigate with caution. It would be best to sneak between asteroids and dwarf planets to avoid being discovered."

"Noted. Continue on," Commander Rogers said.

"Commander Rogers, we are following the multiple objects we saw earlier," Star said. "They are moving quickly from the orbit of Uranus towards our current position here on Pluto."

"Any idea confirmation of who they are, Star?"

"No, sir, but most likely the Sarkos. And they will reach us soon."

"Jen, alert all passengers to fasten their seat belts. We will be crossing into the Kuiper Belt at maximum speed."

"Yes, Commander Rogers." Jen turned to her communications board. "Attention all passengers, we are entering a zone of frozen objects, rocks, and asteroids called the Kuiper Belt. Stay inside your living quarters and fasten your seat belts. It could be a bumpy ride."

JEN

A few days later, the people on the *Dunamys* were free to walk outside their quarters again. They were still inside the Kuiper Belt zone and nearing the Heliosphere, the last zone of influence of the sun and the outer layer of the Solar System. Their path was free from frozen objects, planetoids, and asteroids. On the bridge, the crew scanned for enemy ships as well as for an exit from the heliosphere, which was like finding a needle in a haystack.

"Commander Rogers, Dr. Mendel needs a meeting with you," one of the crew members announced.

"Ok. Jen, with me!" Commander Rogers motioned for Jen to follow him to the conference room.

"Any new information on the excessive mass issue," Commander Rogers asked as soon as they were all seated.

Dr. Mendel shook his head. "All I know is there has been an exponential increase in mass, but I still don't know the reason why. But it is urgent that we find the answer because even if we finish all the repairs, the rate of increasing mass will make navigation very difficult."

Commander Rogers frowned. "Keep working on it, Dr. Mendel. The crew is searching for a way out of the Solar System. It's hard to read the itinerary after the Kuiper Belt. We need to get out before the enemies catch up with us."

Just as they returned to the bridge, Star approached Commander Rogers. "Sir, I was just coming for you. The Sarkos. They've found us."

Commander Rogers ordered the navigator to turn the ship to face the armada, but this order was followed by an alarm.

"What's wrong, Star?"

"We're surrounded, sir!" She pointed to the screen. "Look!"

Thousands of enemy ships stood just beyond the window. She switched the view on the screen and they saw several distant shimmering objects approaching from behind, getting closer, moving like bats in a straight formation and shimmering with a metallic brightness.

"Dragon spaceships!" cried Dr. Mendel.

The crew and senior officers checked every square inch on their screens, analyzing data, and checking possible scenarios and outcomes.

"Even with the weapon systems we've found, I don't think it'll be enough. There are so many of the Sarkos's ships, and the dragon ones move extremely fast. Both are more advanced than us. It doesn't look good, Commander."

Jen almost was able to hear Commander Rogers's racing heart as he breathed deeply. She knew he tried to show confidence for the sake of his crew, but it was obvious he was as frightened as they were.

"We need to call Joshua right away," he said. "No time to lose. In fact, we all need to call him—each person. Every passenger, crew member, pilot. Everyone. We need his help urgently. Jen, I know you're the closest with him, but I know he hears all of us."

Jen nodded. "He's always been friends with all of us. And remember, he told us, 'I will be with you always.'"

Jen opened the *Dunamys* intercom channel, cleared her throat, and spoke. "Attention everyone. I know we've all been discouraged during these last months, especially after losing so many people who went back to Earth. Our enemies are approaching, trying to stop us from leaving the Solar System. But Joshua, our friend, has never abandoned us. I'm pretty sure he didn't bring us to this point for us to just go back. So, we want to make a special request. It may be strange for some of you, but we need to ask Joshua to help us. Let's call his name, each of us individually."

"I hope people will do it." Commander Rogers walked away from Jen's post.

Jen switched from camera to camera, every scene showing people crying out, "Help us, Joshua! We need you!"

Immediately Joshua appeared on the bridge.

"Oh, thank you! Thank you for coming!" Commander Rogers approached him. "Please let everyone on board, every passenger and crew member, hear your words for themselves. We know you are way too advanced for us to comprehend your knowledge. I know you've been looking after us all this time, and you planned this journey to Zion, but look, our enemies have us surrounded. Will you please help us? We need you more than ever! Honestly, we are powerless against this great armada, and we don't know what to do. But we are ready to follow your instructions."

Joshua hugged him. Immediately Jen opened the channel for everyone to hear.

"Each of you need to decide if you want to continue this journey," he said softly. "If you are willing to die to the lifestyle you had back on Earth and let go of your past so you can move forward, then come with us. Remember, this is voluntary. You are free to go back to Earth, as others of your friends and family have done. Or you can stay and continue this journey. But think carefully. Are you willing to pay the price?

"The reward is an infinite life with the One who created the cosmos, the universe itself. You will live where He lives. So, this is it. You decide if you are in, or you are out. If you want to keep going, you must lay down your life for your neighbor, for your friends and family. You must look after one another, think about others before yourself. Again, consider carefully."

There was a long silence. Then Commander Rogers looked Joshua steadily in the eyes. "Where else can we go? Earth is not an option for us anymore, knowing its imminent destruction. There is nothing for us there now! I know everyone on board feels the same way. And you are the original pilot and captain of this vessel, so please lead the way."

Joshua put his hand on Commander Rogers' shoulder. "Don't be afraid, and don't be discouraged by this great armada. For my father will take care of this situation as you prepare for the battle. After all, my father is the one who sent me on this mission to rescue you. He invited you to Zion."

"Who is your father and how can we thank him?"

"He is the Creator of the Universe, of everything that exists! I have been preparing you for this moment. All you have gone through and everything that has happened, every mission in your itinerary, every resource you have gathered, all will serve as a preparation. Now, you have the resources to survive and finish the repairs of the *Dunamys*. Then I will instruct you on how to use this ship in its full capacity. But for now, you must assemble all the squadrons on a planet called Gulgolet to prepare for battle. I will take care of the rest."

"*Gulgolet?* I've never heard of it," Jen said.

"I think many on Earth call it Planet X or Planet 9, it is another dwarf planet," Dr. Mendel explained. "It is between the end of the Kuiper belt and the beginning of the heliosphere."

Everyone on the bridge looked shocked. Joshua had given them specific instructions of what to do. Then Joshua disappeared. But Commander Rogers seemed at ease knowing Joshua would help them.

*****

The following day, Jen went to the botanic garden in the *Hearing Place* to collect some of the *rhema* fruit from the *logos* tree, but to her surprise all of the passengers were gathered close to the garden to pick some of the fruits. According to Dr. Mendel, the *rhema* had very strong energy readings.

After waiting patiently, Jen got a basket of rhema and brought it to the bridge to share it with the crew. Jen felt the effect of the fruit right away. A few minutes later, after everyone had eaten, the crew seemed more focused and assertive, which encouraged Jen, giving her hope for the battle ahead.

Suddenly she felt an urge to look to her right. She noticed a small circle with a point of light in the middle. "Open, show me!" She said out loud, wondering why those words popped in her head at that moment. Immediately several new controls appeared, and new information about the *Dunamys* was displayed on the screens.

"How did you do that, Jen?"

"I don't know, I just spoke and it all showed up. It seems more information has been accessed."

Commander Rogers scrolled through all the new data finding maps and names of places outside the Kuiper belt and information about many other solar systems.

Then they found the name of one object barely bigger than Pluto, at the edge of the heliosphere. The screens indicated that the name of that planetoid was Gulgolet, the place Joshua told them about.

"Use the new coordinates and set a course for Gulgolet," Commander Rogers ordered. "We'll move into its orbit."

Upon arrival they found a dark planet. The telemetry indicated no life forms and a very thin oxygen atmosphere.

Suddenly, the Dunamys shook violently.

"Ok, people, talk to me. What is going on?" Commander Rogers asked.

"Sir, a wave of fire attacked the *Dunamys*." Star sounded panicked.

"Where is it coming from?" he asked.

"Here, sir." Star pointed at her screen as more fire came at them.

"It's the Sarkos!" Dr. Mendel cried.

"Damage report!" Commander Rogers barked.

"Shields are holding," reported Star, "but the ship was shaken badly."

"We have an incoming transmission, sir." Jen put her headset down.

"Patch it through."

"Yes sir."

"...I repeat, you are in violation of the Piprasko treaty. You can't leave the solar system. Surrender and return to Earth immediately. If you keep going this path you will face pain, suffering, hunger, and the wrath of our Majesty and his armada. Turn around. There is no escape. I repeat, you are in..."

"Turn it off, Jen." Commander Rogers walked to the front of the bridge and faced the crew. "Ladies and gentlemen, this is it! We will now proceed with Joshua's plan." He turned to Jen. "Call the free Ommites on the frequency Desperado provided."

315

15
KUIPER

WILL

Will heard the voice of Joshua on the intercom in his living quarters, it was like a small drop of hope. He was still sharing the room with David since neither of them ever had a chance to request a relocation.

He carefully considered the high stakes of venturing into the unknown. Not that he didn't like adventure and new challenges, but during this journey people had died. They had almost been taken as slaves twice. And they had risked their lives in very harsh conditions on every planet so far. And that was within their own solar system! What would be expected when they arrived at those stars beyond? He had already lost the possibility of being in a relationship with the girl of his dreams. But his love for flying jets and fighting for those he loved would never change.

By the time the enemy forces grew closer to them, he knew exactly what he wanted to do. He requested to join the squadrons in the upcoming battle. The officer in charge allowed him to attend the meetings but never gave him a definite answer.

"This is not a drill," came a voice over the intercom. "All squadrons prepare for battle against the enemy. Remember, we are following Joshua's plan. Stay within your designated areas."

All pilots were dispatched to their fighter jets.

Iram and Joseph rushed to their planes while Will stood by, waiting for orders. He couldn't stand it any longer. He marched directly to the bridge to discuss the situation with Commander Rogers.

"So far our shields are holding, sir, but—"

"Sir, they're getting closer. It's a massive armada!"

Will looked out the window and at the screens. The Sarkos were in front of them in waves of attack, while on the opposite side the dragon spaceships were on a stationary route to block their way of escape. The Sarkos immediately started fired warning shots to force them to surrender.

"Jen, please open the channel to the intercom," Commander Rogers instructed.

"The channel is open, sir."

"This is your commander. Our enemies are trying to stop us, but we are proceeding with Joshua's plan. Don't be afraid. We have commanded all our squadrons to prepare for battle on this planet, as Joshua instructed. We trust that the Creator of the Universe is guarding us, and he will protect us." Commander Rogers sat back down and prepared to monitor the progress of the battle.

"Please, sir," Will pleaded. "Send me into battle. Allow me to help my friends, my family!"

"You are not totally recovered, Will, and you haven't shown up for your check-ups and recovery sessions. You are in no condition to fight, so the answer is no."

At that moment a fighter jet exploded right in front of them—and the Sarkos' fleet crept closer.

"Please, let me go!" Will insisted.

"I can't be responsible for what happens to you, Will."

Jen crossed the bridge and put her hands on her brother's shoulders. "Please don't go. I don't want to lose you."

"I have to, sis. I need to make a difference. Please let me go."

Commander Rogers paused for a moment looking at the battle outside. "Go. But you will report to Iram. He's in charge. And you will not take unnecessary risks."

"Aye, aye, sir." Will turned to Jen, who was holding his jacket and crying. "I'm sorry Jen. I'll be alright. You know me."

Then he left to find his jet.

JEN

The battle had already lasted over an hour. Jen did her best to stay focused on her duties, but it was getting harder and harder. Finally, she stood up and paced around the bridge.

"Jen, how are you holding up?" Star asked.

"I need a break."

"This is not a good moment, Jen," Commander Rogers said.

"I know, but I can't concentrate."

"I will cover for her, sir," Desperado volunteered.

"Fine. Jen, take 30 mins. Come back immediately after that. Desperado, let me know when our new friends respond to our proposal."

Jen hurried off to find David and Elizabeth at *Expression Place*, the biggest open space for the passengers situated in the very middle of the ship. Windows surrounded the space, giving it a view of the outside all around. When she got there, a big group had gathered with David and Elizabeth. They both tried to encourage Jen, but she was totally overwhelmed. In contrast, it seemed, with her friends who appeared calm even as they watched the battle from the windows.

"Oh, please, God, save us all!" Jen heard one of the people in the back cry after everyone witnessed several explosions outside the windows.

Jen fell on the floor and began to cry silently, feeling hopeless and anxious.

"Come on, guys. We won't give up." David stood on a table and spoke to the gathered crowd. "We've been through rough times before. We will survive this one." He sat down and look at Elizabeth.

"I'm sorry for being so pushy and selfish, you are right we have more things at stake here, now let's do our part." He gave his guitar to Elizabeth, and with a big smile she hugged him and began to play softly as the battle continued outside. Then David accompanied her singing.

Jen listened for a moment, then went to the storage area where the audio equipment was kept for events. She connected a few mics and a couple speakers and patched into the ship systems. Not a complicated set up. Then she called Doris, who had joined them. Jen prepared three mics, and they continued singing.

"Let's do this!" Jen said.

But as they were about to start the next song, the *Dunamys* shook under intense fire. David walked out in front of the crowd holding one of the microphones.

"Hi, everyone. We all know the enemy has surrounded us, and maybe they are too many, maybe they are too powerful, but we are on our way to freedom and the new world promised to us, so if we must battle them to get there, we will."

Elizabeth joined him with her mic. "Today we learned something wonderful. We learned that the Creator of the Universe is the one who sent Joshua to rescue us and invite us to a new paradise world. Joshua is the son of the Creator himself. It is amazing how someone more powerful and ancient than the universe cares so much about us that he sent this lifeboat to save us all. This is one more reason why we love to sing to God, the Creator of the Universe. We have done this since we were back on Earth—because he is still watching over us!"

"We want to invite you to sing with us," David finished. "We have a special song we've been working on for this journey. We've reserved it for a special occasion, and we believe this is it!"

Jen flipped the switch to transmit the audio into every room on the ship. As soon as they started singing, she recognized the song right away, the very song Elizabeth had been working on with David, for a while already.

Tonight, we heard your voice saying
"I knew you before,
Before creation, before the world, I thought of you."
Like a good father, like a hero,
You rescued me!
Thanks, we will give from our hearts,
For your love
That endures forevermore!
You have given us the victory!
Oh our God!
You are the only One
The great God!
Our defender and our guide

You are our captain!
And by your love.
We are free!

The people began to sing along as they picked up the words of the new song. Then Jen began to sing with them. She remembered how her dreams as a little girl came true, how they were led and protected during their journey across space. The singing grew louder and louder.

"Jen," she heard from her communicator. "We need you now."

She hurried away to the bridge.

WILL

"There are too many! How are we going to beat them all?" Joseph's panicked voice came through the communicator as they continued to engage the enemy.

"We'll be ok. Let's trust the plan will work," encouraged Iram.

Suddenly, a big explosion hit the area, shaking the *Dunamys*.

"We got these guys," Will said to his friends. "After all, the Creator of the Universe is with us!"

"Will, you were supposed to be standing down," Joseph said.

"No, my place is with my buddies, so let's go!"

Iram and Joseph destroyed enemy ships left and right, but the battle intensified. Many pilots were hit.

Will saw a couple of the Sarkos getting closer to Iram. He immediately intercepted and destroyed the enemy.

"Thanks, Will. You saved my life!"

"That's what friends do!"

Then Will noticed the dragon ships drawing closer. "Guys, we need to destroy these fighters before the dragon ships arrive."

He immediately notified the bridge, which confirmed it on their monitors.

The dragon ships approached rapidly. Then they attacked the *Dunamys* directly, shooting long-distance fire, like dark-reddish lasers. The activated shield of the *Dunamys*, which looked like a cloud, held strong, but the whole spaceship shook. Finally, the cloud began to transform. It turned into a ball of flames that moved between the *Dunamys* and the dragon ships. The fire trailed away from the Dunamys, farther and farther, pushing the dragon ships away from the battle.

Meanwhile several other Sarkos ships got closer to the *Dunamys*. They lined up to attack the passenger area.

"I need some assistance," Will said to the squadron, but many of them were already engaged with enemy ships. Only three jets answered his call to defend the *Dunamys* from the imminent threat.

He blasted some Sarkos ships in front of him. Two of them were destroyed, but the rest continued coming closer. Will zoomed his jet in view of the projected target area, the place where the Sarkos were heading— the *Expression Place* neighborhood.

He noticed David through the window, singing. There was very little time to act, perhaps a few seconds, and the Sarkos were very difficult to hit. In that moment Will realized the only way to protect David and the rest of the civilians was to move his jet as fast as possible between them and the attack.

He pushed his jet to its limits hitting one of the Sarkos ships sending it spinning into another. Suddenly an alert warned him of an incoming fire. Will tried to react but it was too late; he was hit, then his jet began to shake uncontrollably.

Without hesitation, he responded to the enemy fire the best he could, destroying several more Sarkos ships in the process. Finally, the ones remaining limped away. Will relaxed. He had prevented the attack, but his ship had suffered extensive damage.

All of the sudden, he began to cough. And have difficulty breathing. He looked at his hand. It was covered with blood.

"Dunamys, I'm injured. I need to return immediately," he said to the bridge. If only he could stabilize his jet first.

JEN

Jen returned to her post at the communications board. They could all feel the tremble of the battle inside the ship. The shaking grew more intense at the aggressive attacks of the Sarkos. Were they willing to kill them at all costs or just scare them enough to go back to Earth or to slave them? Jen didn't know. But at the moment, her major concern was her brother and the rest of the pilots engaged in the fierce battle.

Jen picked up another transmission. "Sir, we have another communication."

"The Sarkos?"

"No sir, it's from somewhere else."

"Patch it through."

"We are the free Ommites," the voice said. "We accept your invitation to join you in battle. We also want to go to Zion with you."

"Please open the channel," Commander Rogers said.

Jen did as he asked.

"This is Commander Rogers. You are very welcome to join us, and thank you for fighting alongside us."

"Thank you, Commander. Joshua told us you would grant our request. He said he came to set us free, and we prefer to die free than be slaves for the rest of our lives."

"I'm so glad you became friends with Joshua too. Listen, many on board here are singing to the Creator, to thank him for his protection along our journey. Would you like to join them?"

"Yes, that would be an honor."

Commander Rogers ordered Jen to transmit David and Elizabeth's music through the frequency for the free Ommites. She lowered the volume. Now it could be heard not only by the free Ommites but also by everyone on the bridge without disturbing their concentration. But instead of disturbing them, the music seemed to energize and encourage them.

Jen watched the footage from the plaza from a small camera located with a wide-angle view of the place. Everyone in there was watching the explosions and battles taking place outside the windows, and as they sang, enemies were destroyed one by one. People appeared to be singing more enthusiastically even as the bombardment against the *Dunamys* became more and more aggressive.

Jen was amazed at what was happening outside the ship, too. Several of the Ommites' ships were joining the *Dunamys*' jets to battle the Sarkos. But still the Sarkos were still too powerful, even with the Ommites help.

Then Joshua appeared again on the bridge.

"Command all the battleships to return," he said firmly.

Commander Rogers didn't hesitate. He immediately called all the fighter jets to return, including the Ommite ones. Soon they were all hovering close to the *Dunamys*.

The fire that had been holding the dragon ships away suddenly turned into a foggy cloud. It enveloped all the dragon ships as well as the rest of the Sarkos ships.

At the same time, the people inside the *Dunamys* sang as one, with a loud voice.

CARLOS MORENO

Thanks, we will give from our hearts,
For your love
That endures forevermore!
You have given us the victory!

Oh our God!
You are the only One
The great God!
Our defender and our guide
You are our captain!
And by your love.
We are free!

Suddenly, explosions became visible behind the cloud. Lasers and other weapons detonating behind its foggy mass.

"Go to the other side of Gulgolet and wait there," Joshua instructed. Once all of the pilots returned the *Dunamys*, Commander Rogers proceeded with Joshua's instructions.

Jen watched as David and Elizabeth continued to sing with the passengers. Kids were hugging their parents, wives their husbands. Friends gathered in circles and hugging each other while the explosions and trembling continued.

After several hours, Commander Rogers ordered the launch of a probe to see what was on the other side of the planetoid. As the probe approached the surface of Gulgolet, they studied the images it sent. They found brand new craters full of debris, spaceships, and other big metallic objects. They saw the head of a metallic dragon floating around. But there was no sign of the enemy living. It was over.

Commander Rogers requested a count of the casualties. Immediately Star retrieved the information.

"Sir," she said "Amazingly, all the pilots came back, but several of them were hit, and a number of the pilots were injured. I don't have any names yet."

Jen stood up. "Sir, may I go to check on my brother?"

"Go ahead, Jen, but keep your communicator on."

"Jen, wait." Star took her hand. "I was told one name. Will's. He is still alive, but he was taken to the medical bay emergency section. They are working on him as we speak."

"Nooooo!"

Tears sprang to Jen's eyes, but she nodded.

"Why don't we go to see our friends David and Elizabeth?" Desperado got closer to her.

Jen agreed and went with Desperado to *Expression Place*, looking for David and Elizabeth. By this time, the music had ended, and everyone was gone, except for David, Elizabeth and Doris, who were taking everything down.

"... I agree, I think this is the best." Jen heard David talking to Elizabeth.

Elizabeth was in front of David. She reached for his hand giving him a friendly handshake. Then she noticed Jen. She stood up and ran to Jen, hugging her.

"It's so good to see you! It's been a long night."

David put his hand on his pockets and looked at

the ground. Jen wondered what was going on with them. But she turned her attention back to her friend.

"I know. So many things have happened," Jen responded.

"You have no idea!" David hugged her and Elizabeth goodbye.

"Thank you again for everything," he said to Elizabeth after she returned the guitar to him. Then he left.

"We heard about Will. Any report on his condition?" Elizabeth asked.

"I'm going to check on him later. Do you want to come?"

"Count me in!" Elizabeth smiled.

Desperado stepped in and hugged both of them, a huge smile on his face. "I have been a slave almost all my life, and now..." He stopped, overcome by emotion.

They talked for a while, then Jen decided it was time to check on Will. Elizabeth went with her, as promised, while Desperado remained, talking with Doris and about her experience after taking the cure from Joshua's blood. He seemed fascinated by her story.

Elizabeth, and Jen arrived at the medical bay a few minutes later, but they couldn't see Will. They were only told was in a coma. Suddenly, alarms went off, alerting the passengers to get to their quarters. An announcement came from the speakers.

"We are about to enter the Oort Cloud, which is filled with debris and comets. This is the final boundary of the Solar System. The trip might be bumpy. Please, everyone, go to your quarters immediately."

A nurse approached them. "Excuse me, you can't remain here. You heard the orders."

"Yes, ma'am." Elizabeth saluted politely. "I'll see you later, friend." Elizabeth hugged Jen goodbye.

"Can't I stay here, please?" Jen begged the nurse.

"He's, my brother."

"Okay, but you will be confined to the medical bay."

"I don't mind."

For several days, Jen remained stuck in the medical bay while they exited the Oort Cloud. Will's vitals were stable, but he remained unconscious.

Finally, an announcement freed everyone from their living quarters. But Jen stayed where she was, watching over Will. *Why isn't he waking up?* she thought. *It's been days since he lost consciousness.*

Then a nurse came into the room. She put her hand on Jen's shoulder. "I have to tell you the truth, Miss Morant. Will's previous injuries have turned into severe internal bleeding, not to mention several fractures from the most recent battle. We are doing everything we can, but he might not−"

"Please, stop right there, I'll get the picture." Jen leaned against Will's bed and cried.

"I hope he'll be okay," a soft voice said.

Jen felt a hand over her shoulder and turned to look. Star. She set a card on the table by the bed.

"Were you the one who−"

"Yes, I brought the other card last time. But please don't tell him. Let's keep it our secret. For some reason, I know he'll be okay."

"I hope so." Jen began crying again. "I told you not to go, Will! I told you!"

Star held her as she cried. Then she encouraged Jen to get some rest. She walked Jen to her living quarters before returning to the bridge. Jen tossed and turned, but finally fell asleep.

"It is in the blood," she heard as she saw a blood cell turn from black to red and then to white. "Take it and all will be made new." Then she heard the slow pulse of a beating heart.

Her communicator beeped, waking her from the strange dream.

"Jen, we need you on the bridge as soon as possible," Star said.

Jen got out of bed and slipped on her shoes. "What's going on?"

"We'll tell you when you get here."

Jen arrived at the bridge hoping it wasn't bad news again.

"Hey, Jen. How are you?" Star greeted her as if she hadn't just called her with such urgency.

"I'm fine, just a little restless."

"What about Will?" Commander Rogers asked.

"Honestly, not well. He's still unconscious. But what's going on? It sounded urgent."

"A friend asked for you," Commander Rogers said, smiling.

Jen turned around to see Joshua, who seemed more tangible than ever. He looked exactly the way she remembered from when she met him the first time.

"Everything will turn out fine, Jen. Don't be afraid," he said.

Jen gave him a hug. Then Commander Rogers asked her to open the channel for everyone to hear what Joshua had to say, including the Ommites who had come on board.

She signaled Joshua and he began to speak. "Slavery has filled this universe, but you've been set free, like many others before you. Now you will be able to help others to be set free, too. Take the cure, you will need it to be able to stand the speed of the journey. Be sure you choose the route that is narrow, because the wide one leads to destruction." Then he vanished before their eyes.

"I know what the cure is. It is the same he gave to Doris made with his blood, that is what the dream was all about!" Jen said after remembering her dream.

"See, that is why we need you, Jen." Star reminded her.

"Where are we?" Commander Rogers asked, realizing they were in a different sector of the space. The crew members returned attention to their stations since everyone had been paying attention to Joshua.

"We just crossed the Oort Cloud," Star told him. "We are on the other side."

The commander gazed out the window. "It's amazing!"

"Sir, look at this." Star zoomed in on a point from the big screen. "Two Einstein–Rosen bridges,"

"What?" Jen asked.

"The technical names for the two wormholes in front of us. I don't know how, but they are far away from each other," Dr. Mendel told them.

"Give me full zoom on screen," Commander Rogers said.

"Aye, aye, sir." Star magnified the images, then gasped. "One is huge, and the other—it's just too small!"

"Joshua said to take the narrow path," the commander said. "That is what we are going to do. But there is something we need to do first."

Commander Rogers ordered Dr. Hacket to distribute the cure among all passengers, pilots, and crew, including the Ommites and everyone in the medical bay.

EPILOGUE

WILL

W ill felt everything inside his body moving. He heard his heart beating like strong drums. Every fracture, every scratch, every damaged part of him was mending, being renewed and put back together. He was feeling like something alive was running through his body, through his veins. Like rivers of living water, refreshing, cleaning and restoring. It felt like he was being immersed into a pool of water or a lake.

Then he began to remember every encounter with Joshua since the first time they had seen the spaceship landing. The conversations at the coffee shop, the dreams he had, his broken heart about Elizabeth, his goal of becoming a pilot, the space battles, Joshua's words of encouragement, the departure from Earth. The images were out of order, but very vivid. Then he saw himself on the Dunamys with everyone else. He saw the battle with the Sarkos and all the passengers singing. He saw the last time they were on Earth, saying goodbye to friends, to his parents and loved ones.

He continued hearing the beat of his own heart. Then he saw a bright, golden light engulfing everything—the Plaza, the coffee shop, the bridge. Everything. A golden wind full of brightness and music and happy voices of people laughing and having a good time. He felt the light as it surrounded him. Then love, lightness, and joy filled him. The light shone so strongly that he could barely see. Then he sensed a familiar presence, a feeling of comfort and happiness. The son of the Creator was there, speaking to him.

"I always knew you were alive," said Will. He felt the sensation of getting out of the water, as if he had submerged for a long while.

He opened his eyes and realized he was in a room, but it wasn't the medical bay. It wasn't even the Dunamys. Or anywhere in space. It was a cabin built of wood, or at least something that looked like fine wood. He felt more alert than ever before. His eyes observed every small detail on the structure, like he was looking at it with a powerful magnifying glass or a microscope. He felt moisture in the air, heard the sound of the wind running across the room from a nearby window. It seemed he was more awake than ever before in his life. He stood up and walked across the room until he found the door.

Slowly but surely, he opened the door. The smell of something similar to fresh forest grass drew him outside. The light was very strong now. He closed the door behind him and walked forward, feeling the dust and grass under his feet. Had they returned to Earth?

"Oh, finally! You're awake!" a familiar female voice said.

Will's eyes adjusted to the light.

"Elizabeth?"

"Yes, it's me! I'm so glad you're well!"

Then Will looked up at the horizon. They were surrounded by mountains. He looked down at the ground. He and Elizabeth were each casting two shadows instead of one. In fact, everything was casting double shadows. He turned his face to the sky and saw two suns, one the same as on Earth, the other the size of the moon, a reddish color, on the opposite side in the sky.

"Welcome to the Alpha Hodon System." She approached him with a smile. "Or the Teegarden, as we call it around here."

"I never heard of that star system." He responded.

"It is an orbiting star system located 144 light years from Earth. How are you feeling?"

"I just remember a huge battle and a very strong golden light everywhere in the *Dunamys*. And then Joshua..." Will looked again at his surroundings.

"Everyone on board had a similar experience, Will. We all took the cure, same as you did. We all witnessed God the creator fighting for us as we all sang to him. We've all had a one-on-one encounter with Joshua, and every individual's experience was unique and different. But the message from him was the same for everyone."

"Wow!" Joy overwhelmed him.

"Do you remember the message?" she asked, giving him a strong hug.

"You have been reborn. The old has gone, the new has come. Go and grow—and help others to be set free. Your journey has just begun."

ABOUT THE AUTHOR

Carlos Moreno has been a writer since elementary school, winning his first competition when he was eight years old. Since then, he has pursued writing and creating many kinds of media for teens.

In 2011, he began teaching filmmaking workshops for teens and preteens, producing several short films with moral and life lesson content. He has also directed and edited several short films. More recently he has written and directed the pilot for a miniseries called "Welcome to Eden."

Carlos has produced several podcasts and helped create successful YouTube channels.

In 2022 he founded Wonder Light Productions, LLC, a content creation company dedicated to storytelling in different forms and mediums.

Milton Keynes UK
Ingram Content Group UK Ltd.
UKHW020111181024
449757UK00012B/785

9 798330 397921